David Boon's cricketing career spanned from 1984 to 1996 and in that time he became the quintessential sportsman, and one of the most popular and respected cricketers of his, or any, generation. His career peaked in 1993, when he scored centuries in the second, third and fourth Tests in the 1993 Ashes series in England.

DAVID BOON's BIG BOOK of Great SPORTING JOKES

HarperCollins*Publishers*

HarperCollins*Publishers*

First published in Australia in 2007
by HarperCollins*Publishers* Australia Pty Limited
ABN 36 009 913 517
www.harpercollins.com.au

HarperCollins*Publishers*
25 Ryde Road, Pymble, Sydney, NSW 2073, Australia
31 View Road, Glenfield, Auckland 10, New Zealand
77–85 Fulham Palace Road, London, W6 8JB, United Kingdom
2 Bloor Street East, 20th floor, Toronto, Ontario M4W 1A8, Canada
10 East 53rd Street, New York NY 10022, USA

National Library of Australia Cataloguing-in-Publication data:

Boon, David, 1960– .
   David Boon's big book of great sporting jokes.
   ISBN 9780732285241 (pbk.).
   1. Sports – Humor. 2. Sports – Anecdotes. I. Title.
A828.402

Cover design and illustration by Matt Stanton
Typeset in 11/16 Berling Roman by Kirby Jones
Printed and bound in Australia by Griffin Press

79gsm Bulky Paperback used by HarperCollins*Publishers* is a natural,
recyclable product made from wood grown in a combination of
sustainable plantation and regrowth forests. It also contains up to a 20%
portion of recycled fibre. The manufacturing processes conform to the
environmental regulations in Tasmania, the place of manufacture.

5 4 3 2 1   07 08 09 10

I would like to dedicate this book to
my mother Lesley and my sister Vanessa,
who have always enjoyed a good story.

Contents

INTRODUCTION

SPORT HAS ALWAYS BEEN a popular place for jokes. There are plenty of jokes out there that can easily be put in a sporting context, and while many sports jokes are familiar, I am still constantly amazed by the ingenuity of fans who come up with a new joke to fit the latest controversy or adapt an old line so they can laugh about themselves, their team or, best of all, their opponents.

One of the most often-told sports jokes is a yarn that has starred different characters and teams across the world but always ends with the punchline, 'They never beat anyone.' In America, the joke most often features one of the Chicago teams — baseball's Cubs or football's Bears. In Australia, it might feature the Geelong Cats, the ACT Brumbies or the Wests Tigers or any other footy team. During the 2006–07 Ashes Test cricket series in Australia, as England slumped to a 5–0 defeat, it began appearing this way …

*An eight-year-old boy was at the centre of a
courtroom drama when he challenged a court
ruling over who should have custody of him.*

*The boy had a history of being beaten by his
parents, so the judge awarded custody to an
aunt, as he wanted to preserve family unity as
best he could. However, the boy informed the
court that his aunt beat him as much as his
parents and he refused to live with her. When
the judge then suggested that he live with his
grandparents, the boy maintained that they also
beat him.*

*'Well, who can you live with then?' sighed the
judge.*

*'I'd like to live with the English cricket team,'
said the boy. 'They never beat anyone.'*

Then, just weeks later, after India were beaten by
Bangladesh at the 2007 World Cup, the same joke re-
emerged on subcontinental websites and chat rooms
… only now it was the Indian cricket team that was
gaining custody.

In this book, we've focused on the most talked-
about spectator sports in Australia — cricket, golf,
racing and the major football codes — but you'll also
find yarns about sports fought out on two wheels and
four, in the pool and in the ring, and on the court and
the high seas. And there are not just jokes, but also

some funny true stories and the odd sporting myth or two. Most of these tales are from Australia, but occasionally we came across a story from foreign fields that was just too good to leave out. All up, we've come up with what we believe is the biggest collection of sports laughs ever published in Australia.

They've come from a variety of sources — books, magazines, newspapers, personal memories and especially from the Internet. The web has become an extraordinary resource for yarns good and bad, and the advent of e-mail has seen jokes flying around the world, forwarded from one inbox to the next, with the best saved in archives and memories to be told and retold whenever a group of like-minded souls gets together for a chat and a laugh or two.

SO WHAT KIND OF jokes will you find here? There are the 'oldie but a goodie' jokes that have been told in many guises across the sporting world, though it must be stressed that what one bloke considers to be an old joke might never have been heard by the man or woman standing next to him. An example of this type of joke is the one that has been cracked many times — relating to cricket Tests, the Olympics, World Cup Finals, FA Cup Finals, the Superbowl, the World Series, the NRL and AFL Grand Finals — basically every sporting event that occurs regularly and is usually sold out ...

Five minutes before the start a man is sitting quietly beside a vacant seat. It seems crazy that on such a grand occasion someone would buy a ticket and then not turn up, so the bloke on the other side of the empty place leans over and says to the other man, 'Strange how this seat is empty.'

'Actually, it belongs to my wife,' says the man a little mournfully. 'We've been coming to the big day together every year for 35 years, but unfortunately she died.'

'Oh, I'm so sorry,' came the reply. 'But couldn't you find a friend or relative to take your wife's place?'

'Normally, yes,' said the man, 'but they're all at the funeral.'

While it is true that some jokes are old, they are still classics, so I was keen to include them in this collection, no matter how many people might or might not have heard them. The same is true of some of the factual stories in the book. Just as many sports jokes now fall into the 'oldie but a goodie' category, so too do some events that definitely did occur — these terrific yarns gradually evolve into legend as they get told and retold over the years at presentation nights and sportsmen's lunches. A favourite from my career concerns, inevitably, Big Merv Hughes ...

During our tour of South Africa in 1994, we played Orange Free State in Bloemfontein and on the last day Hansie Cronje smashed us all over the place, making 251 out of an innings total of 396. We still won the game, but my overriding memory is of Hansie hooking our fast bowlers time and again, and of Merv's response. He'd been under an injury cloud since the 1993 Ashes series, when he'd bowled bravely and magnificently, and now, after he bowled a delivery, he suddenly collapsed in a heap on the pitch. He was moaning and groaning as he lay there and we were all really concerned ... even Hansie, who walked up the wicket to see how the big bloke was. Soon, he was standing right over him, asking, 'Are you all right?'

Merv took one last painful half-roll down the pitch, so that his backside was pointing straight at Hansie, and then let go one of the biggest farts in history. 'Hit that for six!' he said matter-of-factly, then added, 'Ah, that feels better.' And then he got up and began walking back to his bowling mark. For a moment, we couldn't believe it, and then every one of us — Hansie most of all — just cracked up. It was a long while before play could continue.

I've heard that story told many times in many ways, and read it in a few books, but that's how I remember it. I think it's funny just about any way you tell it.

BESIDES THE 'OLDIES BUT goodies' are the 'you had to be there' yarns — the jokes or true stories that were definitely funny at the time, or the first time you heard them. I'll always remember my Australian cricket team-mate Tim May as a fantastic off spinner and as a very, very funny man. He was also, it must be said, a fairly ordinary fieldsman — at least by Test-match standards — and hardly the most co-ordinated bloke in the world; the kind of guy who'd get his feet in the wrong order and trip himself up when he was trying to prevent a short single.

In Australia's match against the West Indies at Madras (now Chennai) during the Nehru Cup in 1989, 'Maysie' was fielding down at third man when he ran down to collect a ball that had been hit in his direction … and he just fell over. Naturally, we all started yelling at him to get up but he wouldn't, even though the ball was sitting there just a few metres away and the batsmen were contemplating taking another run. At this point, I guess we should have been showing concern, but given Maysie's propensity for making people laugh and also his reputation for appearing ungainly in the field, we couldn't help but have a quiet chuckle.

Then, when he slowly lifted his head and started to crawl towards the ball, like a wounded animal trying to find a hiding place before the hunter shoots again, we just broke up. Eventually, someone had to run from slip to third man to help him get up — and prevent the Windies batsmen running a dozen! — and it turned out he'd actually 'done' his knee. So it wasn't funny at all, but geez we laughed at the time. You had to know Tim, and *you had to be there*. I know this'll sound more than a little unsympathetic, but when I get the picture in my mind of him trying to get to that ball, I still laugh. I bet all the boys do. Even Maysie!

OF COURSE, IT'S ENTIRELY possible that a joke one person finds hilarious someone else will find a little distasteful. These are the 'one man's meat' jokes, from the old saying, 'one man's meat is another man's poison'. Take one episode I always remember with a laugh from a big match involving Australia that was played on the subcontinent. Not that I want this to be an introduction full of fart jokes … but on this day I was having a conversation with captain Allan Border. We were talking about whether a bowler (who shall remain anonymous) should keep going or have a rest, when I suddenly stopped and thought, *Where is that stink coming from?* Then we looked over at the bloke in question and saw that there was this massive stain over the back of his creams. The question had to be asked: 'Mate, did you shit yourself?'

'Yeah, I did,' our comrade replied. 'But don't take me off, I'm bowling beautifully. I did it five overs ago, and I'm as dry as a bone now!'

I was cringing! Others were chuckling. It's a bit the same with jokes that some find risqué but others see as 'tame', and also those 'dreadful' corny jokes such as the ones we used to swap in the school playground when we were kids …

> *If you have a referee in rugby league, rugby union and soccer, and an umpire in cricket and AFL, what do you have in bowls?*
> *Corn Flakes …*

Maybe you prefer the one about the chickens who were sent off in the Grand Final … for fowl play. Or the ice skater who did a runner on his wedding day … because he had cold feet. Some people hate such jokes — just see them as being silly. Others love them. There's a chapter of them here.

THEN THERE ARE THE practical jokes. In many set-ups there has to be a victim, but if the play is a good one, even the wronged party will see the funny side of things. Take, for instance, the little boy dressed in rags sitting on the side of the road, with a cheap fishing rod in his hand and the line running down the drain …

> *A woman walked by and, feeling sorry for the poor little bloke, threw a two-dollar coin in the*

bucket that the kid had optimistically brought
with him to collect any fish he might have caught.
Seeing this, an old man strolled up and quipped,
'How many have you caught today, son?'

'That lady was number 23,' the boy chuckled,
as he stuffed his latest 'catch' into his wallet.

As far as practical jokes go, I think Stephen Waugh was the No. 1 culprit during my time in the Australian team. Steve was a cricketer capable of pulling off a prank so well that few knew he was responsible. So it is somewhat ironic that he managed to complete one of his finest stunts without even knowing he was doing it.

It happened in Perth one year, when Steve 'took' Dean Jones' suitcase. Steve always claimed that it was the concierge's fault, that the bag was delivered to his room by accident and that he never knew it was there until he discovered it when he was packing up to go home, but for a long time I wasn't so sure. Neither was 'Deano'. In Steve's defence, he was the most untidy tourist imaginable and his room could get so messed up, with clothes and playing gear going in all directions, that maybe a large suitcase *could* get lost in there. But it was a big bag! Deano — a bloke who cares about his appearance and who likes things to be neat and orderly — had to go out and buy new clothes so he could survive for the week, all the while badgering the hotel staff to see if the case had turned up and moaning to anyone who'd listen about how tragic it all was.

Steve was rooming with Peter Taylor at the time, and — as he tells it — it wasn't until it was time to leave the hotel that he and Peter realised that the mystery bag in their room didn't belong to either of them. It was one of those classic situations where Steve said, 'Hey, you've forgotten your bag,' and 'PT' said, 'I thought it was your bag.' And then they reported it to the hotel staff. Deano was probably a few hundred bucks out of pocket, but at least he had some nice new gear to remember this particular Perth trip.

Another time, in the West Indies, Steve and Mike Veletta came up with the idea of running a trail of breadcrumbs from the grounds outside a hotel room all the way to a sleeping player's pillow, a scheme that worked like a charm. The birds really seemed to enjoy it, though the startled Aussie cricketer woken from a heavy slumber by the local wildlife didn't seem quite as happy … at least not until he realised how he'd been done.

IN THIS BOOK, YOU'LL find jokes that have a go at various football teams across all codes, and sometimes the supporters of those clubs, but I hope no one finds any of them malicious or cruel. They're not meant to be. One of the things about being a sports fan is that you have to take as well as give. From my experience, most Aussies are good at that.

Throughout, we have adapted jokes to fit in with the sporting theme, and given many of them an Australian feel. You can do this with jokes. There is, for example, a story that's been told against Tasmanians for years, but it's never been told quite like this …

A ventriloquist was working in a pub outside of Hobart, but instead of his usual doll he was using the world-famous 'Boony Doll' as his partner. The guy's act was basically a long string of Tasmanian jokes, and after a while this got too much for one man in the audience.

'Listen, mate,' the bloke shouted out. 'You've been bagging us Tasmanians all night long! We're not all stupid, you know.'

'Relax,' said the ventriloquist. 'They're just jokes!'

'I'm not talking to you, sir!' the Tasmanian replied. 'I'm talking to the midget in the yellow shirt sitting on your knee!'

He's actually a good little bloke, the Boony Doll, even if he did cause a bit of grief for some people in the winter of 2006. As I think every one knows, the Dolls were given away with cases of VB beer during the

2005–06 Australian cricket season, the idea being that they would respond to signals activated by Channel Nine technicians at appropriate moments during Nine's telecast of the cricket throughout the summer. And that should have been it; the figurines were supposed to 'shut down' at season's end. However, there was a hiccup of some kind in the microchip (don't ask me to be any more technical than that), and the battery came back to life.

My daughter Lizzie had a Boony Doll in her room, which she refused to give up, even when it started chatting during the night, waking every one in the house but me. I kept a box of them in my office at the Tasmanian Cricket Association, in case I ever wanted to give one away, but one day when the office was empty the whole box went off like a drunken choir, which did nothing for the nerves of one long-serving employee, who had no idea what was going on. The poor woman was searching everywhere for intruders, without having a clue how many there were or what their motive might have been. It was only when the culprits were discovered that every one thought it was hilarious, though for a little while there were a few people walking around as if they'd seen (or at least heard) a ghost. Maybe they had ...

The Boony Dolls were a bit spooked out by the experience as well. One of them went down to

the pub down the road for a calming drink, and
after he entered he said to the bloke behind the bar,
'Geez, mate, I need a scotch. I just had the people
up at the TCA telling me I was some kind of ghost.'
'I'm afraid I can't help you,' the barman
answered. 'We don't serve spirits here.'

For the 2006–07 Ashes summer, the people at Carlton & United brought the Boony Doll back, and introduced a 'Beefy' Botham Doll to keep him company. By all accounts the promotion was as successful as the first campaign, the only 'negative' (my word, not that of the advertising people) being that there were no malfunctions. That took a little of the fun out of them.

Amazingly, there were web pages with no connection to VB that were devoted to the little guy. In one chat room, a guy told of how he was close to getting a new job, and it all depended on one final phone interview. Things were going well, until the two dolls he kept on his window ledge started jibbering away, and all he could do was meekly apologise and explain it was Boony and Beefy talking while the executives on the other end of the line laughed themselves silly. Another bloke changed the batteries on his original Boony Doll, but for weeks there was nothing. Then, suddenly, the figurine muttered, 'Anyone seen my thongs?' Before the summer was out, the Boony Doll even had its own page at *Wikipedia*!

That's got to be some kind of joke.

In one sense, I reckon, this book is a bit like an encyclopaedia — please stay with me on this one — in that it's not a publication I'd be reading from cover to cover, but one I'd be dipping into any time I needed a quiet chuckle, or maybe a good comeback for the bloke at the bar or the footy club who likes to start a conversation with, 'Have you heard the one about …?'

If you have as much fun reading the jokes — and sharing some of them with your mates — as we've had collecting them, then I reckon the time it took to create this *Big Book of Great Sporting Jokes* will have been very well spent.

1. HOWZAT!

Cricket Heaven

An avid 105-year-old cricket fan named Jock died happily, and having been a good and sporting man all his life, he went straight to heaven. On his first day there, one of the archangels took him to heaven's cricket museum, and Jock's face lit up when he came across an old piece of willow. 'Is that … can that be … it's Victor's bat, isn't it?' he gasped.

'That's right,' said the angel. 'That's the bat Victor Trumper used when he scored 185 not out at the SCG in 1903. Vic is a wonderful man. He's been up here since 1915.'

'And that Sykes bat?' Jock said. 'That's Don Bradman's bat!'

'Right again. That's actually the blade Sir Donald used during the bodyline series. He brought it with him when he came here in 2001.'

Jock really was in heaven. He saw Stan McCabe's bat, Archie Jackson's bat and Charlie Macartney's bat.

But then he came across a modern Kookaburra bat, and his heart sank. 'Oh no, that looks like the bat Ricky Ponting uses,' he cried. 'You're not telling me Punter's died and gone to heaven?'

'Oh no, Jock, calm down,' replied the angel. 'That's actually God's cricket bat. He just lets Ricky use it down on earth during the Test matches.'

Ticket Please

Three Australian lads and three Kiwis were travelling by train from London to Cardiff for a game during the 1999 World Cup. At the station, the Kiwis each bought a ticket and watched as the Aussies bought just one ticket between them.

'How will the three of you be able to travel on just one ticket?' asked one of the New Zealanders. 'Watch and learn,' responded the first of the Australians. Soon after, the train arrived, and they all jumped aboard.

The Kiwis took their allotted seats, while the Aussies crammed into a toilet at the far end of the carriage and then closed the door behind them. Not long after the train set off, the conductor arrived to collect the tickets. He tapped on the toilet door and said in a loud voice, 'Ticket please!'

The door opened just enough for an arm to emerge with a ticket in hand. The conductor took it and continued on his way, and the three Black Cap fans were most impressed.

At the ground, the lads went their separate ways but they caught up again at Cardiff station for the trip home. The Kiwis were in a good mood for their boys had earned a rare win over the mighty Australians, and now it was time for the three of them to buy a ticket — just the one — for the return journey. To their astonishment, the Aussies didn't buy a ticket at all.

'What's the matter, boys?' one Kiwi asked. 'Lose all your money backing the wrong team?'

The Australians said nothing.

As soon as the train arrived, the New Zealanders watched the Aussies cram into a toilet in one carriage, and then they squeezed into another in the adjoining carriage.

The train was on its way. Almost immediately, one of the Australians left his hiding place and walked up to the toilet where the Kiwis were waiting. Then he knocked on the door and said with great authority …

'Ticket please!'

Ins and Outs

An old farmer from the Queensland outback built quite a reputation as a character as well as a tough and durable opening batsman. During one game, he dislocated his shoulder while fielding and, at the hospital, a doctor decided to try to manipulate it back into place without the aid of an anaesthetic, a process that made the 'bushie' scream with pain. The nurse had little sympathy.

'I thought you were tougher than that,' she said coldly. 'There is a woman in the next room having a baby and she is not making half the fuss you are.'

To which the injured man replied, 'No, but I bet she would be if they were trying to put it back.'

The Catch of his Life

Steve was an outstanding wicketkeeper: the star of the local team. One day, during pre-season training, he was jogging down the street when he saw a big apartment building on fire. A woman stood trembling on a sixth-storey ledge, holding her pet cat in her arms, while rescuers on the ground yelled at her to stay calm. Help, they explained, was on the way. In the distance, the sound of wailing sirens could be heard.

Steve, being a confident young chap, pushed through to the front, and yelled out, 'Hey, lady, it's OK. Throw me your cat.'

'No, I can't,' she cried. 'It's too far.'

'I'm a great wicketkeeper. I haven't dropped a chance in three years. I can catch anything.'

'Do it, lady!' yelled out someone in the crowd.

'Don't worry, dear,' roared another. 'Stevie's a champion; he's a magician with the gloves.'

Smoke was pouring from the windows, and then there was an explosion out the back of the building.

The keeper's arms were outstretched ... waiting ... waiting ... and then, finally, the woman waved to Steve, kissed her cat goodbye, and dropped it down towards the street.

Steve kept his eyes locked on that cat as it came hurtling towards him. It seemed to dip just before it arrived, but he was up to the challenge, grabbing the feline with the softest pair of hands imaginable. The crowd roared, the woman on the ledge offered a nervous, relieved smile ... and Steve gave an enormous cheer, almost an appeal, and then he threw the cat high into the air before running into the arms of the friends around him to celebrate.

Don't Tread on the Ducks

Lloyd, Ian and Phil were driving home from their cricket club's presentation night one year when they had a terrible car accident. All three men died and went to heaven. Because they were all such top blokes, St Peter quickly let them in, saying, 'We only have one rule in heaven. Don't step on the ducks!'

Sure enough, there were ducks all over the place. 'Geez,' said Lloyd, 'a lot of blokes didn't score a run!' Very droll! It was almost impossible not to step on a duck and, although they tried their best to avoid them, soon Phil accidentally stepped on one. In a flash, along came St Peter with the ugliest woman anyone had ever seen. St Peter chained Phil and the woman together and said, 'Your punishment for stepping on a duck is to spend eternity chained to this ugly woman.'

The next day, Ian accidentally stepped on a duck and along came St Peter, who doesn't miss a thing, and with him was another extremely ugly woman. He chained them together, offering exactly the same rebuke he'd given Phil.

Lloyd had observed all this and, not wanting to be chained for all time to an unattractive woman, was very careful where he stepped. He managed to go months without walking on a duck. Eventually, St Peter came up to him with the most gorgeous woman anyone had ever laid eyes on: a tall, tanned, curvaceous, sexy brunette. St Peter chained Lloyd and her together without saying a word.

Lloyd looked at his new friend with great satisfaction. After a while, he whispered quietly to her, 'I wonder what I did to deserve being chained to you for all eternity?'

'I don't know about you,' the beauty replied. 'But I stepped on a duck.'

Nick Off

During an Ashes Test, the great Bill 'Tiger' O'Reilly hit the pads of one of England's top batsmen with a superb top-spinner and roared an appeal. The umpire said not out, but judging by the angry look O'Reilly gave both the batsman and the ump, it was clear that he was not happy with the ruling.

At the end of the over, Tiger snatched his cap from the umpire and began to walk away. 'Sorry, Bill, but he nicked that one,' the umpire said quietly, to which the disappointed bowler spun around and glared at him.

'I know he nicked it,' O'Reilly roared. 'That's where the bloody rule's wrong!'

Whit

One of the most popular cricketers to play for Australia in the last 30 years was the NSW left-arm fast bowler, reliable No. 11 batsman, raconteur, Gladiators referee, TV presenter and all-round good bloke, Michael Roy Whitney. Now 'Whit' is a bloke with a million funny stories from his cricket career, such as the day he came out to face the fearsome Patrick Patterson in Jamaica with the crowd chanting 'Pat-rick! Pat-rick!' only to discover — when the bowler was halfway to the wicket for the next delivery — that they were actually cheering for a HAT-TRICK. No one had told him that wickets had fallen from each of the previous two balls, and he was so put off he had to tell the bowler to abort the delivery, which was not always a wise thing to do with a big paceman such as Patrick Patterson.

Batting at the other end when this was going on was one D. Boon, who was actually past his hundred.

He had, as Whitney remembers it, already given the new batsman the following advice: 'Just concentrate on the ball and you'll be OK … otherwise you're going to get hurt.' Not surprisingly then, when the No. 11 somehow and finally managed to get bat on the first ball from Patterson, and better still squeeze it into the vacant cover region, he raced for a single and the non-striker's end so quickly and determinedly that one, there was no way Boon could stop him, and two, he ended up 30 metres past the stumps to make sure there was absolutely no chance in the whole wide world that they'd be running two. Imagine Whitney's disappointment then, when he heard umpire Steve Bucknor say with a slight chuckle, 'Over!' Now he'd have to face Courtney Walsh!

From when he was a boy Whitney had got into the habit of writing his name on all his cricket gear, to make sure it could never get lost or confused with anyone else's. So when the gold-and-green uniforms were handed out before the World Cup in Australia in 1992, he went straight to work on the inside collar of his shirt. 'What are you doing, Whit?' asked Dean Jones, in reply to which he explained the whole process.

'Mate, have you looked on the back of that thing?' asked Jones.

Right across the back of the shirt's shoulders, in letters big enough that you could've read them from the pitch to the boundary, was the following: W-H-I-T-N-E-Y. As discreetly as he could, the No. 11 snuck his pen back into his kitbag.

Nervous Nineties

A batsman was batting beautifully and had reached 99 not out when his partner was dismissed. This brought their captain to the wicket. Almost immediately, the man in the nervous nineties pushed one into the offside, and the skipper yelled, 'Yes!' and charged down the wicket. But the man at the batting end said, 'No, get back!' and it was all the new batsman could do to turn around, sprint and then dive back to make good his ground.

As he dusted himself off and brushed the dirt out of his hair and off his face, the captain stormed down the wicket to talk to his partner. 'I'll have you know, son,' he roared indignantly, 'that I'm the best judge of a run in this competition. If I say there was one there, there was one there.'

'Mate,' his partner replied. 'If I'm 99 not out, I'm the best judge of a run on the whole bloody planet!'

Trueman v Hall

In a match at the Scarborough Festival in the early 1960s, Freddie Trueman was facing the great West Indies' fast man Wes Hall and he managed to snick four consecutive balls through the slips for four.

After the fourth, Hall stood in mid-pitch, hands on hips, and with a smile asked, 'Where did you learn to bat? Edgbaston?'

Bloody Beauty, One for None!

One of cricket's most repeated yarns is an old classic originally told by the former Queensland cricketer Bill Tallon. Bill was the brother of the outstanding Queensland and Australian keeper Don Tallon, who was, of course, one of Sir Donald Bradman's Invincibles. This story involved Sir Donald and a game between Queensland and South Australia at the Gabba, and begins with Bill Tallon relating how he took the new ball and bowled an inswinger to: 'a bloke named Nitschke, a left-hander. Bloody good bat.'

The delivery took the edge of Nitschke's bat. 'Bloody beauty!' said Bill Tallon, according to the version that appears in a book by Fred Trueman and Frank Hardy called *You Nearly Had Him That Time … and Other Cricket Stories.* 'Me brother Don caught it in front of first slip.'

South Australia were 'one for none'.

The new batsman was Badcock, whose first name was Clayvel, which might explain why he preferred to be known as 'Jack'. In Bill Tallon's opinion, he was another 'bloody good bat', but he went for a drive and got a thick edge, and Bill's brother Don took the catch in front of second slip.

Two for none.

Out walked the great Bradman. Bill Tallon tried a short one, and Bradman went for a hook. 'He hit it so high,' recalled Bill Tallon, 'that fine-leg ran for it, square-leg ran for it, mid-on ran for it, I ran for it meself and I got a sunburnt mouth waiting for it to come down.

'Bloody beauty. Me brother Don got under the ball first and caught it.

'Three for 284!'

It's a great yarn, but unfortunately, it can't have been true. Bill Tallon played against Bradman twice, both times in 1938–39. The first time was at the Adelaide Oval, when Tallon bowled third change in South Australia's only innings, and finished with 1–90 from 18 overs, that wicket being the SA No. 5, Ron Hamence, caught and bowled for 17. South Australia's openers, Dick Whitington and Ken Ridings, did both go cheaply and Bradman then made 225 before he was the fifth wicket to fall, dismissed by the left-arm finger spinner, Charles 'Chilla' Christ. In the return match at the Gabba two weeks later, Bradman scored another hundred, this time 186, his fifth successive first-class hundred (he'd make a sixth in his next knock), and it came after Whitington and Ridings had both made centuries of their own. At least Tallon did dismiss Bradman this time, but unfortunately his brother was off the field, having hurt his thumb while keeping the previous afternoon. Instead, the legend was caught by Christ, which could happen to anyone.

'Slinger' Nitschke, who later achieved fame as the owner of the champion racehorse Dayana, played his final first-class match for South Australia in January 1935, almost four years before Bill Tallon made his first-class debut and the season before Don Bradman transferred from New South Wales to South Australia. Jack Badcock did play for SA in those games in 1938–39, batting four and scoring 100 in Adelaide and one and four not out (opening up in the second dig) at the Gabba.

The point of putting up all these facts is not to be smart, but to ask the question: in terms of the humour, does it really matter? Bill Tallon obviously saw a lot of The Don in action in those two games; maybe he thought up the joke while he was fielding or afterwards when he was recovering in the dressing room. The scenario in Adelaide wasn't too far out, and the thing with Bradman is that if you'd made the punchline *three for 584!* the story would have remained totally realistic!

Even though the facts are skewiff, it's still a bloody good yarn guaranteed to raise a laugh. And it also captures something of the greatness of The Don, not least by the way *everyone* gets the joke as soon as it's told. That, surely, is no bad thing.

Two Aspirin

A cricket umpire from the bush had been invited to come to the city to officiate in the first-grade competition and accepted, hoping that he might graduate from there to the first-class arena and maybe even international matches. His only problem was that he had a terrible winking problem. So here he was sitting across from the chairman of the grade umpire's appointments committee, winking away, while his prospective new boss read through his résumé.

'I've never seen an umpire whose performances have been praised by so many people,' the chairman said. 'You are clearly a superb decision-maker. Ninety-nine times out of 100, we'd give you a first-grade game on the spot, but being an umpire is a highly visible position. You'll be on the field with highly-strung, temperamental cricketers, many of whom have ambitions to play for Australia. I can imagine you turning down a huge appeal from a big fast bowler, and then you winking away — that could cause an incident I'd rather not hear about.'

'But wait,' the umpire responded. 'If I just take two aspirin, I stop winking.'

'Really? Can you show me?'

So the still-winking umpire reached into his coat pocket, and started pulling out all sorts of condoms: red condoms, blue condoms, ribbed condoms, flavoured condoms, large and small condoms, until finally he found a packet of aspirin. He ripped it open, took two pills, and the winking stopped.

'Well, this is all fine, isn't it?' said the chairman. 'I don't know what sort of morals you adhere to where you come from, but in our umpiring community we don't like our men womanising everywhere they go!'

'Womanising? What do you mean? I'm a happily married man!'

'Well, how do you explain all these condoms?'

'Oh,' he sighed. 'What can I do? Have you ever walked into a chemist, winking, and asked for aspirin?'

Dress Code

When the Australian cricket team toured New Zealand in 1990, the manager was a fellow named Dr Cam Battersby, who was in the role for the first time. The team flew in and played their first game. The following morning they were due to fly to a new location. It was at this point that the new manager suddenly realised that he didn't know what the dress code was for the team when it was flying from city to city within New Zealand. There was nothing in his notes, and no one had briefed him, but of course there were a number of players in the squad who'd done plenty of overseas touring. So Battersby thought it best to quietly ask the captain exactly what the protocol was.

'Jeans,' said Allan Border flatly.

Next morning, Cam Battersby turned up at the hotel reception clad in his team polo shirt and best pair of Levis. The players, of course, were all wearing ties and blazers.

Lost and Found

If you've ever lost a crucial piece of cricket gear, the easiest way to find it is to go out and buy the most expensive version of the lost item. The misplaced object will turn up almost as soon as you've purchased its replacement.

I Declare

A few seasons back, in Sydney grade cricket, it had become fashionable for captains to declare their first innings closed, or even to forfeit an innings, in the hope that such a decision or decisions would lead to an outright result. Often, this process would start with the two captains getting together to 'make a deal' that might benefit both teams — the team that won on the first innings could not chase the extra points that would come with an outright win, while the losing team might get something out of the contest, even though for most of it they'd been outplayed. Of course, like in any negotiation, a key component is that the captains needed to retain any advantage they could while the deal was hammered out.

One day, however, this process came unstuck because one of the skippers, who had played Sheffield Shield cricket, didn't quite have the intricacies of the process in hand. On the first day, Team A ran up a big score, and then on day two, Team B was struggling, six or seven wickets down for not very many. Suddenly, without a word of warning, the captain of the batting team waved his boys in, yelling out to his opposite number, 'I'm declaring.'

When the teams came off the field, the skipper who'd just called his batsmen in went up to the other captain and said, 'OK, I'm happy to bowl my mug bowlers. How many runs will you set us in a run chase?'

'A run chase? What run chase?' came the reply. 'I'm enforcing the follow on.'

2. BAD LIES

The Wedding

It was mid-afternoon on a beautiful sunny day. A male golfer in his early 30s was on the first tee, preparing to drive. After a few practice swings, he stepped up to his ball and was just about to launch his drive on the first hole when a woman in a wedding gown came running down from the car park. There were tears falling down her face. As she reached the area in front of the pro shop, she looked out to the first tee and screamed, 'I can't believe it! How could you do this to me?'

The golfer calmly took his swing and slammed the ball straight down the middle of the fairway. He gathered his tee, put his driver back in the bag, and then looked up at the distraught woman. 'Darling,' he stated flatly, 'I definitely said, "Only if it rains."'

The Inheritance

Dean knew for years that when his aged father died, he'd inherit a fortune, which was handy because all the money he'd made during his golf career had been squandered on wine, women and song. Finally, the day came when he was told that his dad only had weeks to live, and quickly he realised that this could be a chance to revive his old lifestyle in more ways than one.

One night he went back to the same nightclub where he and his former golfing mates used to do their thing. Soon, he spotted the most beautiful woman he had ever seen, and he decided to try his luck. He sidled up to her and said with a smile, 'I may look like an ordinary bloke but I can tell you that in a few short weeks my father will die and I'll inherit at least 100 million dollars.'

'Is that right?' said the girl with a gleaming smile. 'And what might be your name?'

'Dean,' he replied, 'or to use my full title, Dean Johnson, the third.'

The beautiful woman was clearly impressed. He bought her a drink, she asked about his ailing father, they swapped numbers and addresses … and a fortnight later she became his stepmother.

A Rough Caddy

'I think we've found it, sir,' the caddy cried out to his golfer as he stood over a ball in the trees, a long way from the fairway.

'That can't be it,' replied the golfer, 'it's too old.'

'Well, it is a long time since we teed off,' said the caddy.

An hour or so later, and the group had made it to the next hole and were walking towards the green. But the golfer was getting frustrated at the way his caddy kept looking at his wristwatch. 'Will you stop doing that,' he cried, 'it's too distracting. I don't care what time it is.'

'Sorry, but it isn't a watch, it's a compass.'

Relative Earnings

A young professional was back in Australia after his first year on the US PGA tour. He hadn't won a tournament, but he'd gone pretty well and easily made it into the top 125 money-earners on the tour, which meant he had his 'card' for the following season.

'Do you realise,' asked a reporter at a media conference before his first Australian tournament of the season, 'that you now make more money in a year than the Australian Prime Minister?'

'So I should,' replied the golfer. 'I'm a much better player than he is.'

Good News and Bad News

Bert and Harry were two of the worst golf addicts in Australian history. They played together whenever they could, they loved to walk around golf stores together, they went to the major tournaments together. Often they'd have breakfast together on a Monday morning so they could watch the final round of the latest USPGA Tour tournament on pay-TV. They could talk for hours about golf courses they'd played or hoped to play. Holidays were about resort courses, or maybe one day a trip to Augusta for the Masters. Their wives hated golf with a passion, only because their husbands were so obsessed. Craziest of all, Bert and Harry had made this ridiculous pact: if one of them died, they'd do everything they could to come back to earth to let the other know if there was golf in heaven.

Then one day it happened. While comparing putters in the pro shops after playing 36 holes in pouring rain on Bert's wedding anniversary, Harry collapsed and died. A couple of nights later, Bert suddenly woke up in a cold sweat. He could hear a voice, and not any voice … it was Harry, calling from 'beyond'.

'Harry, is that you?' Bert asked nervously.

'Yes, mate, it's me.'

'This is fantastic!' Bert exclaimed. 'So you've got to tell me, Harry, is there golf in heaven?'

'I have some good news and some bad news.'

'What's the good news?' Bert enquired.

'Mate, the good news is that there is most definitely golf in heaven. The courses are fantastic.

The clubhouses are beautiful. There's no rough. Every one breaks par. Only this morning I played nine holes with Bobby Jones, and he was a terribly nice bloke. A good loser, too!'

'Oh, that is so wonderful! What could possibly be the bad news?'

'We're playing a foursome together tomorrow at noon.'

Pressure

The great Lee Trevino defined pressure this way: 'You don't know what pressure is until you've played for five dollars a hole with only two dollars in your pocket.'

Early Retirement

'It's a pity you didn't take up golf earlier in your life,' said the caddie to the man whose clubs he was carrying.

'Why?' replied the golfer. 'Do you think I'd be a better player?'

'No, you would have given the game away by now.'

The Longest Drive

In his book *The Golfer Who Laughed*, the great Australian golf writer Phil Tresidder told the story of AC 'Titanic' Thompson, whom he described as 'golf's most famous hustler'. One of Titanic's more famous stings occurred after he claimed that he could drive a ball 500 yards, a claim that was derided to the point that he had $10,000 resting on his being able to prove his boast true.

He took the men who'd bet he couldn't do it down to a course that was located on the edge of a lake. It was in the middle of winter, and as they got closer they could see that the water had iced over, which meant that when Titanic hit his driver, the ball skidded off the ice and kept going and going and going. As Tresidder put it, the ball 'was still travelling when the bets were paid off.'

The Old Gum Tree

A young bloke who loved his golf — and thought he was pretty good at it — found time one afternoon for a quick nine holes. He'd have to hurry, because he'd booked a table at a flash restaurant for dinner with his gorgeous new girlfriend, but things were looking good when he arrived at the first tee and there was no one else in sight. However, just as he was about to hit his opening drive, an old gentleman emerged and asked if he would like some company on the round. The young fella could hardly say no, and the pair set off together.

Fortunately, the old man played pretty quickly. He couldn't hit the ball far, but he was always straight down the middle, and when he got to the green it was one practice putt and then he invariably rifled the ball straight into the hole.

In what seemed like no time at all they had reached the ninth tee. They hadn't been keeping their scores on a card, but the young man was a competitive type, and he knew that he was one shot in front. His veteran partner seemed oblivious to this, as he hit another short but dead straight drive down the fairway. The young guy's drive was just as straight but 100 metres further down the short grass, setting up the chance for him to maybe go for the green on this par five in two. The old man's second shot, a three iron, whizzed another 130 metres down the fairway, and then the two of them stood beside the young man's ball. There was a large gum tree directly between his ball and the green. Perhaps safety was the best option, especially — as the young man kept reminding himself — given the fact that he had that one-shot lead.

The evening engagement was forgotten, as the young man spent several minutes debating how to hit the shot. Maybe a fade to set it up for pitch and run into the green. Of course, he could just go for the flag, which as the crow flies was only 180 metres away. Or should he leave himself a full sand wedge in? Finally, the old man broke the silence. 'You know, when I was your age I'd have hit that ball right over that tree,' he said.

The young man looked coldly at his rival. He pulled out a four iron, and swung as hard and as fast as he could. On contact, he thought he'd made it, but when he looked up he saw his ball crash into a branch near the top of the tree and rebound into the deep rough only 30 metres in front of them, with no option left but to take a drop and still have no shot at the green. Given his partner's skill with the putter, he knew the round was lost.

'Of course,' the old man said as they walked up the fairway, 'when I was your age that gum tree was only 10 feet tall.'

The Best Caddie in Queensland

In 1929, the great American professional Walter Hagen came to Australia for a series of exhibitions with the Australian Joe Kirkwood. In Brisbane, the pair were due to play at the Royal Queensland Golf Course. In *The Australian Golfer's Handbook*, published in 1957, Norman Von Nida described what happened next:

> *I was an under-sized, underweight caddie at the club, but I was the No. 1 caddie. When I stepped forward to take Hagen's bag, which was almost as big and heavy as I was, he raised his eyebrows in surprise. But before he could say what I knew he was thinking — that I was too small, it had been said often before — I spoke up.*

'That's all right, Mr Hagen,' I said. 'I am to carry your clubs. I am the best caddie in Brisbane.'

Hagen looked down at me. 'OK, son, then you and I are a pair,' he said, 'because I'm the best golfer in Brisbane.'

Norman Von Nida went on to be one of Australia's greatest golfers, good enough to even beat the great Walter Hagen.

Safe but Sorry

Harry and his best mate Tom were playing a round of golf with their wives early one Sunday morning. At the 10th, Harry hooked his drive into the trees and when they got to where it had fallen he found that it was in an awkward position, with his best option being to simply chip out onto the fairway and hope for a bogey. But his wife looked at his predicament and said, 'C'mon dear, what are you, man or mouse? There's a narrow gap between those two trees right in front of you. Go for it.'

So Harry went for it, but the ball crashed straight into the tough old gum tree just a few metres away, and then ricocheted back into his wife's forehead. She collapsed to the ground, but despite her husband's frantic efforts and the sterling work of the paramedics when they got there, there was nothing anyone could do. The poor woman was dead.

Harry was devastated and didn't set foot on the golf course for weeks after his wife's funeral. But eventually he was coaxed back, and next time he played the 10th he hooked his drive into around the same place he'd hit the fateful drive on that awful Sunday morning.

There were tears in his eyes as he tramped up the fairway. As he stood over the ball, he knew he had no option and he reached for his wedge. But one of his partners had walked up with him and he said quietly, 'There's a narrow gap between those two trees right in front of you. Why don't you go for it?'

The man stopped, then turned quietly to his colleague. 'You cannot be serious,' he said in a bitter tone. 'I did that last time and finished with a triple bogey!'

Value for Money

A golfer walked up to a gaggle of caddies standing in front of the pro shop. In his hand was a crisp $100 note. 'Boys,' he said, 'I need a caddie who can keep an accurate score. What's three plus four plus five plus six?'

'Fifteen!' spurted out one of the caddies.

'Excellent answer,' replied the golfer, 'You seem perfect.'

Boned

The thing with the eighth hole was that on the left-hand side was a ravine in which you could find all kinds of scrub and thorns and bushes and who knows what else? If you hooked your ball in there, the best advice was to take your medicine, drop a new ball, and continue on. One day, Dave and Norm were on the eighth tee and, sure enough, Dave promptly duck hooked his ball deep into the ravine, but instead of taking a penalty and hitting another ball, he grabbed his six iron and marched up to the embankment near where his drive had disappeared.

Down Dave went, through the bushes, constantly stopping to disconnect his shirt or trousers from a tentacle of lantana or an errant branch. As he went, he'd kick at the scrub, stomp on some grass or smash away with his club, hoping against hope that he'd come upon his Titleist, but though occasionally he'd stumble across someone else's old ball his was nowhere to be found. Then, suddenly, he saw a glimpse of light through the gloom and as he got closer he realised that what was shining was the sun's reflection off a golf club, and that the club in question was in the hands of a skeleton. A very old golf ball lay at the skeleton's Niblick-clad feet.

Dave took one look at the scene in front of him and dashed frantically for the surface. He scurried up the bank, and then yelled at his golfing partner in a panicked voice, 'Hey Norm, get over here. I'm in trouble.'

Norm rushed over and cried, 'What's the matter?'

Dave yelled back, 'Quick, get me my five iron! I'll never get out of here with a six iron.'

Foul!

A young nun is deep in conversation with her Mother Superior. 'I'm afraid I used some awful language this week. I feel sick about it,' she said.

'When did you sin, my dear?' asked the elder nun.

'Well, you see, I was enjoying a round of golf and I hit a superb drive, if I do say so myself. It looked as if it was going to go more than 250 metres, right down the middle, but it struck a seagull that was flying across the fairway and dropped straight down into the rough after going only 100 metres.'

'Is that when you swore?' Mother Superior asked sternly.

'Oh, no, Mother,' the nun replied. 'Suddenly, a possum raced out of the scrub and grabbed my ball in its paws and scurried away!'

'Is THAT when you swore?'

'Oh, no, Mother. As the possum ran for cover, a big crow flew down, pecked at the possum, which dropped the ball, and the crow then took the ball in its beak and sailed away!'

'THAT'S when you swore?'

'Oh, no, Mother. As the crow flew away past the green, an errant drive from the next fairway clipped its wing and it dropped my ball.'

'Did you swear then?' asked Mother Superior, becoming a little irritated.

'No, Mother. The ball fell into a big clump of rocks, ricocheted out, over the bunker and onto the fringe of the green, from where it rolled up no more than a metre from the hole.'

For a moment, there was silence. The Mother Superior looked aghast. 'Don't tell me you missed the fricking putt!'

How Much for the Mobile?

A group of golfers are in the change rooms after a hot summer's day on the fairways. Suddenly, the fancy ring tone of a mobile phone starts ringing, and quickly one of the men steps forward to engage the hands-free speaker function on a phone lying on a bench. He begins to talk, while every one in the room stops to listen.

''Ello,' the man with the mobile says.

'Sweetheart, it's me,' says a woman's voice at the other end of the line. 'Are you still at the club?'

'Yes, dear.'

'I'm doing a little shopping and I've discovered this gorgeous leather jacket, but it's $2000. Oh darling, I love it. Is it all right for me to buy it?'

'My darling, go for it if you like it that much. Put it on my card.'

'Thank you, sweetie. You won't regret it. Also, you know I said I was going to stop off at the Porsche dealership, to have a squizz at their latest models. I absolutely love the new Boxster. It would be perfect for my image.'

'How much is it?'

'$200,000!'

'Geez, that's plenty. For that price it would want to have all the extras. But if you really want it, who am I to stop you being happy?'

'Oh, thank you, darling. I'll go back and order a gold one, or maybe red. What do you think?'

'I've always thought of you as a golden kind of girl.'

'And what about the house? They still want $2.5 million, but can you picture us on a summer's night, watching the sunset over the Harbour Bridge, a chilled glass of chardonnay in our hands? Is two-and-a-half million too much for something as beautiful as that?'

'You're right. It's a once-in-a-lifetime opportunity. You tell them we'll take it and I'll find the money somehow.'

'OK. I better go. Much to do! I love you so much!'

'I love you too, honey.'

The man hangs up, and then looks up to see his golfing mates staring at him, jaws dropped in astonishment. He just smiles, and then says cheerily, 'Does anyone know who owns this mobile?'

Handicapped

A keen golfer was driving through the Northern Territory when he came across a golfing oasis in the middle of the desert. He didn't even know this course existed, and couldn't resist going in and seeing if he could have a round. The guy at the pro shop said he could as long as he was a member at a registered course. The bloke said he was, so the man checked on the computer and saw that he was off 12 at a flash Sydney layout, and guided him out to the first tee. 'Just one thing, mate,' he said, 'I'll need you to use one of our local caddies, if you don't mind.'

'No problem,' the visitor responded. 'No problem at all.'

It was a terrific course, and the gentleman was quickly at the peak of his game. But then at the fourth hole, just as he was about to play his second shot, a dingo emerged from the bush and charged straight for him. Fortunately, the caddie saw this, pulled out a rifle and shot the dog between the eyes.

At the seventh, a big angry buffalo raced out and headed for the golfer. But again the caddie was alert to the danger, and a crack from the rifle saw the buffalo drop dead at the man's feet. Then, at the 12th, the man was attacked by a huge crocodile, but this time the caddie did nothing. The man's leg was severed above the knee. Writhing in agony, with blood pouring from his wound, the golfer yelled out, 'Why didn't you do anything?'

'Sorry, boss,' the caddie replied, 'but you don't get a shot on this hole.'

This story reminds us of a yarn told by the late Phil Tresidder about two golfers, Noel Hunt and Warren Humphreys, and a round they played at the Elephant Hills course near Victoria Falls in Zimbabwe. Hunt found his ball near the edge of a pond, but he wasn't keen to go near it because there was a large crocodile sleeping just a couple of metres away. Eventually, he summoned up the courage to hit 'the quickest wedge shot of my life', with his playing partner as his 'bodyguard'.

As Tresidder wrote so cleverly in The Golfer Who Laughed, *'Humphreys protected Hunt's rear with an eight iron, which was probably not enough club.'*

The World's Worst

The golfer stood on the fairway, looked down towards the green, and then said to his caddy, 'Do you think I can get there with a five iron?'

'Eventually,' the caddy replied.

These sorts of remarks continued throughout the round, to the point that on the 17th tee the golfer muttered under his breath, 'You would have to be the worst caddy in the entire world.'

'I doubt that's true, sir,' the caddy responded. 'It would be too much of a coincidence!'

3. THE BIG JOKES FLY

You Don't Always Get What You Want

A man in a Sydney Swans guernsey walked into a bar carrying a Sydney Swans sports bag. He sat down and placed the bag on the counter. The barman came over, took his order and asked what was in the bag. The Swans fan went into the bag, pulled out a little bloke no more than 30 centimetres tall and stood him on the bar. Then he reached into the bag again, pulled out a miniature piano and placed it on the bar. Then he got out a tiny bench, which he put in front of the piano. The midget then sat on the bench and began playing the tune of the Swans theme song!

'That's fantastic!' exclaimed the barman. 'Where did you get him from?'

The Swans fan didn't say a word. Instead, he reached into his bag again and brought out a lamp. He handed it to his new friend and said softly, 'It's magic, give it a rub.'

The barman did as he was told, and straight away a genie emerged from a cloud of smoke. 'Hello,' said the genie. 'I can grant you only one wish.'

This was exciting. The barman looked at the Swans fan, who simply nodded his head. 'Well, um,' he hesitated, 'I'd like ... I'd like a million bucks!'

The genie looked at him a little strangely, and then waved his arms. Suddenly, a duck walked into the bar, then another and another and another. Soon, you couldn't move for ducks. The barman grabbed the lamp and rubbed it and rubbed it, but nothing happened. Then he turned to the Swans fan and said, 'You know, I think your mate's a little deaf. I said "bucks", not "ducks".'

'And you think I asked for a 12-inch pianist?' replied the Swans fan.

Fast Food

Sam the ruckman was an excellent exponent of his art, but he had a problem — he loved food and was constantly being harassed by his coach about his girth. Still, he got through the season OK, and on the end-of-season trip the lads found a pub out the front of which a sign read: 'Today's special — all the beer you can drink, all the pies you can eat, and all night with the woman of your dreams ... five bucks!'

Sam saw the sign first. He raced into the pub and up to the barman and asked excitedly, 'Are the pies hot?'

Wedded Bliss

Finally, after nearly 30 years, Richmond made the Grand Final, but it was such a surprise that many Tigers fans couldn't get a ticket. In desperation, one supporter put this advertisement in his local newspaper:

> *Man offers marriage to woman who can provide*
> *Grand Final ticket. Offer completely genuine.*
> *Replies must enclose photograph of the ticket.*

Skipping Lunch

The pies gaffe aside, Sam enjoyed a good off-season, but when he turned up for the first training of the new year his coach was ropeable. Rather than let him work with the rest of the team, he sent him straight to the doctor to get a diet prescribed.

'I'd like you to eat normally for two days and then skip a day,' the doctor advised. 'Repeat this for three weeks, and then come back and see me.'

When the ruckman returned, even the doctor was astonished. Sam had lost 25 kilos.

'You lost all that weight simply by following the diet?' the doc asked.

'Absolutely. But I gotta tell you, that third day nearly killed me.'

'What? The hunger?'

'No, the skipping.'

Feelin' Lucky

An AFL club had just fired their head coach halfway through a season, and quickly needed a replacement. The consultant hired to facilitate the employment process ruled that there was no one on the old coaching staff who was capable of turning the top team around, and made the bold suggestion that they should put an advertisement in the 'Positions Vacant' section of the national newspapers. Not surprisingly, hundreds of applications arrived — which was good in one way because it meant that the club now had a vast range of potential coaches to pick from, but bad in another because there really wasn't time to give due consideration to all the applicants.

When the committee sat down to begin the sifting process, the chairman immediately split the applications into two piles and threw the larger pile into the bin.

'What did you do that for?' someone asked.

'We need to avoid unlucky people,' he replied.

Charity Begins at Home

The staff at a high-profile local charity were chatting one day when the fact came up that Hamish Lincoln, player-manager to the stars, whose office was just around the corner, had not donated even one cent in all the years they'd been located close to each other.

The man in charge of celebrity donations decided to give him a call. Unannounced, he knocked on the player-manager's door, and after being ushered into Lincoln's velvet-lined office he said confidently, 'Sir, our research shows that while you earn at least $2 million annually representing sports stars and organising charity nights, you don't actually give anything to charity. Wouldn't you like to give something back to the community, and help those who aren't as lucky as you?'

Lincoln pondered the concept for a moment and then gave the charity worker the same steely stare that he'd given plenty of club chief executives and company sponsorship managers over the years. 'Listen, mate,' he said firmly, 'did your research also tell you that my mother is dying from incurable cancer, and has medical bills hundreds of times her annual pension?'

Embarrassed, the charity worker mumbled, 'Ah ... no ... we didn't know that, but ...'

'And are you aware that my poor brother was an elite VFL player as a teenager — until he was drafted to go to Vietnam? That was the end of him. Now he's severely disabled, almost blind and stuck in a wheelchair.'

The charity worker just wanted the world to end.

He began to offer an apology when Lincoln stood up, and like a lawyer at the High Court, interrupted him indignantly. 'Or that my sister's husband was crushed to death in a car accident that was none of his fault, leaving her broke and battling to raise four beautiful children?'

'I'm sorry, sir, I had no idea …'

Lincoln cut the charity worker off again. 'So if I don't give any money to them,' he sneered, 'why on earth should I give anything to you?'

A Bad Line

Having just moved into his new office, the newly appointed Minister for Sport was keen to impress all around him with his knowledge of all things athletic and his connections in the sporting world. Soon, there was a knock on the door and as he motioned for the young man to enter at the same time he grabbed the telephone and said confidently into the handset, 'Yes, Leigh, I'd be delighted to come up to Brisbane and address the boys. I'm not sure if there's anything I can teach them, but as you know I have picked up a few things about leadership and man management over the years, and I have been watching football since the days when you were winning premierships at Hawthorn, so maybe one or two of my ideas on tactics might appeal to you … excellent … I'll see you then … good to talk to you again, Leigh … goodbye.'

Then the minister looked up at his visitor and said, 'Sorry sonny, just organising a meeting. What do you want?'

'Nothing important, minister,' the man replied. 'I'm just here to connect your phone.'

The Sleepover

It is apparently a true story that after the 1984 Grand Final, the Essendon team partied long into the night. As Paul Salmon relates in his book *Fish Tales*, at 4 a.m. the great footballer Paul Van Der Haar decided he needed a 'bit of a lie-down'.

The next morning, there was a phone call at the club from a family that lived near the Essendon offices at Windy Hill, to say that Van Der Haar was asleep on their couch. They had left the front door open for when their teenage son came home, and the Bombers champion had obviously seen the light on. 'They weren't concerned that he was there,' wrote Salmon of the family, 'they were just worried that someone might be wondering where he was.'

A Simple Explanation

There was this group of young backpackers on a tour bus somewhere in Europe. To kill time between stops, the French guide on the bus asked if someone on the bus could tell every one else a joke, whereupon a girl volunteered to tell a 'Port Adelaide joke'. Straight away, a bloke up the back of the bus cried out, 'That's not fair, I'm a Port Adelaide fan.'

'That's all right,' said the guide, 'we'll explain it to you afterwards.'

Till Death Us Do Part

After many years as Australia's most effective advocate at AFL judiciary hearings, Norman Ashcroft-Jones QC was in horrible trouble. The legal practitioner who had got more footballers off charges after they'd been reported or cited than any other man in history, even when the evidence was totally damning, had been diagnosed with terminal cancer. His specialist had confirmed he only had weeks to live.

Soon after receiving this awful news, Ashcroft-Jones was visited by one of his clients, who was surprised to see the famous lawyer furiously flicking through the Bible. 'What are you doing, Mr Ashcroft-Jones?' the man asked. 'I never saw you as the religious type.'

'Searching for loopholes,' the QC replied.

Pebbles Before the Sand

An AFL coach had built an enviable reputation over the years as a wise philosopher; a motivator who could inspire seemingly ordinary players to do extraordinary things. He'd been successful at every club he'd been with, sometimes turning previously poor teams into champions. Now he was facing his most difficult assignment: he'd signed up as the new coach of last year's wooden spooners.

At the new season's first training session, he asked the coaching staff to bring in a bag full of Sherrins, which he promptly threw in the garbage bin. 'Before we get to football,' he said soberly, 'we have to get our priorities right, we have to get a bit of spirit in this joint. Men, are you with me?'

'Yes sir,' said the players in unison.

The coach then produced a large glass jar from under his desk, and proceeded to fill it with stones, each of which was about five centimetres in diameter. He lifted the jar above his head so every one could see it, and then asked, 'Gentlemen, is this jar full?'

'Yes sir,' roared the players.

The coach said nothing. Instead, he picked up a handful of small pebbles and poured them into the jar. Then he shook the jar lightly and the pebbles fell into the open spaces between the stones.

'Now, gentlemen, is this jar full?'

Some players shouted in the affirmative; others simply nodded their heads. A few said nothing. One or two chuckled, but the coach's stern look soon put a stop to that.

He said nothing. Instead, he produced a small box of sand and poured it into the jar. The sand filled the gaps between the stones and the pebbles. The players stared in amazement; no surprise the man was a 'wonder coach'.

'This jar is your life,' he asserted. 'These stones are the crucial things, the vital things — your health, your family, your friends, the things so precious that if everything else was lost and only they remained, your life would still be full.

'The pebbles represent the other thing that REALLY matters in your life: your FOOTBALL. People say football is more important than life and death, but that's nonsense. However, it is VERY important to us, gentlemen, and we have to give it our full attention.

'The sand is everything else. The little stuff. The stuff that you wouldn't really miss if it didn't happen. Late nights, laziness, junk food, mindless computer games. If you put the sand in your jar first, there will be no room for the pebbles or the stones. If you waste all your time and energy on the small stuff, you will never have room for the things that are crucial to you, and the things that are important to you.

'I need you to pay attention to the things that are critical to your happiness. Play with your children. Love your wives and partners. Take time to get your health right. But you must also focus on your football long before you worry about the little things. Set your priorities …'

Then the coach lifted the full jar again. 'Remember, men,' he shouted, 'the pebbles before the sand.'

At this point, the club's leading ruckman, a tattoo-clad veteran with a reputation as a partygoer, emerged from the back of the room. He had a can of beer in his hand. He walked to the front of the room and took the jar from the new coach. Then he poured his beer into the jar. Of course, the sand absorbed the beer. None of it overflowed.

'What's your point?' asked the coach indignantly.

'No matter how much is going on in your life,' the ruckman answered, 'there will always be room for beer.'

Best on Ground

Two dads are in the outer watching their boys play, when one suddenly says, 'There's no doubt my lad is the best player on the ground.'

'You're probably right,' said his mate. 'I just wish he'd get up once in a while and get involved in the play.'

Winner Takes All

After many centuries of fighting, God decided it was time to try to make peace with the Devil. So he gave him a call, to see if there was any way they could sort out their differences. But talking was no use, and eventually the debate turned to how they might resolve their ongoing conflict once and for all.

'May I propose a game of Australian Football, the national game of Australia?' said the Devil. 'Winner takes all.'

God, as fair as ever, replied, 'Satan, I'm not sure what you're thinking. I have all the best exponents of that fine sport. It wouldn't be a contest.'

'Don't be so sure, God,' the Devil responded with an evil grin. 'I've got all the umpires.'

Three Wise Men

Hamish Lincoln, player-manager to the stars, went on a shooting trip to the country with his lawyer and his stockbroker. Out in the middle of nowhere, their Mercedes broke down. Fortunately, there was a farm nearby, on which was a small house and a fair-sized barn. The farmer let the city slickers use his phone, but unfortunately the local towing company couldn't get anyone out there until the morning. They'd have to stay the night.

That was OK, said the farmer, but he only had two spare beds, so one of the flashy trio would have to sleep in the barn. 'It's all right, gentlemen,' announced the lawyer. 'I grew up on a farm. I'm used to doing it tough with the animals. I'll go out there.'

So every one went to sleep, but after about 15 minutes, there was a banging on the front door of the house. It was the lawyer. 'I'm terribly sorry,' he muttered, 'but it's bloody disgusting out there. Nothing on our farm ever smelled like that. And the animals are crazy. I can't possibly sleep in those conditions.'

'OK then,' said the stockbroker. 'You may not know this, but my father worked in a slaughterhouse. I saw some disgusting things when I used to go to Dad's work, and he brought some horrible smells home with him. There hasn't been an animal born that could intimidate me. I'm sure I can handle it.'

But within 15 minutes, there was another banging at the door. 'It's hell out there,' groaned the stockbroker. 'The stink is ugly, the beasts are frightening. There was nothing in Daddy's slaughterhouse as appalling as that.'

The player-manager just shook his head. 'What a bunch of wimps,' he said. 'I'll sleep out there.'

Fifteen minutes later, there was yet another knock at the front door. It was the barn animals.

Happy Days

Winning the Grand Final wasn't supposed to feel like this. Jack had just woken up with the worst hangover of his life. The previous day he and the boys had won the club's first premiership in 28 years, and boy had they celebrated — at the ground, the club, into the city, God knows where else. 'How the hell did I get home?' he muttered to himself. He bravely put his hand out beside him, but the wife was long out of bed. His head hurt, his throat was the Sahara, he knew he'd throw up eventually. He was wearing only his trousers, and his belt was unbuckled.

Jack forced himself to open his eyes. The first thing he saw was a couple of aspirins next to a glass of water on the bedside table. That was weird enough; what was much weirder was that next to the glass was a single red rose!

Next he forced himself up on an elbow to look around at the carnage that would be his side of the bedroom. But it was spotless. Where were the shoes, socks and shirt he assumed he'd thrown on the floor as he stumbled into bed?

As Jack moved ever so slowly into the bathroom, he saw that the entire house seemed crisp and clean. Sadly, his face didn't match that serenity — a huge black eye was forming on the right side of his face, but what had caused it, he had no idea. In the kitchen, he found his son sitting silently at the table, the coffee maker ready to go, and the Sunday paper, conveniently turned over so he could read the important pages first. On the fridge was a note, written in red and ending with a lipsticked kiss from his wife. 'Honey, I've gone to get the groceries,' the note read. 'I assume you won't feel like breakfast just yet, but I'll cook you some bacon, eggs and sausages when I get back, if that's what you want. I love you.'

Something was terribly wrong. Or so it seemed.

'Hi, Dad,' said his son quietly, as if he was acting under instructions. 'How are you?'

'Son, what happened last night?' Jack asked.

'Well, you came home after 3 a.m., drunk and out of your mind, and you woke the whole house up,' the boy responded. 'You fell over the coffee table in the lounge room and broke it, you watched five minutes of English soccer at full volume and then you puked in the hallway. You got that black eye when you ran into the bedroom door.'

It was all coming back to him. 'So, why is everything so perfect? Your mother even left me a rose, and she never gets me a Weet-Bix in the morning, let alone bacon, eggs and sausages. Is she buttering me up before she kills me?'

'No, you'll be right,' the son explained. 'After you smashed into the door, Mum came out and picked you up and tried to drag you into the bedroom. But you wouldn't let her.'

'I wouldn't?'

'But she got you in, and then she tried to take your clothes off …'

'She did?'

'But when she came to taking your trousers off, you started screaming, "Leave me alone, lady, I'm married!" She hasn't stopped smiling all morning!

Staying Solid

This woman's husband, a former star of the VFL, had been falling into and out of a coma for many weeks, yet she had remained at his bedside day after day. At one point, when he regained consciousness, he beckoned her, his childhood sweetheart, to come closer.

As she sat there, as close as she dared, he choked back tears and whispered, 'My darling, you have been with me all through the bad times. When I got dropped for the Grand Final in my rookie year, you stuck by me. When I lost the Brownlow by one vote, you stayed with me. When I had to retire because of that damn knee, you were there. When the pub went belly-up, you never lost faith in me. Even when we lost the house, and the kids left us, and then there was that drama with the barmaid, you stayed right by my side. Now, with my health failing, you're still here … And you know what?'

'What, dear?' she softly asked, a sad but beautiful smile forming on her lips as her heart began to swell with pride.

'I think you're bad luck.'

Family Feud

A young boy from a family of West Coast Eagles fans turned six and for his birthday his father took him down to the local sports store and said, 'Son, I've got $100 in my pocket. You can have anything you want that all up costs no more than that!'

The boy's face lit up, and he dashed to aisle one while his dad stayed at the checkout, talking to the store manager about the 2006 Grand Final. Unfortunately, though, things went awry when the kid came back with a broad array of Fremantle Dockers merchandise, including a football, T-shirt, socks and poster. The man was horrified, but he had to keep his word, so he paid for the items as discreetly as he could, made his son keep them in the plastic bag all the way home, and just hoped like hell that none of the neighbours saw anything and that nothing had been recorded on the shop's security cameras. If word got out, the embarrassment would kill him.

At home, the boy raced to his room to try on his T-shirt and put up his new poster. Soon after that, his elder sister walked in and asked, 'What are you doing?'

'I've become a Dockers fan,' her brother replied.

This was too much for the girl, who stepped forward, ripped the poster off the wall and smacked him across the head. The boy, in tears, raced down to his parents, but on the way his brother saw the Dockers T-shirt and tripped him so he fell down the stairs. When the birthday boy complained to his mother, the woman spat back, 'You dug your grave, you brat, you lie in it.' And then when he found his dad alone in his shed, rather than sympathy the boy got belted again, this time with a strap. 'I hope you've learnt something from this little stunt of yours,' the father shouted.

'I sure have,' the boy replied tearfully. 'I've only been a Dockers supporter for half an hour and I know that all you Eagles fans are bastards.'

Pushing It

A man and his wife were woken at 3 a.m. by a loud pounding on their front door. The husband got up and staggered to the door, which he opened to see a drunken stranger standing in the pouring rain. The drunk asked if the man could give him a push.

'No, go away,' the man said angrily. 'Don't you know it's three in the morning?' He slammed the door and went back to bed.

'Who was that?' asked his wife.

'Just a piss-pot wanting a push,' he replied.

'Did you help him?' she asked.

'No, I didn't! It's three o'clock in the bloody morning and there's a cyclone raging out there!'

'Well, you sure have a short memory,' said the wife, suddenly wide awake. 'Don't you remember driving home from the MCG last year after your beloved Magpies thrashed Melbourne? Your BMW broke down and it was Demons fans who got out in the rain and helped you. But now it's too dark and too wet for you to do the right thing. You should be ashamed of yourself!'

The man didn't say a word. He got up, dressed and headed out into the storm. At the front gate he looked out, and called into the gloom, 'Hello, are you still there?'

'Yes,' came a voice from behind him — from his own backyard.

'Do you still need a push?' the husband called out.

'Yes, please!'

'Where are you?'

'Over here, on the swing!' replied the drunk.

4. A LEAGUE OF THEIR OWN

Big Animals v Small Animals

While every one knows that the AFL and the NRL have their annual Grand Finals, it is a little-known fact that once a year in the Australian bush the animals have a rugby league Grand Final of their own. It's the annual 'Big Animals' against the 'Small Animals' extravaganza, and this season — just as has occurred every year since the event's inception — the big animals were giving the small ones an absolute hiding. At half time, old Cec the Bandicoot, the Small Animals' coach, was making a passionate speech, trying to rally his tiny charges.

And straight away, it seemed Cec's words had made an impact. Right after the resumption, the Red Kangaroo got the ball but was tackled without making even a metre. From the play-the-ball, the Big Animals' front-rower, the Saltwater Crocodile, charged forward, but was met by a crunching hit for no gain. The Emu dashed from dummy half, but was clipped from behind and fell flat on his beak. When he didn't get up, the referee stopped the clock so the medicos could rush out, while the Small Animals formed an excited huddle.

'Hey fellas,' said the Small Animals' captain, the wily Joe Kookaburra. 'Who stopped the Kangaroo?'

'I did,' whispered Mike the Centipede.

'Who smashed the Crocodile?'

'That was me,' said the Centipede.

'How about the Emu? Who nailed the Emu?'

'Ah, that was me, too,' said Mike.

'That's great play, Mikey,' muttered Joe Kookaburra, 'but where were you when we needed you in the first half?'

'Sorry, skipper,' Mike replied. 'I was getting my ankles taped.'

Team Play

A rugby league side had two excellent goalkickers who used to practise together most nights after training. There was no jealousy or ill-feeling between them; if the coach or captain asked one to take the kicks ahead of the other, then that was just the way things went.

Then, without warning, one of the pair developed a horrible shank in his kicks, and no matter how hard he tried nothing could stop the ball from spearing well wide of the posts. After another kick went all wrong, the poor fellow threw his arms in the air and sighed, 'I guess I'll have to give the kicking away.'

'No, don't do that,' said his good mate. 'I remember once I had a similar problem. Do you know what fixed it? I stopped kicking and started making love to my wife three times a day, seven days a week. Within a fortnight I was back kicking them sweeter than ever. You should try it.'

Two weeks later, the two lads got together for another practice session. And, sure enough, the fellow who had previously been in horrible touch was now striking them beautifully.

'So you followed my advice, eh?' said the 'kick doctor'.

'Yeah, I did,' his friend replied as he piloted another shot right between the posts. 'I enjoyed it. Your wife was really good about it, too.'

Dead Unlucky

The team had a bye, so the two front-rowers decided to go out to the bush on a hunting trip. They'd been out there for hours, and covered plenty of miles with no success, when suddenly the older of the two just collapsed. His mate didn't think he was breathing and he couldn't find a pulse, but luckily, though they were in the middle of nowhere, he could still get some reception on his mobile, and was able to get through on the emergency line.

'My friend is dead! My friend is dead! What can I do?' he shouted.

The operator responded calmly, 'It'll be OK, settle down. The first thing we've got to do is make sure that he is actually dead. Can you do that for me?'

'Right,' the young prop answered.

There was silence for a moment, and then the operator heard the crack of a rifle shot. Back on the phone, the front-rower muttered, 'OK, what next?'

The Lord

The coach of a prominent first-grade team was sitting in his room, head in his hands. His team had once been one of the finest in the land but now they were running last, and the club president had told the coach that if things didn't turn around in a hurry, he'd be out of a job. It seemed that nothing could save him, so he closed his eyes, put his hands together, and prayed: 'Dear Lord, please save me and my team. You are my only hope.'

He might have been imagining things, but he thought he heard a whispered voice say, 'Yes, my son, I will help you.'

A few minutes later, there was a knock at the door. The coach slowly climbed from his chair, stumbled to the door, and opened it to find none other than Andrew Johns standing there with his manager.

'Coach,' Johns said, 'My doc says I'm OK to make a comeback. And I'd like to make that comeback with you. Saving a once great club really appeals to me.'

'Joey, mate,' the coach replied. 'We'd love to have you, but we're right on the salary cap limit. And anyway, I think we'll be OK. The Lord is going to save us.'

So Joey Johns left, a bemused smile on his face. A few minutes later, the club CEO entered the coach's office. 'I've been on the phone to England. The English Rugby League has agreed to send us the entire Great Britain pack for a few games, on a free loan. It'll give them a bit of experience in Aussie conditions. They'll foot the bill, so we can afford it, and some of those Pommie forwards will give us that bit of class and experience we've been missing.'

'No, mate, I can't agree to that,' the coach said. 'I want to stick with the young blokes. I know they'll come good. And don't worry, we've got the Lord on our side.'

The CEO looked at his coach in amazement. Then he shrugged his shoulders and left, but as he walked down the corridor he was almost knocked over by one of the coach's assistants, who ran in with an envelope in his hands. 'Coach, you won't believe this, but one of our supporters just dropped in this envelope. It's the Bulldogs' game plan for this weekend. If we go through this, we'll know everything they're going to throw at us.'

'No, mate, that wouldn't be right,' the coach answered. 'And we don't need to cheat. The Lord will save us.'

The assistant walked out, shaking his head. Two days later, the game was on, and at full time Canterbury had won by 38 points to nil. That night, alone in his office, the coach is both depressed and angry. 'Oh Lord, how could you forsake me?' he cried. 'You said you would help!'

Then, from above, came a voice, 'Geez, mate, what did you want? I offered you Joey Johns, the Great Britain forward pack and the Bulldogs' game plan, but you knocked them all back!'

The Tombstone

A high-profile rugby league referee named George Strange died, and his only friend, his agent, was given the job of organising his tombstone. 'I would like the inscription to read,' the agent said to the manager of the cemetery, '"Here lies Strange, an honest man and a good referee". What'll that cost?'

'We charge by the word,' replied the cemetery boss. 'Perhaps I can save you a little money. Why don't you just say, "An honest man, and a good referee"?'

'But how will they know who it is?' asked the agent.

'Simple, sir. Whenever anyone walks up to the headstone, they'll read it and think, "That's Strange."'

Correct Weight

'I caught a 10-kilo flathead last weekend,' exclaimed Mike, as soon as he arrived at footy training.

'Any witnesses?' his mate Jack replied.

'Plenty,' Mike said, a tinge of sadness coming into his voice. 'If there hadn't been, it would have been 20 kilos!'

Tragedy

This is a true rugby league story. It happened at the Sydney Sports Ground in 1931. It was an Easts home game against Balmain, and at half time in the reserve grade a paperboy started walking around the ground crying, 'Get yer paper! News of terrible Balmain tragedy! Afternoon paper! Paper!'

Naturally, a number of Balmaniacs rushed to get the latest news, but when they searched for the big story they couldn't find anything. Thinking they'd been dudded, they rushed after the paperboy and said, 'Hey, kid, where's that Balmain tragedy story?'

'Have a look at the stop press,' the lad replied. 'It's got the final score in the third grade.'

Easts had thrashed Balmain in the thirds by 23 to nil. The beaten fans were not amused.

Cold Comfort

During the 1967–68 Kangaroo tour, the Australians were required to play Rochdale on a cold, wet night. Outside the ground were two young boys, soaked to the skin and clinging firmly to their autograph books. They didn't have enough money to get in and watch the game, but they still hoped to obtain a couple of prized signatures. Perhaps because of the night, most people had left it late to arrive, so there was a traffic jam outside the main gates. Suddenly the boys saw what looked like the Kangaroos' team bus stuck in the queue of cars waiting to get into the parking station. They ran towards it and knocked hopefully on the front door. Their dream was that the driver would take their autograph books and hand them on to the players before the bus moved inside.

Better than that, after consulting with the team's management, the driver motioned the boys in out of the pouring rain. The books were duly passed on to the players, and then the bus started moving. Of course, the driver could have kicked the two boys off, but he didn't. Instead, he told them to keep their heads down, and they ended up not only getting the autographs of all the footballers on the bus, but watching the game in style as well!

Courage

The boss was angry. His staff had been abusing their sick leave entitlements and the most flagrant example had occurred only yesterday. He had asked for Jason Jackson to be marched into his office, but who was this fellow in the flash suit walking in with him?

'Good morning, sir,' said the 'suit'. 'My name is Hamish Lincoln, player-manager to the stars. I am looking after young Jackson's sporting career.'

'Why are you here?'

'I believe there is a problem with the boy's work?'

'Well,' said the boss, 'there is. I'm having problems with my workers taking days off and claiming them as sick leave. Yesterday, Jackson called in ill, yet this morning his photo is in the sports pages of the paper, scoring the winning try in yesterday's junior rep final. I'm afraid I'm going to have to make an example of him and give him the boot.'

'Good man, don't you think you are a little quick to judge?' asked Lincoln.

'I am?'

'I ask you to think of Phar Lap winning the Melbourne Cup after gangsters tried to murder him. Or Grant Hackett winning gold medals when suffering from a collapsed lung, John Sattler playing in a Grand Final with a broken jaw and Steve Waugh scoring a hundred on one leg. This kid got off his deathbed to do his bit for the team …

'Imagine how well he would have played if he'd been 100 per cent fit!'

Always Keep your Glass by your Bed

The old rugby league front-rower was lying in bed one night and was just about asleep, when his wife rolled closer and whispered, 'Remember how you used to hold my hand when we were younger?'

Wearily, the former champion moved his arm towards her and held her hand for at least a second or two. And then he tried to get to sleep.

It was no use, though. A few moments later, she said, 'Remember how you used to kiss me?'

A little annoyed, he leant across and gave her a gentle peck on the cheek. 'Good night, dear,' he said.

Maybe a full minute went by. Then she cooed, 'Remember how you used to nibble my neck?'

With that, the husband angrily tossed back the blankets and — as recklessly as he could — jumped out of bed.

'Where are you going?' she cried.

'To find my teeth.'

The Lighter Side

Easts was walking along the street with Penrith when he reached into his pocket and pulled out a packet of cigarettes. Straight away, Penrith offered a lighter.

'How come you don't carry matches?' Easts asked.

'I'm always losing matches,' Penrith replied.

The Graduate

A man had been enrolled at the rugby league academy for five years — easily the longest time anyone had stayed there — and still it seemed he had no chance of graduating.

Eventually, the head of the academy called him in. 'Son,' he began, 'I've been going through your reports and speaking to the coaches and tutors. The said truth is you don't have the physical capabilities to be a decent rugby league footballer. You're not quick enough, tough enough, skilful enough, strong enough. You have no feel for the game, no nous, the game just seems to pass you by. You can't count. Your sense of anticipation is negative, you don't get along with the other players, we can't teach you anything, and you've got that damn awful habit of getting obsessed with some trifling matter while important things are happening right before your eyes.'

'What are we going to do?' the player asked mournfully.

'I'm recommending that you become a first-grade referee.'

Spewing 'Blood'

As the great Arthur Beetson recalled in his autobiography *Big Artie*, the atmosphere was tense, befitting the occasion — an important game at the Sydney Cricket Ground in the early 1970s. The

Eastern Suburbs team had just made its way onto the field. As John Peard, the Easts five-eighth, jogged to his position for the kick-off he was stunned to see his captain, Beetson, throwing up. It was coming out bright red.

'Geez, Beetson, you'd better go back in … you're spewing blood,' Peard advised.

'It's all right, mate,' came the reply, from a man with a reputation for having a healthy appetite. 'It's just the Cherry Ripes I had last night.'

Ultimate Revenge

The manager of a prominent rugby league player received a call saying that one of his stars from an interstate club had got himself in serious trouble, and that the player-manager was needed there immediately. He asked his secretary to book him on the earliest available flight, packed his briefcase and had just enough time to call his wife before the cab arrived to get him to the airport.

When he rang home, the couple's new maid answered. 'Hello, look, I don't have time to chat, I'd like to speak to my wife immediately, please,' the manager spat down the line.

'Ah, um …' the maid hesitated. 'She, ah … she can't come to the phone right now.'

'Is she there or not?' the player-manager shouted. 'Put my wife on now, please.'

'I'm sorry, sir, I cannot lie to you.' The maid burst into tears. 'Your wife is upstairs in your bedroom with a footballer.'

The player-manager was furious. 'I want you to go to my office, take the revolver out of the top drawer of my desk, and I want you to go upstairs and shoot that cheating bitch and her bastard boyfriend.'

Of course, the maid protested but the player-manager was now beside himself with rage. He yelled down the line that under local law such a crime was legal, given his wife's adultery, and that, as his servant, the maid had to do as he'd ordered. If she didn't, he could get her deported. So the maid put down the phone, and soon after the player-manager heard a shout and a woman's scream, and then two shots were fired. After a short break, the maid returned to the phone.

'It's done,' she wept.

'Excellent work! And what have you done with the bodies?' the player-manager asked.

'I threw them in the pool,' the maid replied.

'The pool?'

'Yes, sir, in the pool,' the maid sobbed.

'But we don't have a pool,' the manager said somewhat sheepishly. 'What number is this?'

Safe Houses

The best player from a Sydney-based team wasn't very bright, but he was the best player so it came as a great disappointment when he put in a transfer request. He wanted to move to the North Queensland Cowboys, he said. Why? He'd read that 80 per cent of accidents occur within five kilometres of home, so he thought if he moved to Townsville he'd be a lot safer.

Jury Duty

Mrs Thompson was called up for jury duty but asked to be excused because she didn't endorse capital punishment. 'I don't want my personal prejudices to impinge on the proper running of the court,' she said.

The judge admired her ethics, but said, 'Madam, this is not a murder trial. It's a simple civil lawsuit. A Manly supporter painted the message "Tigers can't play" on the walls of the Balmain Leagues Club, and the club has sued the perpetrator for damages.'

Mrs Thompson had been an avid Balmain fan for 50 years. She even liked the Wests Tigers. And she hated the Sea Eagles. 'I see your point, your honour,' she said. 'And I guess I could be wrong about capital punishment.'

Snow White

A little-known sequel to the story of *Snow White and the Seven Dwarfs* is that when the Princess left for her new life with her new man, the dwarfs gave her a camera as a farewell present. Now as well as owning a magnificent castle, her boyfriend was also the first-grade captain and president of the local rugby league club, so when it came time for the annual team photographs to be organised, Snow White was quick to volunteer to take the happy snaps. This she did — the camera worked perfectly — and afterwards she headed cheerfully through the forest and into town to get the film developed.

'Not a problem, dear,' the chemist said. 'Come back in six days and they'll be ready for you to pick up.' (You have to remember that back in these medieval times, the film had to be sent to a photolab in the big city to be processed.)

Six days later she returned to collect her photos, but sadly they had not arrived. This happened again the next day, and the next, by which time Snow White was extremely depressed. She was so keen to impress her boyfriend, and things just weren't working out. She stood there sobbing, her tears falling on the counter. The chemist felt terribly sorry for her, but there was nothing he could do.

'Don't worry, Princess.' He smiled as he put a comforting hand on her shoulder. 'Some day your prints will come.'

A Talking Dog

One day at Australian rugby league team training, a dog walked up to the Australian captain Darren Lockyer, put his front legs on his hips, and said,

'G'day, mate, any positions vacant around here at the moment?'

Lockyer looked at the dog with a slightly incredulous look on his face and said, 'No, mate, you'd be better off trying the circus.'

'The circus? What use would they have for a lock forward?' replied the canine.

A Fairy Tale

'Twas was the week before Christmas, and Santa Claus, a scrupulous player-manager and a respected referee walked through the foyer of a city hotel. Suddenly, a $20 note blew in. Who picked it up?

Santa Claus, of course. Every one knows there's no such thing as scrupulous player-managers and respected referees.

Follow the Leader

On her first day as a school teacher in the south-western suburbs of Sydney, Miss Maybury explained to her class that she was a fan of the local Wests Tigers rugby league team and she invited her students to raise their hands if they were Wests Tigers fans, too. The kids were only seven and eight years old, and this was the start of a new year with a brand new teacher, so they wanted to impress and they enthusiastically shot their hands into the air. That is, all but one. Little Nikki Goodwin refused to follow the leader.

'Excuse me, dear, what's the matter?' Miss Maybury asked when she noticed that Nikki's hand had stayed down. 'Why are you different?'

'I'm not a Wests Tigers fan,' Nikki said shyly.

'Oh, aren't you,' the teacher said, a little condescendingly. 'Then what are you?'

'I'm a St George fan,' the tiny girl answered a little proudly.

'But why are you a St George fan? What happened to you?'

'My dad is a St George fan, and so is my sister. So I'm a St George fan, too.'

'But, Nikki, that's no reason. You should make up your own mind. What if your dad didn't know anything about football, and your sister didn't know anything about football. What would you be then?'

'Then,' Nikki said, 'I'd be a Wests Tigers fan.'

One Last Shot

When the great Tommy Raudonikis came to Western Suburbs from Wagga Wagga in 1969 he was a fresh-faced kid, and before his debut game in first grade, his captain, the ultra-tough veteran prop Noel 'Ned' Kelly, came up to him and offered some advice. 'Son, those blokes out on the sidelines with the big bags are photographers,' Kelly said. 'Before you go out on the field today, ask one of them to take your photo.'

'Why?' Raudonikis asked innocently.

'Because you ain't never going to be as good looking as you are today,' Kelly explained.

The Impossible Dream

A clean-living 40-year-old Canberra Raiders supporter was walking in the park in front of Old Parliament House, deep in prayer. Suddenly the sky was filled with dark storm clouds, and in a booming voice God himself said, 'As you have been faithful to me, I will grant you one wish.'

The Raiders fan responded, 'Lord, please build a new road from Canberra to the coast and then a bridge to Fiji so my wife and I can drive there for a holiday whenever we want.'

The Lord said, 'Son, your request is very materialistic. And think of the enormity of the undertaking — the supports required to reach the bottom of the Pacific! ... the concrete and steel it would take! ... the human lives that I would have to protect as the bridge was constructed ... it would almost exhaust all of the natural resources and take up so much of my attention. It is hard for me to justify your desire for such a worldly thing. Take a little more time and think of something that will truly honour and glorify me.'

The man thought about it for a long time. Finally, he said, 'Lord, I see where you're coming from. Instead, I wish that you could allow my beloved Raiders to win another Grand Final in my lifetime.'

The Lord replied, 'You want two lanes on that bridge or four?'

Prognosis: Negative

A footballer was badly injured in a game and that night he was in intensive care with all sorts of tubes and machines attached to him. Eventually, the doctor came in and though heavily sedated the patient was able to get out a few agonised words.

'Doc,' he said, 'do you think I'll recover?'

'Your chances are excellent,' replied the doctor, prompting the footballer to heave a sigh of relief and a slight smile to form on his face.

'History shows that nine out of 10 people suffering your condition end up dying,' the doctor continued. 'You're the 10th person I've treated who's been this way. The other nine have died. On that basis, you should be OK.'

Like Grandfather Like Grandson

One day when was he was very young, little Eddie announced he wanted to play rugby league for Australia … just like his 'Pop' did. Everyone in the family was thrilled, but no one more than Eddie's grandfather, who took the boy aside to give him some advice: 'Every morning at breakfast,' Pop said quietly but firmly, 'put a dash of gunpowder in your cereal. That way you'll grow up to be big and strong like me.'

Little Eddie did as he was told. From that day on, as soon as woke, he snuck out to his dad's garage and found some gunpowder, and then he came back into the kitchen and sprinkled it on his Corn Flakes. Sure enough, he did go on to play league for Australia. After that, he went on the professional wrestling circuit, played on the US Seniors golf tour, and was running marathons well into his eighties. He kept secret the fact he was following his Pop's advice right up till the day he died, aged 103, when his heart gave out while he was powerlifting at the gym.

At his funeral, Eddie left his 19-year-old third wife, eight surviving children, 29 grandchildren, countless great-grandchildren and a 50-metre wide crater in the grounds of the crematorium.

Be Careful

A husband and wife were in bed together. She was reading a book while he was watching his beloved Manly on the TV, when suddenly she put the novel down and asked, 'Darling, if I died tomorrow, would you get married again?'

'No, dear,' the husband replied, keeping one eye on a replay of a disputed try. 'I love you too much to even think about getting married to a different woman.'

'But you love being married, don't you?'

'Yes, of course,' said the husband.

'So, honestly, you'd get remarried wouldn't you?'

The man sighed. He wanted to watch the football, so he decided this was a situation where it would be easier to say what his wife wanted to hear. 'Yeah, I guess I would get remarried eventually.'

'Would you and your new wife live in our house?'

'I guess.'

'Would you let her wear my clothes?'

'If they fitted, I guess I would. You have such good taste. It would be a shame to see some of those classy outfits go to waste. Though, darling, no woman could ever look as good in them as you do.'

'Would you let her wear my shoes?'

'Same story. Don't be silly, dear.'

'Would you take down all the pictures of me and you together?'

'I'd have to, I suppose. But I'd keep our photos in my private drawer.'

He went back to the TV, and she to her book. Soon after, Manly went in for a try, and the husband cheered. The woman looked up, and then asked, 'Would your new wife go with you to the Grand Final like I've always done?'

'No, she's a Cronulla fan,' he muttered, his attention focused on the replay. 'Grand Finals don't interest her.'

Chopped Out

Back in the late 1970s, the old Newtown club was run by the multi-millionaire businessman John Singleton. The club was on its last legs, but with Singleton's backing it enjoyed one last shot at glory, as a group of high-profile players signed with the club and eventually made the 1981 Grand Final. An irony was that one of the members of the Parramatta team who beat Newtown in that game was the great centre Mick Cronin, who Singo had tried ever so hard to lure to his club. In the book *Whatd'yareckon!*, he recalled how he offered to double whatever money Cronin was then earning, and at the start of the '81 season he also offered to make available his helicopter to get Cronin to and from training and games. Cronin was the publican at the Gerringong Hotel, a good two hours south of Sydney, and had been making the journey by car.

'Mate, I hate to tell you but I love driving and I really hate helicopters. They scare the shit out of me.'

Cronin kept motoring to Parra, and appeared in five Grand Finals between 1981 and 1986. Newtown played two more seasons, 1982 and 1983, and was then booted out of the premiership for good.

5. THEY'RE RACING!

A Day at the Races

A father takes his four-year-old daughter to the races. At one point, they head down to the mounting yard — ostensibly so Dad can give his little girl a close-up look at the horses, but actually, of course, so he can check on the fitness of the favourite. As they're watching the thoroughbreds parade past them, one of the horses stops and leaves a large, warm pile of droppings on the grass.

'Dad,' the girl asks innocently, 'where does poo come from?'

Where does poo come from? the man thinks to himself. This is one of those situations where a parent has to think quickly, because a wrong answer could scar a child for life. *Where does poo come from …*

'Well, my dear,' he says, 'can you remember when you had breakfast this morning?'

'Yes, Dad.'

'Well, the food we eat goes down our throats and into our tummies. Then, our bodies use all the good things in the food to keep us healthy, while all the bad things come out of our bottoms and go into the toilet. Those bad things are poo.'

The little girl looks devastated. She stares at her father, then at the steaming pile of horse droppings in front of her. Then she puts her little hand to her throat and then down to her tummy. A few more seconds pass, her eyes tear up, and then she asks, 'And Tigger?'

Bad Timing

In 1882, a former premier of Tasmania named Mr Thomas Reibey was the owner of two horses with some chance in the Melbourne Cup: the four-year-old Stockwell and three-year-old Bagot. He decided to seek the opinion of a psychic as to his two horses' chances in the big race, and was told that Bagot would win the Cup.

This was no good, because he and his friends had backed Stockwell, so he scratched his younger horse, watched Stockwell run second to The Assyrian and then sold Bagot to Mr J.O. Inglis, who promptly renamed the colt Malua. In 1884, Malua won the Cup, which sort of proved the fortune teller right.

Just Wondering ...

Which leads us to the question ...

How come we've never seen the newspaper headline: 'PSYCHIC WINS MILLIONS ON MELBOURNE CUP!'

Unlucky

The jockey took the favourite to the lead from the jump in the Melbourne Cup and by the time they reached the winning post for the first time he was already six lengths in front. Down the back, he led by 10 and he was still well clear as they approached the final straight.

At the 400, the lead was still around four lengths, and he was a length and a half clear at the 200. But then, out of nowhere, he and his horse were struck by a box of biscuits, a small bottle of wine and a satchel of nuts and crackers. He managed to keep his mount balanced, but then they were struck by some chocolates, dried fruit, cashews, potato chips and half a dozen mince pies. By the time he recovered, half the field had dashed past him and the Cup was lost.

In their report on the race, stewards commented that the favourite was severely hampered just after he passed the 200-metre pole.

A Day at the Zoo

Little Jordan and his sister Olivia kept nagging their father to take them to the zoo, but Dad wouldn't be in it until one day their mother got sick of all the crying and said, 'For God's sake, George, please take them. It can't be that hard to have one day out with your own kids!'

So off the three of them went, and they didn't come home until around 6pm, when George pushed the children through the front door, gave his wife a kiss on the cheek and handed her some flowers, and then headed straight down to the pub. Soon the two little ones were sitting at the kitchen table, talking to mother.

'What did you think of the zoo?' Mum asked.

'It was pretty boring, all the animals looked the same,' said Jordan.

'Really,' replied Mum, 'that doesn't sound right. What did your father think of it?'

'He was really quiet at first,' said Olivia. 'But then one of the animals won at 25–1 and he was pretty happy after that.'

Position Vacant

A man applied for a job at the racing stables, and was granted an interview. After a couple of general questions about straw and bridles, the trainer enquired, 'Are you any good at shoeing horses?'

'Dunno, to be honest,' the applicant replied. 'But I once told a pony to piss off.'

Deepest Sympathy

Jack and Harry were just about to cross the road to walk into Moonee Valley for a Wednesday meeting when a funeral procession went past them. It was quite impressive, too — a big, black hearse complete with coffin and wreaths and then about 30 or 40 cars, all with their headlights blazing.

When the last car went past, Jack strolled across the road to the course entrance, but when he reached the other side he stopped and turned, and saw his friend had taken his hat off and was standing to attention, head bowed with his headwear over his heart. He didn't move until the procession was totally out of view. Only then did he scurry towards the turnstiles.

'That was quite a gesture, Harry,' his colleague said when they finally got into the course.

'Oh, it was the least I could do,' Harry replied softly. 'It's true she never liked racing, but she was a good wife and I was married to her for 40 years.'

Alley Oop

A hurdle jockey accepted a last-minute ride on a galloper he'd never seen before, trained by a man he'd never met. Before the race he received some bizarre instructions from the trainer, the sort of advice that jockeys listen to intently, and then forget as soon as they're out on the track. 'All you need to know with this horse,' the trainer had told him, 'is that every time you approach a jump, you have to shout out "Alley oop!" if you want to get over.'

The race begins and as they approach the first hurdle, all the jockey can think of is, *I am not going to shout at this horse*. What would his mates think? So instead he kept quiet, and the horse simply ploughed through the barrier and was lucky to stay on its feet. Same thing happened at the second jump, so at the third the rider decided to compromise. He leant down on the horse's mane and whispered, 'Alley oop,' and the horse managed to lift his feet a few centimetres off the ground. At the next, he spoke a little louder and the horse jumped a little higher, so at the fifth barrier he shouted for all his worth and the horse flew higher than any Grand National winner. This continued for the rest of the race, as horse and rider came from tailed off to take the lead at the half furlong, and win going away.

Back at the bar afterwards, the trainer was congratulating the jockey on his winning ride. 'It was a tough one,' the rider conceded. 'I just wish you'd told me the horse was deaf.'

'Deaf?' the trainer responded. 'He's not deaf. He's blind!'

Time to Pray

A few weeks later, the same jockey got another last-minute ride on a different horse for a different trainer at a different track, this one located not far from the Pacific Ocean. This time it was a flat race (no hurdles), but the instructions were eerily similar. 'He is a very religious galloper this one,' the trainer explained. 'You have to say "Thank God" to get him to go and "Amen" to make him stop.'

'No problems,' said the jockey. 'These sort of horses are my speciality.'

When the starter sent the field on its way, the jockey cried out, 'Thank God!' and his mount jumped to a three-length lead. For the rest of the race, he kept purring 'Thank God' into the horse's ear and he kept increasing his margin until at the post he was 10 lengths in front. It was one of the easiest wins ever seen at the track, but in the excitement the jockey forgot what he had to say to get the horse to stop. So they kept going, past the bemused spectators, through the car park, onto the main road, down the highway and all the way out to the cliffs. After that, all that was left was a 50-metre drop to the sea below. They were only metres away from catastrophe when he finally remembered. 'Amen! Amen! Amen!' he cried, and the horse pulled up just centimetres from the cliff's edge.

'Thank God,' said the jockey.

Dead and Deader

A smart bookmaker from the city decided to go on a bush holiday and take one of the horses he owned with him. When he got to town, he made enquiries about the upcoming Saturday meeting and was told that if he wanted to set up as a bookie for the day he was most welcome. So he entered his horse for the feature race on the program, and went along to do his best.

He was a little surprised to see that he was one of only four bookmakers operating on the local meeting, and a bit disgusted when he saw that all three of his colleagues put up his horse as an odds-on favourite in a field of five when it came time for the race of the day. *Bugger this*, he thought, and he got word out to his jockey that he wanted his galloper to lose. Then he put up 2–1 odds about the horse, and started writing bets.

Eventually, a toffee-nosed character came up and said, 'I'm surprised you're laying the favourite. It's won at Flemington, you know.'

'You're right, sir,' the city slicker replied. 'But you've got to back your judgment in this game. Would you like a wager, perhaps?'

'I think I would,' the gentleman said. 'Will you give me $20,000 to $10,000 about the favourite?'

There was no way he could balance his book with a bet like that at a place like this, but, really, what do they say about a fool and his money? 'Certainly, sir,' the bookie responded in an appropriately sombre tone.

Soon after, the race was on, and it was never in doubt — the bookie's horse led all the way, winning by four lengths in a ridiculously slow time. He could hardly believe it, and was in a filthy mood when the gentleman came to collect his winnings.

'You might think you're clever, mate,' he snorted, 'but the truth is you're a mug. You didn't know I was the owner of that horse and it was running dead. It should never have won.'

'Actually, I did know,' the man replied as he counted his cash. 'What you didn't know was that I owned the other four horses in the field, and they were even deader.'

Seeing Straight

A trainer took his prized greyhound to the vet and said, 'Doc, he's not chasing the bunny like he used to. A mate of mine reckons it might be his eyesight. Is there anything you can do to help him?'

'Let's have a look,' said the vet.

He picked the dog up and looked straight in his eyes. Then he checked his teeth, even lifted him high and stared intently at his chest and belly. Finally, he muttered, 'I'm sorry, I'm going to have to put him down.'

'What, because he's going blind?'

'No, because he's very heavy.'

An Eye for Breeding

A horse trainer went to an eye doctor, and it was discovered that he could hardly read the top line of the chart, let alone the bottom ones. 'I'm afraid you need glasses,' he was told.

'All right then,' the trainer replied, 'what do you recommend?'

'These will suit you,' said the optometrist, as she placed a classy pair of spectacles over his eyes. 'And only $200.'

'Whoa! That's way too expensive!' cried the trainer.

'But they're bi-focal,' said the optometrist.

'I don't care if they're by Danehill. Two hundred dollars is way too much.'

The Tale of Captain Paddle

A true story ... in the spring of 1876, the SS *City of Melbourne* sailed for Melbourne with 12 classy thoroughbreds aboard, among them the ruling Melbourne Cup favourite. South of Jervis Bay, on the NSW south coast, a storm hit but for too long the wonderfully named Captain Paddle, the ship's skipper, refused to take shelter. Only one horse survived — a promising unnamed colt that had already won the AJC Derby and which was later given the rather apt title of 'Robinson Crusoe' — and Captain Paddle was condemned by all but the bookmakers, who'd made a fortune owing to the fact that all the horses were now out of the upcoming big races such as the Derby and the Cup. When Paddle made it to Melbourne, the bookies presented him with a cash prize as a token of their appreciation for the role he played in the catastrophe.

The Dead Greyhound

The greyhound trainer carried his favourite dog into the vet's surgery. The dog seemed lifeless, and the trainer had tears in his eyes. 'I found him this morning, doc,' he explained. 'He was just lying in his bed. Can you help him?'

The vet grabbed his stethoscope and put it to the greyhound's chest, then shook his head and looked up at the trainer. 'I'm sorry, Ron,' he said quietly, 'your champion is gone. He's dead, passed away.'

'Are you sure?' asked the trainer. 'You seemed to draw that conclusion a bit quickly for my liking.'

'I'm sorry …'

'How can you be so sure? He might be in a coma or a deep sleep or something.'

The vet shook his head. He looked at the trainer and realised he'd need some convincing. So he walked out to his back office, and then came back with a Labrador dog on a lead. He motioned to the Labrador, and he stood up on his hind legs, put his front paws on the examination table and sniffed at all parts of the greyhound. He then looked at the vet and the trainer with mournful eyes and shook his head. The vet patted the Labrador and then returned him to the back room.

When the vet came back, he had a cat in his arms. The cat also sniffed the greyhound from nose to butt, even nudged at the dog's head with her nose, before sitting back on her haunches, meowing softly, and shaking her head.

'I'm sorry, Ron,' said the doctor. 'But this is most definitely a dead, deceased, demised greyhound.'

With that, he went to his computer, clicked a few keys, hit the print button and then handed an invoice to the greyhound trainer. 'You'll find another good one, Ron. Be strong,' he said.

The trainer had a soft tear running down his cheek. Then he looked at the bill. 'Geez!!' he cried. 'You've charged me $300 to tell me my dog is dead!'

The vet shrugged his shoulders. 'I am sorry,' Ron,' he said. 'If you'd taken my word for it, it would have set you back 25 bucks. But lab reports and cat scans are expensive these days; that's why it's cost you $300.'

Out of Line

They were just about to go into line for the final of the Inter Dominion Pacing Championship at the Harold Park trotting track in Sydney, when one of the horses farted. 'Sorry about that, fellas,' shouted out the driver with a grin.

'That's all right,' replied one of his rivals. 'We thought it was your horse.'

The Only Dangers

It was a new chief steward's first day, and he was determined to make his mark. Before the first race, he had his eyes and binoculars focused on the mounting yard, waiting (and hoping) to see something untoward. And then it happened — he was sure he saw one of the trainers slip something into the mouth of his horse.

'Oi, you,' shouted the new chief steward. 'What did you do then? I saw you give your horse something.'

'No, sir,' asserted the trainer, 'it was just a cube of sugar. Old Jack here loves his sugar. There's nothing in it. See, I'll even have a cube myself.'

And the trainer popped a sugar cube in his mouth.

'Look, mate, it's not that simple,' said the steward. 'Here, give me one of those.' He swallowed one of the sugar cubes whole. 'I'll soon find out if there's anything in them.'

Soon after that, the jockeys came out, and as the trainer legged his rider onto his horse, he muttered, 'Listen, son, this horse is a certainty. Get him back third or fourth early, and then take off as soon as you hit the straight. If you hear anything coming up from behind, don't worry. It'll either be me or the new chief steward.'

Needs More Ground

The trainer and the jockey were talking after the race about their horse, which though well-bred had just finished well back in a race over 2400 metres. 'He was just getting warm at the finish,' said the jockey. 'I think he'll run two miles.'

'That's good,' the trainer replied. 'But how long will it take him?'

Still, the guys in the press box were somehow impressed by the run, and they were keen to tip the horse to anyone who would listen when his next race was over the 3200 metres (two miles by the old measure). Their confidence was boosted even further when the trainer was interviewed. 'He'll walk it in,' he said.

Which is exactly what happened — only trouble was all the other horses were still galloping, so he finished 20 lengths last. Afterwards, those same reporters asked whether the trainer was disappointed.

'Not really,' he replied. 'It took 12 horses to beat him.'

A Walk-up Start

A couple of Sydney-based punters bought into a pretty good greyhound, and then came up with a devilish scheme to make a dollar or two. They found a race out at Bathurst, maybe three hours' drive out of the city, where their 'dish-licker' was likely to start as an odds-on favourite, another greyhound would be 6–4, and the rest of the field would be 10–1 or longer. If they could stop their dog, they reasoned, the second favourite would be a certainty.

Their drive from home to track took about six hours, because every 20 minutes they'd stop, get the dog out and give it a long drink and a walk around. Then, when they got about 15 minutes out of Bathurst, they stopped and took the dog for another walk, this one at some pace and at least five kilometres long. The poor thing was exhausted by the time it got to the boxes, its only rival was backed in to 5–2 on, and the new owners looked pretty pleased with themselves as they found a vantage point near the rail to watch the race.

Later, one of them was asked how the plan unfolded. 'Walk wasn't long enough,' was all he said.

6. RUCKIN' GOOD YARNS

Pass me a Dictionary

The coach was explaining that in this modern world of sophisticated rugby, the team needed code words out on the field so that the opposition would not know what was going on. So this was the plan: if the captain wanted the team to move the ball to the left, he would shout out a word beginning with the letter P. If he wanted to move the ball to the right, he would yell out a word beginning with the letter D. Did every one understand?

One of the coaches, a former rugby league international, asked if this system might cause a problem. What if a player gets confused?

'Son,' replied the coach, 'this is rugby union. We're all educated people here.'

First game, and the system seemed to be working brilliantly. Then, at a scrum on halfway, the captain cried out, 'Physics.'

The half-back looked at his No. 10 and said, 'Phuck, what do we do now?'

The Fox Hat

The Wallabies were on tour in New Zealand, and found themselves in a town called Kaitangata, which is located about halfway between Dunedin and Invercargill on the South Island. It was bitterly cold, and the Australians were in the foyer of their hotel waiting to head off for a function, when their captain emerged wearing the official team uniform, including blazer and tour tie, but also, bizarrely, a strange piece of headwear that appeared to have been made from the hide of a fox. It was something Davy Crockett might have worn, complete with flashy tail down the back.

The players could hardly keep a straight face, and then one of them said, 'Hey, skipper, what's with the fancy beanie?'

'Well, before we left Australia,' the captain responded, 'I was called into the ARU offices and one of the big-wig administrators asked me where the first official dinner of the tour was being held. "Kaitangata," I replied, and he said, "Wear the fox hat."'

Improper Advice

It was late in the 1991 World Cup final at Twickenham, and the Wallabies were leading 12–6 over England, but the Poms were mounting a last desperate attack. Finally, Australia got hold of the ball in their own quarter, and from halfway, and high up in the grandstands, coach Bob Dwyer shouted out some advice …

'Kick it to the bloody shithouse!'

'There was no way any of the Wallabies could hear me,' Dwyer recalled in his autobiography, *Full Time*, 'but those within immediate range — including Her Majesty Queen Elizabeth II — certainly could.'

Good Question

The boys were on an Irish tour when the bus driver announced over the intercom, 'And now, gentlemen, we are passing the biggest pub in all Ireland.'

'Why?' came a voice from down the back.

A Can of Worms

The rugby coach was concerned about the drinking habits of some of his players. He didn't want to single anyone out, so instead he called all the players into the dressing room and explained that he was going to teach them a lesson. He stood behind a table, on which he had placed a glass of water, a glass of beer and what appeared to be two worms in a jar.

'Now, lads,' began the coach, 'I want you to observe closely as I put one of these worms in the glass of water.'

With that, he put the invertebrate in the water, and

every one watched closely as it swam happily around the liquid.

'Now,' the coach continued, 'observe the second worm in the glass of beer.'

The players moved close to the table and watched as the worm struggled for a few moments, and then sank, dead, to the bottom of the glass.

'What does this tell you about what alcohol can do to you?' the coach asked triumphantly, to which Scotty, the young half-back, responded …

'If you drink beer, you won't get worms!'

The Electron 2000

Doug decided he needed a new television, so he went to his local electrical goods shop, walked up to a sales assistant and asked to be shown the latest models.

'Certainly, sir,' said the salesperson, 'we've got all the latest technology here, but you look like a man who'd like the Electron 2000.'

'What's so special about the Electron 2000?'

'Well, for starters, you don't need a remote control!'

Doug was confused, for his old remote control was just about his closest friend. He couldn't imagine life without it. 'What do you mean, no remote control?' he asked, clearly unconvinced.

But a smile slowly spread across his face as it was explained how the new set worked. 'Watch this,' the sales assistant explained. 'All I have to do is look at the

TV and say clearly, "Nine", and Channel Nine will come on.' With that, the television changed to Channel Nine.

'Rugby league,' the salesperson said, and the TV switched to coverage of the latest NRL game. 'Cricket,' he uttered, and the TV changed back to the Test match from the Gabba. 'Baseball,' and ESPN was showing a replay of the Cardinals' triumph in the 2006 World Series. 'Racing,' and the two men were able to watch the last from Caulfield.

Doug looked on in wonder. 'How much does it cost?' he asked.

'For you, sir, only $23,000.'

'Twenty-three thousand!' he shouted as he looked again at the TV. 'Preposterous!!!'

Suddenly, the television switched to a highlights package of the Queensland Reds' 2007 Super 14 campaign.

Coasting

A rugby forward went to the pub and bought himself a beer, and then another, and another and another. Eventually, just after he'd bought his eighth drink, he needed to go to the toilet, but he didn't like the idea of leaving his almost-full glass for some other bludger to pinch. So he grabbed a coaster, and wrote on the back, 'I spat in this beer, do not drink!' Then he put the coaster on the top of his glass and stumbled confidently to the gents.

When he returned, he saw that his beer was still full but that some clown had put another coaster on top of his. On it was written, 'So did I!'

For Whom The Bell Tolls

One of the great traditions of the Upper Gulargambone Rugby Club was its huge bell that was rung to signify half time and full time in the four grades every Saturday. None of those modern sirens for the rugby men from Upper Gulargambone!

For 27 years, the same club stalwart rang the bell, but sadly he died from a shock heart attack and the club urgently needed a replacement. Inevitably, there were many people who wanted the job, but the most intriguing applicant was a small man who had no arms. *This'll be good*, the members of the selection committee thought to themselves. *How can an armless man ring such a big bell?* Still, he had many references from footy clubs far and wide, so they took him up to the bell tower on top of the scoreboard, and asked him to give it his best shot. The man looked at the bell, closed his eyes for a moment, and then charged head first into it, which looked ridiculous, and very painful. But then every one heard this glorious sound, as the bell tolled in a way it never had before. The armless man had the job, with instructions to be at the ground on the upcoming Saturday at noon for the fourth-grade kick-off.

At 11.30 a.m., he walked up to the man on the turnstile and asked to be allowed inside. But he was refused entry because he didn't have a ticket. No one had thought to give him one. 'Don't you know who I am?' the armless man asked defiantly, to which the gateman replied, 'No I don't … though your face rings a bell.'

The armless man quit on the spot, which left the club in desperate trouble. Fortunately, the armless man's twin brother had come with him, and he volunteered to do the job. Up he went to the bell tower on top of the scoreboard, and as half time in the fourths approached, he moved towards the bell to wait for the moment when the timekeeper said, 'Now!' But as he got to the window through which all the Upper Gulargambone fans could see their famous bell, he suddenly tripped, stumbled, and fell over the ledge and down 10 metres to the concrete below.

A group of people gathered around the body, and someone shouted, 'Does anyone know this man's name?'

'No I don't,' said the club president when he arrived on the scene. 'But isn't he a dead ringer for his brother?'

One for the Road

The police were on a drink-driving blitz, and as part of this campaign had decided to stake out a local pub. Sure enough, just before closing they observed a man leaving the hotel. He had the laces of his football boots wrapped around his neck, the boots bouncing on his ample stomach; he was still wearing his mud-spattered guernsey; and a sports bag was thrown crookedly over his shoulder. He was so drunk he could barely walk.

It was almost amusing to watch this poor bastard trying to put his key in the lock on the driver's side door. Even with one eye closed he couldn't quite get that damn key where it was supposed to go. Finally, he made it, and then — while a number of other patrons left the pub — he just sat there, or so it seemed. Most likely, the officers chuckled, he was having trouble working out how to get the car started — on the assumption he'd actually made it into the right vehicle.

At long last, the engine revved into life, the wipers went on at various speeds, the horn blared, the hazard lights flashed on, then the high beam, and then he was on his way, first in reverse and then forward, first to the back of the car park and then finally, out onto the open road. How he'd missed hitting any of the other cars that left the pub at this time was a modern miracle.

Only now did the policemen turn their own engine on. They followed the drunk for maybe 400 metres as he crawled up the road, and then they put on the flashing lights, turned on the siren, and indicated they wanted the man to pull over. Then they carried out a

Breathalyser test. Imagine their shock when the test provided a 'nil' result, nothing, zilch. There was no evidence that the man had swallowed any alcohol at all!

'I'm afraid, sir, that you'll have to accompany us back to the station. It appears our Breathalyser equipment must be broken.'

'I don't think so,' said the driver. 'I'm the designated decoy.'

The 'Taxi' Home

The former Wallaby John Lambie, in his book *Well I'll be Ruggered!* (which he co-wrote with Jeff Sayle and Chris Handy), told a terrific yarn about a function in Wollongong a few years ago at which he was the guest speaker. The night ended after the police had to be called to settle down a punch-up.

At the time, Lambie was an ex-school teacher as well as an ex-rugby international, and he recognised one of the officers as a former student. This was handy, because he and John Coolican, the former Wallaby prop, wanted to get out of there, and they asked if the police might be able to give them a lift.

'John and I climbed into the back of the paddy wagon for our trip home,' Lambie remembered. 'It was great fun to stop at the traffic lights and put our fingers through the grille, shake it and talk to the people in the cars around us. Surprisingly, we could not get any conversations started.

'To top the night off, to the shock of "Coolo", I asked the police to turn on their flashing lights so the neighbours would be aware of John's mode of transport home. From all the bent Venetian blinds in his street that night, he was going to be busy explaining himself next morning.'

Bad Timing

There was this Super 14 rugby player from the ACT Brumbies who bought himself a beautiful new watch. There were only two problems: the watch was two hours fast and he had no idea how to change the time.

So he transferred to the Western Force.

Cheap Trick

The English rugby team is touring Australia and every afternoon at training a little boy comes down to watch them. On the first day, one of the English backs befriended this young bloke, but after a couple of days it seemed the friendship was waning as the footballer explained to a group of forwards, 'That Aussie kid has got to be the dumbest kid in the world. Watch this and I'll prove it.'

'Hey, kid, come here,' the back called out and the boy dutifully walked over. 'Remember we did this yesterday ... I've got a two-dollar coin in one hand and two 50-cent pieces in the other. You can have what's in one hand or the other. What'll it be?'

The boy points at the two 50-cent pieces, and they are promptly handed over.

'What did I tell you?' the Englishman exclaims. 'He thinks two coins is more money than one. He's got to be the dumbest kid in the world.'

Next day, the same thing happens. And the next. And the next. Only after a week does the Englishman thinks it's time to put things right. So when the lad comes over, he says, 'Son, I'm sorry, I've been playing a trick on you. The two 50-cent pieces only add up to a dollar. You should have been taking the $2 coin.'

'I know that,' the boy replied. 'But the day I take the two dollars, the game's over! I reckon I'm five bucks in front.'

Just Gettin' Started

A 72-year-old former front-rower had to go in for his annual check-up, but unfortunately his regular surgeon wasn't available, so he had to see a new, much younger doctor.

After the usual tests had been completed, the doctor remarked, 'Gee, you are in remarkable shape for a man of your age. Must be all that football you played. I believe your father was also a fine front-rower in his day. How old was he when he passed on?'

'Who said he was dead?' replied the patient indignantly. 'Why, he's 91 years old and still coaching the colts!'

'Fantastic,' said the doctor. 'Do you know how old his father was when he died?'

'Who said he was dead?' the man answered. 'Grandad is Dad's assistant coach. He's 111 and doin' just fine. In fact, he's about to get married again.'

The doctor was stunned. 'Why would a man that age want to get married again?' he asked.

'Who says he wants to?' replied the grandson.

One Smart Wallaby

It is a little-known fact that on the first tour of South Africa by an Australian rugby union team, the Aussie players took along with them a fair dinkum wallaby as their tour mascot. This was one of those things that seemed like a good idea at the time, but while the players were clever enough to sneak the wallaby through customs at each end of their voyage, after only a day or two on tour, it bounded off towards the sunset, never to be seen again.

The wallaby was quickly lost in the African jungle. He was smart enough to realise that the rugby players weren't likely to 'fess up that they'd smuggled a live animal into the country, so he knew he was on his own. There seemed plenty of grass to nibble on, so dinner wasn't a problem, but what was that leopard doing lurking in the long grass? If the wallaby was right, unless he thought quickly, he was about to become the big cat's evening meal.

Just nearby was a pile of bones, probably some gazelle that had been last week's tucker. So the wallaby started nibbling at them, while keeping one eye on the approaching cat. Just as the leopard was poised to strike, the wallaby said loudly to himself, 'Geez, that was one delicious leopard. I wonder if there are any more in these parts?'

The leopard shuddered to a halt, and snuck away behind the trees. *That was close!* he thought to himself. *That weird looking creature nearly caught me.*

Nearby, a monkey had been watching these goings-on. This, he theorised, might be a chance to get that leopard onside at last: a trade of information for protection. He called the leopard over, and told him what had just gone on. Trouble was, he didn't quite do it quietly enough, and the wallaby was a smart animal. The Aussie native watched the monkey and the leopard having an animated conversation, and wondered what might happen next.

The leopard, of course, was fuming when he found out he'd been conned. 'Monkey,' he said, 'jump on board and you'll see what happens when conniving marsupials try to take over my domain!'

Soon after, the wallaby looked up to see the leopard coming towards him with the monkey perched on his back. He thought about running, but then he had a better idea. He sat down with his back to them, pretending he hadn't seen them, and then, when they were close enough, he muttered, 'Where's that bloody monkey? I sent him off an hour ago to bring me another leopard!'

Family Pride

Today in a classroom in Brisbane all the children were asked to tell the teacher and their mates what their fathers did for a living. First up was young James …

'My dad is a doctor,' James said proudly. 'He works as a specialist at the City Hospital and saves people's lives.'

Next it was Jack. 'My father is a lawyer,' Jack told the class. 'He goes to court and sorts out people's problems.'

'Well done, Jack,' said the teacher. 'OK, Jason, now it's your turn.'

'I don't want to say, miss.'

'Now, Jason, don't be shy.'

'Oh, all right. My dad is …' Then he stopped, and went to sit down.

'It's OK, Jason …'

'All right … My dad hasn't got a job. He's never had a job. He just sits around all day drinking beer and watching TV while Mum works two jobs, 20 hours a day, to get me and my brothers and sisters fed and through school …'

At this point, the teacher cut Jason off and quickly told the class that it was time for some reading. It was half an hour to recess, but the 30 minutes took an eternity until finally the bell went and the teacher was able to intercept young Jason and have a heart-to-heart.

'I'm sorry, Jason,' she said. 'I didn't realise … you didn't have to talk about your dad like that.'

'Ah, no, miss,' Jason replied. 'Dad has got a job. He's down in Sydney working for the NSW Waratahs rugby team. But I didn't want to say that in front of all my friends. I'd be humiliated.'

'Oh, Jason … I am so sorry,' sobbed the teacher. 'If there is ever anything I can do, please let me know.'

Breakaway Pizza

Then there was the breakaway who, whenever he ordered a pizza, always ended the call by saying, 'And remember, we never had this conversation.'

Pay Back

Bill was renowned for his practical jokes, and always seemed to be at the peak of his form when one of his mates from the club was getting married. The only downside was that when it came to his own wedding, he dreaded the inevitable retribution. Footy players are like that. Bill warned his wife-to-be, his prospective in-laws, the minister, the staff at the reception, the members of the band, every one. To be honest, in a macabre way he was looking forward to it, though he hoped no one else would be hurt or killed in the process.

So it was almost disappointing when nothing happened. Before he donned his new black underpants with the words 'Free Willy' embroidered in gold on the front (a gift from Dorothy, his betrothed), he checked to make sure there was no itching powder or 'Deep Heat' daubed on the inside. He wondered if his shoes might have the letters 'H' and 'E' scratched on the left sole and 'L' and 'P' on the right. He left his Volvo at home, having decided to farewell the party in his mother's beloved Datsun 180B — knowing his mum's reputation, there was no way even his mates would touch that. The best man's speech was disappointingly tame; not even a mention of that mass streak at the races the week before, which led to the last on the card having to be abandoned. No mock telegram from the Australian Rugby Union saying he'd finally been selected for the Wallabies. No bomb scare during the minister's sermon in the church; no late change from AC/DC to the Wiggles for the bridal waltz.

Maybe the fact everything went according to plan was the joke. By the time Bill and Dorothy got to the hotel, the groom was shattered. But this didn't stop him from first checking the bed for breakfast cereal or mashed bananas (a couple of old favourites), and then expressing his love to his new wife more passionately than he'd ever done before. It was 6 a.m. before they finally got to sleep, with the alarm set for 7.30 so they'd be up in time to get to the airport for the flight to Port Macquarie. And not long after that alarm rang out, Bill was on the phone to room service, asking, 'Is there any way I can order breakfast for two?'

And then he heard a trio of voices from under the bed: 'Better make that five.'

The Thoughts of Chairman Stan

It was Stan Pilecki, a bloke who looked like a craggy veteran prop from his first game for Queensland, who said of touring New Zealand: 'It's like going to Las Vegas for a weekend of playing roulette. The first time you went there for fun, the second time for revenge.'

On selectors, Pilecki said flatly, 'The position obviously doesn't call for any deep knowledge of rugby.' He saw them as ranking 'just above plankton in the scale of evolution'.

These two quotes appeared in the book *Stan the Man: The Many Lives of Stan Pilecki*, by Max Howell, Lingyu Xie and Peter Horton. Another funny story retold in that tome involved Horton, one of the toughest hookers to wear the Wallaby jumper. While throwing the ball into a lineout in a match in Argentina in 1979, Horton clipped the touch judge, perhaps accidentally, and the official responded by chasing him onto the field, all the while trying to hit him on the top of his head with his flag. 'The memory of Horton fleeing the touch judge,' wrote the authors, 'brings unprovoked mirth to the Wallabies who were there.'

The Crystal Ball

Garry was a good forward, but a bit of a rogue and a terrible womaniser. Sadly, his wife Mary grew to hate him. One day, she went to a psychic, who looked into her crystal ball, stopped for a moment, and then said quietly, 'I am so sorry, my dear, but your husband is going to be killed in terrible circumstances.'

'Will I get away with it?' Mary responded.

A Good Tip

Mick called the police with an anonymous tip-off — Fred Johnson, the president of the local rugby club, was also a drug dealer. He had a truckload of cocaine hidden in a shed at the back of his property, stashed in his wooden logs.

The constabulary was very grateful, and not much later Mick heard the sound of sirens screaming up the road to Johnson's place. He pictured them knocking on the door with a search warrant, then striding out to the shed, barging the door down and then splitting all the timber into small pieces. This is exactly what happened, but there was nothing except splinters to be found. The police officers left embarrassed and angry; if only they knew where that dud information had come from.

Mick, meanwhile, was back on the phone. 'G'day Fred, it's Mick from the footy club. Were the coppers just round to chop up your firewood?'

'Yeah, mate, they were.'

'Happy birthday, buddy.'

The End-of-Season Trip

The rugby club was on an end-of-season trip that had taken three years to organise and had cost each player 10 grand to be a part of. Not surprisingly, Eric, Brian and Roger, the team's famous (at least among themselves) front-row combination were pretty excited when they were allocated the penthouse suite after they arrived at the hotel on their first day in New York. They were also extremely disappointed when they learned that the hotel's lifts were out of action and they'd have to climb up 75 floors worth of stairs if they wanted to get to their new home.

'How about this for an idea,' Eric proposed. 'To make the journey seem less monotonous, I'll crack jokes for the first 25 floors, then Brian can sing songs for 25 floors, and then Roger can tell sad stories for the final 25 floors.'

Brian and Roger agreed this was as good a plan as any, so off they went. When they arrived at the 26th floor, Eric completed his last joke and Brian started up on his first song. Then, at the 51st floor, Roger prepared to tell his first unhappy story.

'I think I'll begin with my saddest story,' he said wistfully. 'I've left our room key in the team bus.'

New York, New York

It took 48 hours and a lot of beers, but finally Eric, Brian and Roger were mates again. They were now having a drink in a restaurant at the top of one of New York's tallest skyscrapers, when they noticed a bloke walk over to the bar, order a huge beer, skol it, and then walk to the closest window and jump straight out of the building. The boys just shrugged their shoulders and kept drinking, with Eric summing it up for all three of them when he sighed, 'That's New York for you.'

Imagine their surprise when a couple of minutes later the man who'd just committed 'suicide' walked out of the lift and returned to the bar. And imagine their total astonishment if he didn't just do it again — order a beer, drink it in one hit, then walk to the window and jump. This time the Aussie footballers dashed over to see his horrible descent and they were stunned to see that rather than plummeting to the concrete below, the man glided to the bottom, landing as if he had some sort of internal parachute. Within a couple of minutes he was again back at the bar, and the boys made a beeline for him.

'How the hell did you do that?' Eric asked feverishly.

'Oh, buddy, it's just basic physics. The beer makes you all warm inside. Hot air rises, so if you hold your breath after you've had a few beers you actually become lighter than the air, so when you jump like I do you simply float to the sidewalk.'

'That's amazing!' Roger exclaimed. 'I've gotta try that.'

He rushed to the bar, ordered their biggest beer, rolled it down his throat and then dived out the window. Given the speed he was travelling, he would have died for sure if he'd hit the asphalt, but fortunately his fall was broken by an awning. Still, he was seriously injured, and had sustained multiple fractures. His tour was over. Later, doctors would pronounce him incredibly lucky.

Meanwhile, back at the top of the skyscraper, the barman was pouring the bloke who'd completed the previous two jumps another beer.

'Geez, Superman,' he muttered, 'you can be a real bastard when you're on the drink.'

7. WHEEL STORIES

Dear Mandy

After 'Mandy' got sacked from her position as a mechanic with a prominent car-racing team, she found a job at the local newspaper, producing one of those columns where readers write in about their relationship problems ...

Dear Mandy,
I have been married, for almost 10 years, to a beautiful man who once played top-level rugby union. Earlier today, I left as usual for work, leaving my sadly unemployed husband at home to do his daily chores. Unfortunately, I had only been driving for a few hundred metres when the car began overheating violently. Steam was coming out of the engine and I didn't know what to do, so I just parked the car and ran back home. Imagine my shock and horror when I got there to find my husband in our bedroom, dressed in my best lingerie and wearing high heels and some

of my most expensive lipstick. After I sort of calmed down, he explained that he was having terrible trouble coming to terms with the fact that his football career was over and he didn't have a job, that he was worthless and hopeless and just didn't feel like a man anymore. I think the poor fellow is on the verge of a breakdown, almost suicidal even, just a pale shadow of the great person I used to know. My marriage could be over. I'm beside myself with worry. What should I do?

Debbie, Sydney

Dear Debbie,
It sounds like a broken head gasket. Don't drive that car. Instead, get it towed to your mechanic's garage. Continuing to drive a car in that condition could lead to many hundreds of dollars in additional repairs.

Mandy

Modern Technology

The Managing Director of a huge computer conglomerate was being walked through the garage of one of the leading V8 Supercar teams.

'You know,' said the computer man, 'if you used the technology that allowed my company to become a billion-dollar enterprise, putting personal computers into millions of homes and offices across the planet, you'd have to be more successful.'

'Oh, I don't know,' replied the chief mechanic. 'I'm not convinced the way your product operates would be any good in car racing.'

'Why not?' asked the computer MD.

'Well, from our experience here in the office, your computers crash three or four times a day.'

Wiped Out

The new Australian Formula One ace had failed to finish in his previous nine Grands Prix. Before the 10th race, the British Grand Prix at Silverstone, he was in the garage when he heard one of the mechanics shout out, 'We'll need some new wiper blades for this race!' To which another man replied, 'We're out of wiper blades at the moment.'

The Aussie, conscious of his poor record for the season and anxious to be of assistance, volunteered to help. He walked down to the local car accessories shop, walked up to the counter, and said, 'Hi, I'm the new Australian Formula One driver, can I get a new wiper blade for my car?'

'Certainly,' said the sales assistant. 'Sounds like a fair trade to me.'

The Seven-ten Cap

After his days racing V8s were over, Kevin opened an auto-parts store. One day a young woman walked in and said, 'Excuse me, sir, I'd like to buy a seven-ten cap.'

'A what?'

'A seven-ten cap.'

Now this bloke was very proud of his knowledge of cars and engines, but he'd never heard of a 'seven-ten cap'.

'What's a seven-ten cap?'

'You know, it's right on the engine,' the woman replied. 'I've lost mine and I need a new one.'

'What car do you drive?'

'A Volvo.'

'How big is this seven-ten cap you're after?'

The woman made a circle with her typing fingers and thumbs, about six or seven centimetres in diameter. That didn't help, so she asked for a piece of paper and she drew a circle of the same size. Then she wrote '710' in the middle of it.

The car expert looked at the diagram ... and looked at it ... and then it clicked. He turned it upside down, had a chuckle and said, 'I think we've got what you need.'

And then he asked for $9.95 and handed her an oil cap.

The No-Armed Man

A car racer had the misfortune to lose an arm in a fiery smash. When he was finally released from hospital, he was terribly depressed. Not only was his driving career over, but there were so many things he used to love doing that were now out of the question: the golf handicap of four was just a memory; no longer could he play old Rolling Stones songs on his favourite guitar; hugging his beautiful girlfriend was now a chore. Eventually, he'd had enough. He climbed the tallest building he could find, intending to jump off and end it all.

But then a strange thing happened. From the 45th floor, as he peered over the ledge, he could see a man with a huge grin on his face skipping — yes, skipping! — along the footpath below. What was unusual and fantastic about this was that the man had *no* arms. None! The ex-car racer suddenly thought, *What am I doing up here, feeling so bloody sorry for myself? I still have one good arm to do* some *things with.*

He dashed down the stairs and caught up with the man with no arms. He told him how he'd spotted him from the roof far above, had seen him with that grin on his face, skipping down the road. He thanked him for saving his life.

It was a little strange, however, that even though the bloke had stopped skipping, he was still dancing around on the spot. And was that a grin on his face or a grimace?

'Actually, mate,' the no-armed man muttered, 'while I'm pleased you're still alive, I've got to tell you that I'm not very happy at all.'

'You're not? So what's with all the skipping and dancing?'

'My bum's itchy!'

In Code

Which reminds us of the cycling club which finally won the big championship but then had the misfortune to have their just-acquired prized trophy stolen. Smith, the time-trial rider who'd been dropped from the team by the club president over a disciplinary matter and consequently missed out on competing on the club's biggest day, was the main suspect, especially when no one heard from him for days after the trophy was stolen.

Finally, the president received a letter from Smith. The hope was that he'd provide details about how the cup could be reclaimed, but instead all that was inside the envelope was a brief coded message: S37OHSSV O773H.

The president couldn't make head nor tail of it. Neither could the chairman of selectors or the club lawyers. Then, the bloke behind the bar asked if he could have a quick look.

'Ah, gentlemen, I think you need to turn the message upside down,' was all the barman said.

False Alarm

The motor racing ace had a problem in that when he became simply 'Joe Citizen' and was driving on public roads, he really struggled to stay below the speed limit. And so it was that he was pulled over by a policeman for speeding.

'May I see your driver's licence?' said the constable.

'I don't have one,' said the racer. 'They took it off me after my fifth drink-driving charge.'

'I see. May I see your rego papers, please.'

'But this isn't my car. I stole it.'

'You stole it?'

'That's right. Though come to think of it, I think I saw the rego papers in the glovebox when I put my gun in there.'

'There's a gun in the glovebox?'

'Yes, sir. I had to put it somewhere after I shot the woman who owns this car and put her body in the boot.'

'There's a woman's body in the boot?'

'I'm afraid there is.'

The policeman wasn't quite sure what to do, but eventually decided to handcuff the driver, put him in the back seat of the police car, and call for back-up. His sergeant said he'd be on the scene as soon as possible.

When the sergeant arrived, he told the constable to uncuff the prisoner so he could ask a few questions.

'Sir,' he began, 'may I see your licence.'

'Here it is,' said the driver.

'Who's car is this?'

'It's mine, sir. Here are the rego papers.'

'Could you please open the glovebox slowly so I can see if there is a gun in there?'

'A gun? There's no gun in there … as you can see.'

'And can you open the boot of your car?'

'Certainly.' There was nothing there except for one small bag and the spare tyre.

'I don't understand it,' said the sergeant. 'My constable was rabbiting on about a stolen car, a gun in the glovebox and a lady's body in the boot …'

To which the car racer responded: 'He probably told you I was speeding, too!'

Racing Drags

If horse racing is the 'Sport of Kings', is drag racing the 'Sport of Queens'?

Don't Get Lost

On the day before the rally was due to begin, ace driver 'Dynamite' Jack Smith lost his regular navigator. Now Dynamite had a reputation for going through navigators at a rapid rate, so there wasn't a long queue of people hoping to get the gig, even though there was a big chance there'd be a winner's cheque to be collected at the end of the event.

Finally, a young bloke named Julian was co-opted into the role, and the two set off on the first stage. But only 20 minutes after they'd taken off, Dynamite dramatically pulled over to the side of the road, leant over to open the glovebox and pulled out a black .38 revolver. He positioned it on top of the dash, fixed his new navigator with an icy stare, and asked, 'Do you know what I use this for?'

'No,' Julian replied, his voice quavering.

'I use it on navigators who get me lost!'

Dynamite put the car back into top gear and exploded back into the race. Julian, meanwhile, picked up the brown bag that had been at his feet, and pulled out a .45 and placed it on his lap.

'What the hell is that for?' Dynamite snapped.

'The thing is, Mr Smith,' Julian explained, 'I'll know we're lost before you will.'

'By golly, you know more about navigation than I thought,' muttered Dynamite Smith.

Good Directions

The former car racing champion was cruising down the new motorway from Newcastle to Sydney when his car phone rang. It was his wife, who frantically told him, 'Lex, I just heard on the radio that there's a maniac going the wrong way on the highway to the city. Please be careful!'

'Geez,' he replied. 'It's not just one car. There're hundreds of 'em!'

Speed Trap

After his track cycling career was over, Clyde took up road racing, but eventually that got a bit testing, too, so he turned to endurance riding. It was lonely being on the road on your own, but for a while it was strangely rewarding, until one day when pedalling down the Hume Highway, Clyde suddenly thought, *I'm too bloody old for this*. He got off his bike and decided to retire right there, on that spot.

His plan was to hitchhike to the nearest town, and then jump on a train and go back to the city and find a real job. So he stuck his thumb out on the side of the road, but for the next three hours no one would stop. And then, finally, a car pulled over, but unfortunately it wasn't quite what he was hoping for — it was a young punk in a flash Mustang convertible with no room for the bike. That bike represented a lot of happy memories and Clyde was loath to part with it, so they came up with a compromise. They found a piece of rope on the side of the highway, and tied one end to the bumper of his car and the other end to the bike. The driver of the sports car then told Clyde to hop on the bike and he'd tow him into town. 'If I'm going too quick, just ring your bell and I'll ease up,' he said.

Clyde didn't see a lot of alternatives, so off they went, and for the first five or six kilometres everything was sweet. But then a flashy BMW screamed past, and the Mustang's owner took that as a personal insult and raced off after it. A few minutes later, the Mustang and the BMW raced through a speed trap, and the policeman on duty almost had a heart attack.

'Sarge, you're not going to believe what I just saw,' he radioed to his commanding officer back at the station. 'I just had two sports cars past here doing 160kmph.'

'That's not that rare around here, constable,' the sergeant replied.

'Yeah, but right behind them was a bloke on a bicycle, desperately ringing his bell, trying to get past.'

Computer Troubles

The Holden Racing team was keen to keep up with the very latest technological developments, so it hired itself a computer expert. On the new bloke's first day in the job, the team's No. 1 Commodore slowed to a halt in the pit lane, and the computer whiz was summoned to offer an opinion.

'Interesting,' he said slowly. 'Can I suggest your driver closes the car's windows, gets out of the car, gets back in, and then re-opens the windows?'

On Your Bike

Sean was the first Australian to win the Tour de France. He won it three years straight, but never really received the plaudits he deserved because of all the drugs rumours that travelled with him. Although he never failed a drugs test, the accusations lingered, so after the third victory he decided he'd had enough and stunned the sports world by announcing on the podium in Paris that he was retiring, as of right then and there, to go and live in Mexico. He'd bought a bar near the American border and was going to run it.

For the first year, his new life serving drinks went pretty well, but then the investments he'd made during his great cycling career went bad — the business wasn't making any money, and he had to sell up. With no formal qualifications in anything but professional sport, Sean fell on hard times.

And then more rumours started, these ones prompted by sightings of him on the road to the border, slowly riding his old racing bike, with what looked like bags of powder slung over his shoulders.

One early morning, a policeman from the border patrol pulled him over. 'I'm sorry, Sean,' the officer said, 'what's in the bags?'

'Sand,' Sean answered.

'That's not what I've been hearing,' the policeman said. 'Off the bike, now.' He took the bags, tore them open, and emptied the contents on the highway. It sure did look like sand.

'I'm going to send this to Washington for testing. You're free to go for now, Sean, but we'll be in touch. I'd be careful, if I was you.'

Sean continued riding up the road, over the border,

and into the US of A. Soon after, the report came back from the lab: pure sand!

A few days later, the same thing happened. Same policeman, same Sean, same bags over the shoulders. The former bike champion was pulled over again, the contents of the bags were tested, and it was pure sand. Again, Sean was allowed to pedal north.

This same charade went on for weeks. The policeman was convinced something was going on, but though he kept getting the contents of the bag tested, nothing was proved. Making things worse, surveillance told him that Sean seemed to be getting back on his feet financially. He was dressing better and eating better, even though he was still out of work and technically bankrupt.

It was almost a year before Sean stopped riding with those bags over his shoulder. Then he bought back his bar. One day, that same policeman walked into the premises and saw Sean hard at work, making cocktails for some guests.

'Hey, Sean,' he shouted. 'You got a minute?'

Sean slowly walked over to him. 'I know you were up to no good, and it's still driving me crazy trying to work out what you were doing,' the policeman muttered. 'It won't go any further than you and me, but what were you smuggling over the border? Cocaine? … Speed? … Amphetamines?'

'Bicycles,' Sean replied.

Sophie's Choice

A racing car driver was in a dreadful accident, but he came out of it OK except for the fact that his 'manhood' had been severely mangled. His doctor was reassuring, and the specialist reckoned he could fix things, to the point that the driver would have a choice: small, medium or large. 'But I should explain,' the specialist said, 'that the cost varies. "Small" will cost you $5000. "Medium" is $10,000 and "Large" is $20,000. And because it's technically cosmetic surgery, it won't be covered by your insurance.'

The driver wondered if he should ask if they were his only options, but he quickly put that thought out of his head. All kinds of questions about whether size really matters started to bother him, but then the doctor offered some good advice. 'Look, this really is the sort of thing you should discuss with your wife,' he advised. 'Why don't you go home, have a yarn with her, and then come back and we'll book you in for the operation.'

'Thanks, doc,' the driver replied. 'I'll call you in the morning.'

First thing next morning, the doctor found the car driver in his waiting room, looking miserable.

'What have you decided?' the doctor asked.

'She'd rather we got a new kitchen,' the man replied.

8. OFFSIDE!

Two Months in Rome

A gifted young soccer player from the inner western suburbs of Sydney was getting his hair cut as usual by Joe the barber at Leichhardt, when he explained that he wouldn't be in for a couple of months because he had just been offered a trial by the famous Lazio club in Rome. He was leaving tomorrow.

'Rome!' Joe the barber cried. 'Why on earth would you want to go there? It's dirty, it's crowded, the food is ugly, the people are rude and the drivers are worse. You're crazy to go to Rome. What airline you flying?'

'Qantas.'

'Oh no! They're due to crash, they're expensive, they're always late, their planes are dirty, you won't touch their food, you'll have problems with the booking. Good luck. Where are you staying?'

'They're putting me up in the Mazzola, a boutique hotel right on the Tiber, not far from the Olympic Stadium.'

'Don't say another word. I know the place! Biggest dump in the world. Small rooms, cement beds, no views, no air-conditioning, rude staff — you'd be better off sleeping in the street. Have they arranged any touristy things for you, or will it be all football?'

'Mostly football. I am scheduled to have a training session with Roberto Baggio!'

'Roberto Baggio! The most overrated player of all time. Cost us the 1994 World Cup. I'll bet there will be you and a million other footballers there, and Baggio will turn up for maybe a minute. He'll just show his face and be on his way. Good luck on this trip of yours!'

Two months later, the young bloke was back, and he made a point of saying hello to Joe. 'How was the trip?' the barber asked.

'Fantastic! The flight over was superb; Qantas couldn't have looked after me better. I'm never flying with another airline. Rome is an amazing city — there was so much to do and every one was so friendly. I've never had so many glorious meals. The Mazzola was a brilliant hotel, especially given that there was a misunderstanding over my booking but they made it up to me by putting me in the penthouse suite for my entire stay. And Roberto Baggio! What a gentleman and what a football brain. I learnt more from him in an hour than I've learned from all my other coaches throughout my career. His skill with the ball is breathtaking. And I'll never forget the first thing he said to me.'

'What'd he say?'

'Where'd you get the dud haircut?'

Passport to Nowhere

During the 1988 Olympics in South Korea, the Australian football team boarded their bus in Seoul to head to the airport for a flight to Pusan, where they were due to play the Soviet Union. As the author Robert Lusetich recalled in his biography of the Socceroos coach Frank Arok, one of the players turned to Scott Ollerenshaw and asked him if he had his passport with him. 'Oh no, I forgot,' Ollerenshaw replied, and he dashed to the driver and told him to stop and turn around. He had to get back to the hotel.

The player who asked the question let Ollerenshaw go, watched him dash into the hotel and was smiling when he dashed back, by which time every one on the bus was in on the joke — except, of course, for the team's officials and coaching staff, who were fuming at the delay. It wasn't until they got to the airport that Ollerenshaw realised that Pusan was actually in Korea, so this was an internal flight and the passport was not required.

Loneliness

A teacher was on her first day at a new school, and after having a pretty good morning she was assigned to supervising duty on the school oval at lunchtime. Not wanting to impose herself, she stayed in the background, just observing, and soon she found herself closely watching one boy who was standing all on his own while the rest of the children were playing soccer up the other end of the field. She felt really sorry for the poor kid. Eventually she could stand it no longer, and she walked out to talk to him.

'Are you all right?' she asked softly.

The boy nodded that he was, so the teacher retreated, but only for a little while. Soon, she approached him again, this time saying, 'Would you like me to be your friend?'

The boy hesitated, said nothing, and looked suspiciously at her. But the teacher wasn't backing off, so he shrugged his shoulders and said flatly, 'OK.'

Finally, the teacher thought, *some progress*. 'So tell me,' she asked quietly, 'why are you standing here all alone while your friends are playing up the other end of the oval?'

'Because,' the little boy replied, with more than a hint of a sneer, 'I'm the goalkeeper.'

In Their Dreams

England's *Private Eye* magazine liked to record silly and bizarre remarks uttered by sporting callers and analysts in a column named 'Colemanballs', named after the commentator David Coleman, who built a rare reputation for saying things such as, 'And for those of you watching who haven't television sets, live commentary is on Radio 2.' Australian commentators just haven't got the class of the Poms when it comes to saying these sorts of things.

Among literally thousands of quotes is this one from the former Southampton manager, Lawrie McMenemy, 'Some of these players never dreamed they'd be playing in a Cup Final at Wembley — but there they are today, fulfilling those dreams.'

Another came from the England international and former Ipswich, Newcastle and England manager Bobby Robson: 'For a player to ask for a transfer has opened everybody's eyebrows.'

And it was commentator Alan Parry who summed up a thrilling game by saying, 'With the very last kick of the game, Bobby McDonald scored with a header.'

Fantasy Flight

The new assistant to the club secretary at a soccer club in Melbourne was given the job of organising the travel arrangements for the team's trip to Sydney for the first leg of the annual 'interstate challenge' match. She obtained the phone number of the club's preferred travel agent, but before that number was dialled she decided to get a little information so she'd be able to make sure the players were on exactly the right flight.

She called Virgin, and asked, 'Can you please tell me how long it will take to fly from Melbourne to Sydney?'

'Ah, just a minute,' said the voice on the other end of the line.

'Thanks very much,' replied the girl.

Ticket for One

It's hard to believe this is a true story, but apparently there was a thief who pinched a ticket for the Brazil–Australia game in Munich at the 2006 World Cup from a woman's handbag and was then caught when he sat down to watch the match next to his victim's husband.

The robber reputedly mugged the 42-year-old woman as she made her way to the stadium for the game, and when he discovered the ticket in her bag he thought it was too good an opportunity to pass up. When someone other than his wife sat next to him in the stands, the victim's husband called security, who then made the arrest.

The Secret Password

A first-grade goalkeeper decided he wanted to become a member of the Wiggles fan club, which involved registering on the group's official website. So he logged on, went to the site, and filled in all the forms. Then it was time to choose his password …

He went for 'MurrayDorothytheDinosaurWagsthe DogJeffAnthonyCaptainFeathersword'.

The password had to have at least six characters.

Flagging

It's stories like this that make us wish we had promotion and relegation in Australian football. Back in the 1960s, Fulham used to fly the flags of all of their first-division rivals at their home ground, Craven Cottage, in London. However, in 1968, they were relegated to Division 2, and the club secretary was asked if he was going to replace all the flags. 'No we won't,' he replied. 'We won't be the second division long enough to justify the expense.'

He was 100 per cent right. Fulham were *relegated* to the third division at the first opportunity. They didn't get back to the top division until 2001.

You Get What You Deserve

Craig was reading the paper over breakfast when he stumbled across a story about a glamorous beauty queen who was dating one of his team-mates, a bloke whose reputation as a total dill was known across the football world.

Craig turned to his wife, Jessica, and said, 'I just don't get why it's always the dumbest morons who get the most attractive women.'

'Why, thank you, my darling,' Jessica replied.

Happy Birthday!

It was 31 October 1993, the day of Australia's World Cup qualifying game against Argentina at the Sydney Football Stadium. The previous day, the legendary Diego Maradona had turned 33. Now he was in the tunnel, preparing to walk out into a blaze of photographers' flashlights and the cheers and roars of a capacity crowd. Standing next to him was Australian captain Paul Wade, ready to play the biggest game of his life. Coach Eddie Thomson had given Wade the job of man-marking Maradona throughout the tie; to a large degree, Australia's chances of progressing to the World Cup finals in the USA depended on him.

Wade looked across at the little genius and wondered what to say. Should he ignore him? Say something provocative? Snarl or smile? He settled for a firm handshake and just two words …

'Happy birthday!'

The two games, home and away, were very competitive: a draw in Sydney and a 1–0 win to Argentina in Buenos Aires, so the 1986 World Cup champions went through. Following the second leg, the Socceroos accepted an invitation to a local bar, but when they arrived they discovered that it was impossible for them to pay for their own drinks. Someone was picking up the tab, and that someone turned out to be a little man perched in a smoke-filled corner surrounded by friends and hangers-on: Maradona. In his autobiography, *Captain Socceroo*, Wade estimated that the bill came to something like $US10,000.

Happy birthday, indeed!

They're Moving in at Hackney Wick

I'm sure this has happened in Australia, but perhaps never before such an important sporting event. When Arsenal strode out onto Wembley Stadium for the 1950 FA Cup Final few people noticed they were without their Scottish international inside-right Jimmy Logie. The walk from the dressing rooms to the area in front of the Royal Box was one of the most famous in football, every British player's dream, but Logie had sneaked out of the dressing room moments before they were called out, because he needed to find out the result of a dog race at Hackney Wick. There was a delay at the boxes at Hackney Wick, and Logie was missing when they entered the arena. Arriving in time for the official ceremony where the two teams were introduced to a member of the Royal Family, he sneaked in between two colleagues and then called out to his compatriot, team-mate Alex Forbes, 'It got beat,

Alex.' Most observers agreed Logie had an excellent game as Arsenal defeated Liverpool 2–0.

A Mixed Bag

When asked to describe his team, the manager replied, 'Fastidious.' Asked to explain, he said, 'Forwards are fast, defenders are hideous.'

Those Were the Days

The former footballer had fond memories of days long gone when the boys used to go away on end-of-season trips, and a few of them would get up to all sorts of mischief. Now that he was in his 90th year, he decided to see what all the fun was about, and he walked into a brothel and said to the madam, 'I'd like a young girl, please.'

Surprised, she looked at the veteran and asked how old he was.

'I'm 89 years old,' he replied.

'Eighty-nine!' shrieked the woman. 'Don't you realise you've had it?'

'Oh, OK,' the old man shrugged his shoulders. 'How much do I owe you?'

Bill Shankly

The late Bill Shankly, former Liverpool manager, and one of the most celebrated figures of British football history, is the man most widely credited with having said, 'Football's not a matter of life and death. It's more important than that.' It's a line Australian coaches and commentators like to use from time to time, not always attributing it back to the great man who said it. What Shankly actually said was, 'Some people believe football is a matter of life and death. I'm very disappointed with that attitude. I can assure you it is much, much more important than that.' Some who heard him say it, after a game in the 1960s, reckoned it was said half in jest, and given events in Liverpool's history such as Heysel and Hillsborough, its relevance does need to be kept in perspective.

Shankly was once accused of celebrating his wedding anniversary by taking his wife to see a game involving the lower-division club Accrington Stanley. 'It's not true,' he pleaded, 'it was Accrington Stanley reserves.' Another time, Adidas wanted to present him with a 'Golden Boot' in recognition of his service to the game, and he was asked for his shoe size. 'If it's gold, I'm a size 28.' When told a rival manager was ill, he said, 'I know, he's got a bad side.' When told an offside decision hadn't been given because the player wasn't interfering with play or trying to gain an advantage, he said, 'Well, he should have been.' Of referees, he explained, 'They know the rules, but they don't know the game.' He was often denigrating the city's other top-flight club, Everton, such as when he claimed that Liverpool had two great clubs: 'Liverpool and Liverpool reserves.'

But a quote that probably best captures the bloke was uttered during the days before he became the Liverpool manager in 1959. At www.shankly.com, a former Carlisle United goalkeeper named Jim McLaren is quoted recalling a day when Shankly, as Carlisle's manager, hopped off the bus on the edge of Tranmere to ask for directions. But the person he asked couldn't help. Shankly returned to the bus shaking his head. 'Can you believe that?' he asked with a real sense of shock and wonder in his voice. 'Imagine not knowing where the football field is.'

The Confessional

The 80-year-old owner of a football team from the eastern suburbs of Sydney walks into a church. He stops at the entrance, looks around, and then strides to the confessional boxes.

'Forgive me, Father, for I have sinned,' the old man says.

'I know,' replies the priest. 'I have seen your team play.'

'No, no. Not that.'

'Oh, go on.'

The man continues: 'Father, I have been married for 45 years. I am the father of six children, I have many grandchildren and great-grandchildren. But in the last 48 hours I have slept with two different beautiful young women.'

'My son,' says the priest. 'That is a serious sin. How long has it been since your last confession?'

'This is my first, because I am Jewish.'

'Jewish! Then why are you telling me this?'

'I am 80 years old. I'm telling every one!'

Definition: 'Five Minutes'

If a wife or partner says 'five minutes' when she is getting ready to go out, she means 'half an hour'. Husbands need to understand this. It is a totally different 'five minutes' from the 'five *more* minutes' you have been given when she asks, 'How much longer is that bloody game? I need your help to clean up the house!'

The Cup Goes Flying

The 1973 FA Cup Final was a supposed mismatch between the finest team in Britain, Leeds United, and second-division Sunderland, but the outsiders famously stunned their opponents and the football world by winning 1–0. Four days later, the new Cup champions were back at their home ground, Roker Park, for a league game against Queen's Park Rangers, and not unnaturally they decided to show their new prize to the club's supporters.

After a parade around the ground, the glistening trophy was carefully placed on a table at the side of the field, near the halfway line. The local fans were very excited, but they couldn't have known that a few of the QPR players had made a £10 bet among themselves as to who would be the first to knock the Cup off the table. It didn't take long. As Stan Bowles, their gifted forward, remembered in *The Guardian* in November 2006, 'With the ball at my feet, I tear off straight across the park. Every one on the pitch is just staring at me — and then, bang! The FA Cup goes shooting up in the air.'

Every one knew that the silverware had been knocked over on purpose, and not surprisingly the Sunderland fans were enraged. Making things worse, their heroes were thrashed 3–0, with Bowles, of all people, scoring two goals, so it wasn't all that surprising that at the end of the match there was something of a pitch invasion. 'At least I got my tenner, and my picture on News at Ten,' Bowles remembered. 'And all because I was just having a bit of a laugh.'

Good Question

'You're not a referee's bootlace,' the veteran supporter yelled out at the man in charge of the football match.

'Why would I want to be a bootlace?' the ref replied.

Party Time

A couple of players from the local football team, which had not been playing well, were dining at a local restaurant.

At a nearby table, another man was putting away the drinks like there was no tomorrow. He seemed happy enough, though he was clearly extremely drunk.

'Do you know him?' asked the younger of the two footballers.

'Yeah, I do,' the other answered. 'He used to play for us. But five years ago, he was transferred to another club, and he's been on the drink ever since.'

'Gee,' said the first player. 'I didn't know it was possible to celebrate for that long.'

Sportsmanship

After the game, when his team had been beaten 3–0, the coach called one of his nine-year-old players aside and asked, 'Son, do you understand what co-operation is? Do you know what a team is?'

The boy didn't say a word, just nodded his head. His bottom lip was quivering.

'Son, do you understand that what matters is that we win or lose as a team, and that we shouldn't argue, curse or attack the referee, or call him or the volunteers running the lines "dickheads". Do you understand all that?'

Again, the boy nodded. Tears welled in his eyes.

'And do you understand when I take you out of the game so another boy can get to play the last 20 minutes, it's not good sportsmanship to call your coach a dumb so-and-so and threaten to kick the coach's wife up the bum?'

Again, the little boy agreed. He started to say something, but then thought better of it.

'That's good, son,' said the coach. 'Now can you go over and explain all that to your grandmother?'

Blind Loyalty

A Melbourne Victory fan desperately wanted to watch his team play their away game against Sydney FC, but he couldn't afford the flight north, he didn't have pay-television and he couldn't go to any of his local pubs to watch the game because his new girlfriend had asked him to mind her pet dog, a dachshund named 'Fang', and he knew all the hotels in the area had strict 'no dogs' policies. But then he came up with an ingenious plan.

He found a pair of very dark sunglasses and the dog's lead, and set off on a long walk to a pub he had never been to before. There, he carefully walked up to the entrance, 'felt around' for the door, stumbled in, knocked over a chair and then clambered on to a bar stool close to a TV showing the football. The dog sat down next to him. But within a minute a barman came up and said, 'Hey mate, can't you read the sign? No dogs allowed! Please get that mongrel out of here.'

'I'm sorry,' the soccer fan replied softly. 'But I

can't read any signs. I'm blind. This is my seeing-eye dog.'

'Mate, you're not fooling anyone,' the barman sneered. 'Since when have dachshunds become seeing-eye dogs?'

'They gave me a dachshund?' the Victory supporter asked incredulously.

Blind Date

His fellow midfielders had lined him up with a blind date, which meant Neil didn't know what to expect. By the time the lift reached the 38th floor of the city apartment building, where he had to get out, he assumed he'd be dining with a girl who looked like his late great-grandmother, so you can imagine his surprise when his knock on the door was greeted by a voluptuous blonde with a gorgeous smile and what seemed to be a bright, charming personality.

'I'll be ready in a sec,' she said softly. 'Why don't you play with Keano, my pet Irish Terrier, while you're waiting. He can do some amazing tricks.'

So there was Neil, picturing his glamorous partner changing into her frock, and playing games with the cutest little mutt that had ever lived in a 38th-floor apartment. Keano could play dead, sit up, shake hands, roll over, and if you made a hoop with your arms, he'd leap right through it. But Neil quickly grew tired of this frivolity, so he walked onto the balcony and began to admire the view. Of course, the dog followed him, and started gnawing at his leg, so Neil said, 'Sit, Keano.' Then, 'Roll over, Keano.' And then, 'Jump through my arms, Keano.' And the Irish terrier leapt through Neil's arms, and straight over the balcony railing. Just then, Neil's date emerged.

'Isn't Keano the loveliest, happiest puppy you've ever met?' she giggled.

'To be honest,' Neil answered, 'I thought he seemed kind of depressed.'

The Wise Man Knows

Snow White, Popeye and Darth Vader ran into each other one day while they were on tours of Australia promoting their latest movies. During their conversation, Snow White said, 'I think I'm the most beautiful woman in Australia, but how can I find out for sure?'

Popeye then said, 'I think I'm the strongest man in Australia, but how can I find out for sure?'

Vader said, 'I think I'm the most despised person in Australia, but how can I find out for sure?'

'You could go and ask the Wise Man,' advised Snow White's agent.

So off they went to Launceston, to the Wise Man's tent. First, Snow White entered, and soon after she came out all smiles, saying, 'I am the most beautiful woman in Australia.'

In went Popeye, and after about 10 minutes he came out, beaming, 'I am the strongest man in Australia.'

Then it was the Star Wars villain's turn. Into the tent went Darth Vader, but when he reappeared he had a confused look on his face, as he asked, 'Who the hell is Fabio Grosso?'

The Diver

Fans who long for the good old days like to tell us that soccer professionals of seasons long gone never tried to con referees in the way modern stars do. But a story (told in the book *The Wit of Soccer* by the great commentator Kenneth Wolstenholme) about the old Glasgow Celtic forward Jimmy Delaney lends a little of the lie to that. Delaney played for Celtic from 1934 to 1946, and during one 'Old Firm' clash with the Rangers he tried to dribble through the defence on the edge of his opponents' penalty area. But there was no way through, so Delaney dived while the Celtic crowd roared.

Now one of the rules of the dive that has never changed over the years is this: stay down and pretend that you're injured. Delaney lay there in the mud as if he'd been pole-axed, and then out of the corner of his eye he saw a boot, and presumed it was a team-mate checking on his welfare. 'Has he given it yet?' he asked.

'Not yet, Laurence Olivier, and he won't,' came the reply. 'So you may as well get up.'

The boots belonged to referee Peter Craigmyle.

Penalties

They did, though, breed them tough in the old days. Wolstenholme tells the story of the famous 1923 FA Cup Final, the first held at Wembley, when there was such a crowd turn-up that the game was delayed as fans poured onto the pitch and police on mounted horses were needed to force them back. When the game finally started, spectators lined the sidelines.

Not surprisingly, the players' nerves were tighter than ever, and one player affected more than most was Bolton Wanderers' young winger Billy Butler. At one point he walked up to his captain, Joe Smith, and muttered, 'Joe, I'd die if anyone asked me to take a penalty kick today.'

To which Smith replied kindly, 'And what makes you think anyone is going to be mad enough to ask you?'

9. BALLS OF ALL SHAPES AND SIZES

Hardly Yorkers

It was Stan McCabe, the legendary Australian cricketer of the 1930s, who said he couldn't see what was so hard about hitting in baseball. 'After all,' he said to a team-mate during a charity game in South Africa in 1935–36, when describing what the opposition pitcher was throwing at him, 'they're all full tosses.'

Size Matters

A survey of Australian society has shown that the most popular sport of the poorer sections of the working class is football, in any of its many forms. Those who are still working class but better off than their football-loving comrades follow cricket. The middle class, it seems, likes tennis, while the rich prefer golf.

The people conducting the survey have come to the conclusion that the wealthier you get, the smaller your balls become.

Why women like netball is still to be determined.

Snookered

A professional snooker player went down to his local club to have a couple of quiet beers and maybe a frame or two if the table was empty. It was, but he'd only just set the balls up when a stranger walked into the room and asked for a game.

'Well, I suppose so,' said the pro, 'but will you give me a start?'

'Listen, mate,' replied the stranger a little rudely, 'I've never seen you play. I'm not going to give you a start.'

The pro broke by smashing the pack, and one red dropped into the centre pocket. From there he proceeded to clear the table — all reds and blacks, then the colours, a maximum break of 147, completed in nine minutes. It was a breathtaking performance, and the pro couldn't help thinking that it was sweet retribution for the bloke's surly attitude when he joked about the start.

'Can we have another game?' the stranger asked. 'Only this time, I'll break and I think I'd like a start.'

'A start?' cried the pro. 'Sorry, mate, I can't give you a start. I've never seen you play.'

Dress Sense

Norma Matthews was renowned as the craftiest, most devilish netballer to ever play the sport. As a coach, she was just as shrewd and just as successful. There were plenty of incidents on the court that epitomised this fact, but an episode that occurred on the eve of her eldest daughter's wedding captured her cunning best of all.

It started when the bride-to-be came home in tears. She had just discovered that the groom's mum had deliberately bought the very same expensive dress that Norma had selected for the big event, which was devastating — she loved her mum and wanted the day to be perfect for her as well as for herself.

'Don't you worry about it, darling,' Norma said. 'I'll just have to go out and buy another one. Remember, everyone will be looking at the beautiful bride, not your husband's new in-laws.'

'But, Mum, what will you do with the old dress? How will you get your money's worth out of that one?'

'Don't worry, dear. I'll wear it to the rehearsal.'

Coloured Commentary

Though it's been repeated many, many times, it's still a quote too good to leave out. It came from the legendary snooker commentator 'Whispering' Ted Lowe, who said so famously during a live television event around 1980: 'Griffiths is snookered on the brown, which, for those of you watching in black and white, is the ball directly behind the pink.'

Ted Lowe was also the commentator who said, 'Fred Davis, the doyen of snooker, now 67 years of age and too old to get his leg over, prefers to use his left hand.'

Cardinal Hewitt

The Pope met with his Cardinals to discuss a peace proposal from the Prime Minister of Israel.

'Your Holiness,' said one of the Cardinals, 'The Israeli Prime Minister loves tennis. He has challenged you to a five-set match game to illustrate the friendship and spirit of fair play that are shared by the Jewish and Catholic faiths.'

The Pope thought it was a good idea, but he had never held a tennis racquet in his life. 'I cannot play,' he said. 'But do we have a Cardinal who can represent me against the Israeli Prime Minister?'

'None who play very well, Your Holiness,' the Pope was told. 'But what if we made young Lleyton Hewitt from Australia a Cardinal, and then asked him to play the Israeli Prime Minister as your personal representative? By accepting their offer, it will show our spirit of co-operation, and we'll also win the match, which will be good for the morale of the Church.'

Every one agreed it was a good idea. The call was made, and Hewitt was greatly honoured and agreed to play.

The day after the match, Cardinal Hewitt reported to the Vatican to let the Pope know how he'd got on. 'I'm afraid to say, Your Holiness, that I lost in five sets,' he said.

'How could this be? I was assured you were a very good player.'

'I am, Your Holiness, and I hit the ball very well. But you've got to take your chances, and sometimes the bounce of the ball just goes the other bloke's way and you've got to take your hat off to him. At the end of the day, Rabbi Rafter was just that little bit too good.'

Golf and Other Sports

Hank Aaron, one of the greatest home-run hitters in the history of Major League baseball, once said, 'It took me 17 years to get 3000 hits in baseball. I did it in one afternoon on the golf course.'

Meanwhile, Don Carter, a pro ten-pin bowler, had his own take on golf. 'One of the advantages bowling has over golf,' he declared, 'is that you seldom lose a bowling ball.'

Seldom?

Loyalty Comes at a Price

The owner of the local basketball team had forged a reputation over the years as one of the tightest individuals on the planet. He had worked hard, earned plenty but spent very little, and when he died few people lamented his passing. Further hardening his enemies' opinion of him, word got out that on his deathbed, he had asked his wife to make sure he was buried with the team singlet that carried the No. 1, and also with all of his money. If there really was an afterlife, he wanted to be financial when he got there.

Club officials decided he was such a miserable sod, he'd have to make do without the singlet. It wasn't as if his penny-pinching ways had resulted in years of glory for the team. Then, at the funeral, the few people who had bothered to show up waited to see what his wife would do. Before the closed casket was hammered shut, she stepped forward and slipped a sealed envelope under the lid.

Later, she was asked exactly what was in the envelope. 'It was a personal cheque,' she explained. 'If he can cash it, he can spend it!'

One Mistake Too Many

One of the greats of Australian tennis, John Bromwich, was playing a tournament in Adelaide and was winning his match against Len Schwartz 6–0, 6–0, 5–0 when he demonstrated a side of his character that had helped him reach the very top of his sport. It also, it must be said, have looked more than a little funny.

Schwartz was no dummy. He was a finalist in the men's doubles at the Australian Championships and had once beaten Jack Crawford on this same court. Now he played a beautiful volley that had Bromwich at full stretch as he tried to play an impossible cross-court lob. Bromwich's shot was perfect for length, but at the last second it floated fractionally wide, which prompted him to cry at the top of his voice, 'I'll never win this if I keep making stupid mistakes like that!'

A Unique Talent

The man was trying to get his dog on the latest television show, 'Animal New Faces', but things weren't going well.

'What can he do?' asked the producer.

'Listen up,' replied the dog owner. 'Question one: during the last round of the 1996 US Masters, where did Greg Norman spend too much of his time?'

'Rough!' said the dog.

'Terrific,' sneered the producer.

'Wait, there's more. Question two: what makes the Rod Laver Arena unique among venues for Grand Slam tennis finals?'

'Roof!' said the dog.

'Great, mate,' sighed the producer. 'Next, please!'

'No wait. Question three: Who is the greatest baseballer of all time?'

'Rufe!' said the dog.

'Oh please,' cried the producer.

Soon after, the man and his canine were walking mournfully out the studio door. The man kicked the ground and the dog scuffled along, tongue hanging out, tears in his eyes. Finally, the animal looked up at his owner and said quietly, 'I'm sorry I choked on the last question, boss. I should have said "DiMaggio"!'

Kids Half-Price

The women's tennis champion desperately wanted to start a family, but she had two problems: she couldn't find a man to marry her and she couldn't afford the time off the tour to be pregnant anyway. Then one day she went to the movies and saw a sign that said, 'Children half price before 3 p.m: $5.00.' She got out one of her credit cards, raced up to the ticket counter, and asked for a boy and a girl.

Making Millions

At the basketball club's annual presentation night, the owner was on his feet making another of his speeches.

'This club has made me a millionaire,' he told the gathering.

'What was he before he bought the club?' a junior point guard asked.

'A billionaire!' one of the team's veteran players replied.

The Tonic

In his book *The Tennis Player Who Laughed*, Jack Pollard told a story about one of Australia's first great tennis stars, Jack Crawford. In 1933, Crawford won the Australian, French and Wimbledon men's singles titles and when he then made the final of the US Championships he was one win away from becoming the first man to complete the Grand Slam. His opponent in the final would be England's Fred Perry, but by the morning of the game, Crawford felt totally wiped out. Pollard takes up the story …

> *Crawford told his friend Vincent Richards of his chronic insomnia. 'You'll never beat Perry all wound up like that,' said Richards. 'Leave it to me. I'll fix you a nerve tonic I've used myself.' Later, as Crawford went out on to the court to play Perry, Richards handed him a cup of iced tea and said he had slipped the tonic into it. 'Just sip it each time you change ends; you'll forget all about being tense,' Richards advised …*

As Pollard tells it, Crawford believed the tonic worked, even though he had no idea what it was. But maybe the final match score suggests otherwise: Perry won in five sets: 6–3, 11–13, 4–6, 6–0, 6–1. The 'tonic' was straight Kentucky bourbon. It is true that Crawford suffered a broken racquet string at a crucial stage of the match, but even so those last two set scores must make you wonder whether maybe, just maybe, Jack Crawford enjoyed Vincent Richards' tonic just a little bit too much.

Be Careful What You Think ...

A man enters a supermarket, and halfway down aisle three he sees a very attractive blonde woman waving in his direction. He is taken aback, and quite flattered, too, given that it's been such a long time since any woman, even his wife, has paid him the slightest attention.

In the next aisle, their trolleys collide, and quickly he splutters, 'Do you know me?'

And she replies, 'I think you're the father of one of my kids.'

Oh my God! His life rewound before his eyes, all the way back to the days before his wedding, to the only time he had ever been unfaithful to his wife. 'Don't tell me you're the stripper from my buck's party, the girl I had on the cricket club's pool table while your partner whipped me with her leather belt and all the boys cheered me on?'

The woman looked him straight in the eyes. 'No,' she said, 'I'm your daughter's netball coach.'

A Tennis A-hole

This quote appeared not too long ago on a tennis Internet forum. We have deliberately left it exactly as it appeared, in order to protect the innocent ...

One day, I was out practicing serves at the park courts. On the next court, were two guys playing a match. One was outhitting the other and winning. However, the leading player was very rude and condescending about his opponent's lack of ability. After winning the match in a landslide, he blurted out statements like 'gosh you suck' and 'you loser!' So I decided to teach him a lesson. I challenged him to a match and he accepted. My winning score was 6–0, 6–0. Right after matchpoint, I made sure to dance around and cheer loudly. I called the attention of everybody around us. With everybody looking, I criticized his lack of form and talent. I mimmicked his earlier boastful tone and added some of my own when calling him 'the worst tennis player ever' and 'super sucky at tennis.' I even made fun of his short stature and junior racket. He tried to justify his graduated racket length with the fact that he was only nine years old, but I ignored his pleas and continued to laugh and point anyway. He ran home crying. That should teach him a lesson to not be a tennis a-hole ever again. Gosh, what an a-hole!

Tennis Camp

A young boy is enrolled by his ambitious parents in a strict tennis camp high in the mountains. On his first day, the lad is told that he has to focus on his tennis, and as part of this process he will only be allowed to say two words every five years — and only to the great teacher in charge of the camp.

At the end of the fifth year, he is told he will have a face-to-face meeting with the master coach.

'You've been silent for five years since entering our college,' the guru says. 'You have trained hard. Your parents will be proud. What do you wish to say?'

'It's cold.'

Five years pass. At a second meeting, the master says, 'Your progress is excellent. I see a Wimbledon title in the future, some massive endorsements, and many opportunities for your parents to stay in five-star hotels and get plum seats in the stands at major championships. What do you wish to say?'

'I'm hungry.'

Five more years pass. At a third meeting, the great coach says, 'It is almost time. A few more years and you will have a great professional career ahead of you. I have told your parents to talk to Nike, and that they should take media lessons and purchase homes in London and New York. What do you wish to say?'

'I quit.'

'Thank God,' says the master. 'You've done nothing but whinge since you got here.'

Four Fathers

Four expectant fathers were in the hospital waiting room while their wives were in labour. The nurse came in and told the first man, 'Congratulations! You're the father of twins!'

'What a coincidence!' the man exclaimed. 'I work for the Doubleday Book Club!'

The nurse returned a short while later and informed the second man, 'You are now the father of triplets!'

'What a coincidence!' he replied. 'I work for Triple M Radio!'

The nurse returned a third time and told the third man, 'Congratulations. Your wife has given birth to quadruplets!'

'Another coincidence! I'm a producer for the *Four Corners* television series!'

At this point, the fourth man fainted. When he came to, the others asked, 'What's the problem?'

'The problem? I'll tell you what the problem is. I'm the coach of the Adelaide 36ers!'

10. SHORT OF A GOOD LENGTH

A Ripe Old Age

During his career, the former Test cricketer had built up a reputation as one of the most decent, honest sportsmen of his generation. If he nicked it, he walked. He only appealed if he *knew* it was out. In post-match interviews, he always gave credits to his team-mates and his opponents; he thanked the umpires, the administrators, the fans — even the reporters. In his eyes, the selectors never made a mistake — 'Gee, it's a tough job, you know; they can't choose every one,' he would say — and when they finally dropped him from the Test team he personally rang each member of the committee and thanked him for picking him for so long. He refused to be sponsored by a tobacco company or a brewery. His autobiography, a book he dedicated to his parents, wife and six children, was called *For the Love of the Game*.

Now, 30 years after his retirement, he was at the doctors to receive the results of a series of exhaustive tests he'd had to check his physical condition. The overall result, the physician said, was that 'you are doing well for your age'.

The ex-cricketer was a little concerned by that verdict. 'What does that mean?' he enquired. 'Will I live to be 80?'

'Do you drink alcohol or smoke cigarettes?' the doctor asked.

'No.'

'You don't do drugs, do you?'

'Definitely not!'

'Do you eat a lot of red meat?'

'No, I read that too much meat was unhealthy.'

'Do you spend a lot of time in the sun?'

'Well, I do play a little sport, but I'm very conscious of not spending too long in the sun.'

'Do you gamble, drive fast cars or have lots of sex?'

'No, I don't do any of those things.'

'Then why do you care if you live to 80?'

Caught Behind

A cricket umpire went to his doctor and said, 'I don't think my wife's hearing is as good as she thinks it is. What should I do?'

'Try this test to find out for sure,' the doctor suggested. 'When your wife is in the kitchen doing the dishes, stand about five metres behind her and ask her a question. If she doesn't react move a bit closer and try again. If she still doesn't respond, move even closer, and keep doing that until she hears you.'

The umpire headed home and that very evening he noticed that his wife had started preparing their dinner. He stood five metres behind her and said, 'What are we having, honey?'

There was no reaction, so he moved a metre or so closer, and tried again. Still nothing. In a little while he was almost within touching distance, but still there was no answer.

He wondered why she couldn't feel his breathing, but still he said again, 'What are we having for dinner, darling?'

'For the fourth time,' she shouted back, 'I said CHICKEN, you deaf bastard!'

The Heaven XI

Hamish Lincoln, player-manager to the stars, got himself a start in a celebrity cricket match, but unfortunately during the game he was hit on the head while fielding at short leg and was killed.

Soon, he found himself in heaven, and after signing all the papers he was ushered down to a majestic cricket ground, where he was told that he would be captaining the Australian 'Heaven XI', made up of revered figures from the sporting world, in a match against a 'Best of England' side. Sounds good, Hamish thought to himself. The dressing room was magnificent, all the latest cricket gear was laid out for Hamish's personal use, he noticed that among his team-mates were Victor Trumper and Sir Donald Bradman, and he was shown where he should go if he required a massage or some refreshments.

'Fantastic, thanks very much,' Hamish said.

Out on the ground, after he'd tossed with WG Grace, he looked over and noticed that a former Archbishop of Canterbury was rolling the pitch, while an ex-Cardinal from the Sydney diocese was hammering the stumps into the ground. Hamish walked over and said, 'Gentlemen, I'm confused, why are you, two good, devout, holy men, doing such menial jobs, while I have been made captain on my first day? Yes, I was an excellent cricketer in my day, and I made tens of millions of dollars for my cricketing clients, but I'm not sure I deserve all this.'

The Archbishop looked up, mopped his brow, and said, 'Hamish, my son, there are many, many former religious leaders living up here. But we've never had a player-agent. It's no wonder they're treating you special.'

Heals Knows

The most infamous sledge of Ian Healy's great career was probably the time he told Sri Lankan captain Arjuna Ranatunga that he was allowed a runner just for being fat. But a better one-liner was the one recalled by former England captain Mike Atherton in his autobiography — of the day when 'Heals' was captaining Queensland against the touring Englishmen and he asked a fieldsman to come in and field 'right under Nasser's nose'. When the team-mate walked in, he stopped him about six metres away from the batsman. Atherton doesn't record what Nasser Hussain thought of that.

A Killer of a Headache

Ever since his teenage years, Dan had suffered from terrible headaches. How he managed to play cricket for Australia given this affliction was amazing, and there was always the thought that if he was healthier he might have been as good as Bradman. None of the 'traditional' cures helped, and Dan wasn't game to risk any of the weirder 'natural' remedies he'd been offered for fear they'd wreck his career completely.

Finally, on a tour of the West Indies, a medico in Jamaica offered him a cure, but it was so dire that he refused to take it any further. Back in Australia, Dan went and saw his regular doctor, and explained that this bloke in the Caribbean had said that the headaches were caused by his testicles pressing up against the base of his spine. The only way to relieve that pressure was to remove the testicles. The doc said he'd do more tests, and after the results came back he said that the Windies medico might have been right. The cricketer thought about it, and then finally decided that he'd put the operation off until after he retired from the game.

Eventually, that day came, and 24 hours later Dan was on the operating table. When he woke he couldn't believe it — there was no headache, just this glorious feeling as if a vice had been removed from his skull. The following day, he was discharged and was strolling down the street with a rare spring in his step when he saw a flash men's clothing store on the other side of the street. He bounced across the road, walked in and said in a ridiculously cheerful voice to the veteran store manager, 'I feel like a new person, and I'd like to look like one. Can you fit me for a new suit?'

'Certainly, sir, it would be my pleasure. I'd say you're a 102 short.'

Dan was impressed. 'How did you know that? I thought you would have needed to measure me up.'

'Sir,' the tailor replied, 'I reckon I've seen every human shape in my time. I've been in this game for half a century.'

The selected suit fitted perfectly. As Dan admired himself in the mirror, his new friend said, 'Can I suggest a new shirt, sir, to go with the suit?'

'Sure,' Dan said.

'It'd be a 41 neck, 89 sleeve, wouldn't it?'

'That's amazing. How did you know?'

'Like I said, I've been in this game for half a century.'

The same thing happened when Dan decided to purchase a new pair of shoes ...

'Nine and a half E, isn't it?'

'Fantastic!'

'I've been in this game for half a century.'

As Dan walked around the shop in his new shoes, shirt and suit, he truly felt like a millionaire. 'I think I'd like some new underpants as well,' he said triumphantly.

'That would be a size 36,' said the old tailor.

'Well no,' replied Dan. 'I'm afraid I've got you. I'm a 34.'

'Oh no, sir, I don't think so. If you wore size 34, the underpants would push your testicles up against the base of your spine and you'd have a killer of a headache.'

Get a Sack!

During an Ashes tour of Australia between the wars, one barracker wasn't satisfied with telling England's 'Patsy' Hendren to 'get a bag' when the fieldsman dropped a catch. Instead, the fan yelled out, 'You oughta use a great big sack!'

To which Hendren replied, 'I would if I had one as big as your mouth!'

Well Hidden

After Australia regained the Ashes in 2006–07 by winning all five Tests, the concept of a 'boot camp', which Aussie coach John Buchanan had organised for his team prior to the series against England, became the latest fashion. One Brisbane club team decided to organise a similar weekend for its players, and among the instructions for the players was that they should go and buy some 'camouflage trousers' to wear on day one.

The day of the camp arrived and all the players were suitably attired, except for Jason, the young fast bowler. Where was his camouflage gear?

'I went to the store,' he explained, 'and the lady pointed to where they are. But as hard as I tried, I couldn't find them.'

Test of Fire

Much was made of the incident in 1993 when Dean Jones asked Curtly Ambrose to remove his white wristbands during a one-day international at the SCG. Following that request, Ambrose seemed to bowl about 50km quicker, which didn't make Deano look all that smart.

But it's not always the players doing the provoking. In Perth, during Australia's second innings of the second Test of the 1970–71 Ashes series, England's John Snow bowled a harmless bouncer that curved over the back of the batsman, Ian Redpath, but it was still enough for the umpire, Lou Rowan, to admonish the temperamental paceman for bowling too many short ones. One more warning and he'd be banned for the remainder of the Test. Snow copped the rebuke without a word, went back to his mark, and came in and fired down a nasty riser that nearly took Redpath's block off.

Then he turned to the umpire and said calmly, 'Now, that's a bouncer.' And then he strolled down to fine-leg and didn't bowl again in the game.

During the first Test of that series, the Aussie quick Alan 'Froggy' Thomson, had bowled a bouncer that had Snow ducking out of the way. Later, at a reception for the players at Government House in Perth before the second Test, Snow walked up to Thomson and reminded him of that delivery.

'That's a nice haircut you've got there, Froggy,' he said. 'Where would you like it parted?'

Times Change

It started when he was dropped from the Test XI. The coach told him, the captain told him, and the chairman of selectors told him, too — he was too lazy. The media agreed, and some of the editorials and comment pieces were merciless. So were the comments of the few spectators who sledged him as a 'former star' at the Pura Cup games, and after he was dropped from the state side, he copped plenty from opponents in grade matches and from cricket fans who recognised him as he walked along the street.

When Cricket Australia took away his contract, he had no choice but to apply for the dole, but for a while, though the money was terrible, he had to admit that the lifestyle wasn't all that bad. However, then Centrelink contacted him, and said that unless he got fair dinkum about looking for a job they'd have to suspend the cash payments he received every fortnight. This was ghastly news, so down he sauntered to the unemployment office to talk things over.

When his number was called, he marched up to the counter and said matter-of-factly, 'Good morning, madam. Before we start, I just have to say that I hate accepting welfare. I'd much rather have a job.'

The social worker smiled. She recognised him immediately. 'I was there when you got that first hundred,' she said.

Then she continued, 'And fortunately, just like it used to be, your timing today is excellent. We just had a very rich man call in and say he is looking for a former sporting star who might be interested in a position he has which will be based on the French Riviera. He needs a chauffeur who would also act as a permanent minder for his beautiful but slightly wayward 18-year-old daughter. Other than that, servants will be at your constant call. You'd be required to drive around in a BMW convertible, and all clothes, meals and accommodation will be provided. The salary is $200,000 a year, but of course that figure is negotiable.'

The former cricketer couldn't believe his luck had changed so fantastically. 'You're kiddin' me, right?' he said.

'Yes, I am,' the social worker replied. 'But you started it.'

Help Yourself

In the good old days, all a cricketer needed was a cricket coaching book, like the NSW Cricket Association's classic, *Calling All Cricketers*, or perhaps *The Art of Cricket* by Sir Donald Bradman. However, on the 2001 Ashes tour, Australian coach John Buchanan had his players reading books such as *Who Moved My Cheese?* and *The Art of War*. Previously, the only part of a bookshop a cricketer needed to know about was the sports section, and maybe the pulp fiction. Now, it's not so simple.

One day, a cricketer walked into a bookshop, went up to the counter and asked, 'Excuse me, madam, can you please tell me where the self-help section is?'

'Look, sir, if I told you that,' the woman replied, 'it would defeat the purpose.'

Boot Camp

This is from Ricky Ponting's *Captain's Diary 2006*, describing a funny episode that happened in the lead-up to the Australia v World XI one-dayers played in October 2005 ...

A week before the one-dayers started, I was required to go to the Telstra Dome in Melbourne for a promotion and photo shoot in connection with the Super Series. While I was there I noted how cut up and slippery the playing surface was following a hard season of football, so first chance I could I told all our blokes to contact their boot suppliers and get themselves some footy boots. The field was no better on game day, so a number of us batted and bowled in normal cricket spikes but fielded in the footwear that footballers wear, and we had a massive advantage over the overseas fieldsmen — to the point that I could see them looking at our boots and the playing surface, and sense them making a mental note that they needed to catch up for game two. Sure enough, as we went through our warm-ups before the second one-dayer many of the World XI guys were walking around in their brand-spanking-new footwear.

I did my warm-ups in my footy boots, but then I replaced them with my spikes before I went over

to have a hit in the nets. In the next net was
Rahul Dravid, who was facing up to Andrew
Flintoff and Shoaib Akhtar, both of whom were
tearing in. Poor Dravid was having a hell of a
time, as his feet kept slipping from under him just
about every ball … because he was wearing his
new footy boots!

Discretion is my Middle Name

After a tough day's play in the local park competition, a group of six cricketers had a couple of beers and then, when the last of the opposition team departed, commenced a card school in the home dressing room. They were only going to play for an hour, on the basis that in that time they couldn't lose much money and they'd be home in plenty of time to keep their wives happy.

But as these things always seem to work, time got away and the bets kept growing. It was after midnight when Arthur suddenly found himself with four sevens, and he plonked $500 straight down, only to discover that Trevor had four nines. The shock was too much for him, and he groaned, clutched at his chest, and died. Later, the doctors would say he had a massive heart attack, but before then someone had to tell his wife.

They cut the cards, and after George came up with the two of hearts he was on his way. 'Don't be brutal about it,' Trevor advised him, 'be as discreet as you can.'

Discretion, George thought to himself, *is my middle name*. He knocked on the door, and Arthur's wife answered. 'What the hell do you want,' she shouted.

'I'm terribly sorry,' George replied quietly, 'but your husband just lost $500 in one hand of poker and he's afraid to come home.'

'Five hundred dollars! Tell the bastard to drop dead!'

'If that's what you want.'

The door slammed shut, and George was on his way.

What a Catch!

A wicketkeeper was dining on his lonesome in a swanky restaurant when a beautiful blonde sat down at a nearby table. He couldn't help but admire her from a distance, but didn't have the courage to approach her. Then, suddenly, she sneezed and her glass eye came flying out of its socket and across the room towards the keeper, who dived to his right and made a superb reflex catch.

Naturally, he returned it, conversation started and soon they were sharing a very pleasant dinner, which the woman insisted on paying for, given how they'd met.

But this was just the start of a superb night, which ended with the two of them taking a moonlight stroll along the nearby beach, then back to her hotel room for a nightcap and an invitation for him to stay for breakfast. And what a gourmet meal that turned into

— if he wasn't due back at the ground for the start of play he'd still be there now, eating chocolate croissants and sipping chilled champagne and orange juice.

As he left, he thanked her for what had been a fantastic few hours. 'You are an amazing woman,' he said blissfully. 'Are you this nice to every man you meet?'

'Oh no,' she replied. 'You just happened to catch my eye.'

11. A FEW GIMMES

A Natural Slice

A club professional was showing an 18 handicapper the latest model putter, which had an extraordinary range of features that would help him shoot 88 instead of 90. 'It's the best thing since sliced bread!' the pro enthused.

And the mug golfer replied, 'What was the best thing before sliced bread?'

Words of Wisdom ...

Here is some friendly advice from two of the most popular golfers to visit Australia ...

Tommy Bolt: 'Players today throw their clubs backwards, and that's wrong. You should always throw a club ahead of you so that you don't have to walk any extra distance to get it.'

Lee Trevino: 'If you're caught on a golf course during a storm and are afraid of lightning, hold up a one iron. Not even God can hit a one iron.'

Table for None?

The members at the golf club, one of Sydney's finest, were not happy with the attitude of the new people running the restaurant. One day, a member called out to the waiter, 'Excuse me, this coffee tastes like mud.'

'That's not surprising,' came the reply. 'It's freshly ground.'

Soon after, another patron wasn't happy with his meal. 'How do you prepare your chickens?' he asked the manager.

'Nothing special,' was the response, 'we just tell them straight they're going to die.'

Found it!

Why is it that people on the golf course, when searching for their lost ball, always say, 'It's always in the last place you'd look.'

Of course it is.

A Tough Extraction

A husband and his wife rushed into the dentist's office, straight past reception. The man said to the dentist, 'Doc, I'm in a hurry! I have my two best mates sitting outside in my car, waiting for us to go play golf. The engine's running. My wife needs the car this arvo, and I want to get to the course. Let's forget about the anaesthetic and just pull the damn tooth. I don't have time to wait for the drugs to kick in!'

Crikey, the dentist thought to himself, *this is one tough cookie*. 'All right,' he said, 'if that's what you want. Exactly which tooth is it?'

The man turned to his wife and said, 'OK dear, open your mouth and show the doc which tooth hurts.'

A Dirty Secret

A married man was having an illicit romance with the receptionist at his local golf club. One Friday, the day before the Club Championship but also the man's wedding anniversary, they organised a lunchtime rendezvous at her place and made love all afternoon. Exhausted, they fell asleep and were stunned when they didn't wake until 8 p.m.

Of course, this led to one of those typical scenes with the man racing to get dressed as quickly as he could. As he pulled his trousers on, he told his lover to take his shoes outside and rub them in the grass and dirt. This she did, and then he put them on and drove home at top speed.

'Where the hell have you been?' his wife demanded.

'I can't lie to you,' he responded. 'I'm having an affair with a girl at the club. We've been making love since early this afternoon.'

She looked down at his shoes and roared, 'You lying bastard! You've been playing golf!'

A Hopeful Swing

'What do you think of my swing?' the comedian (and golf nut) Bob Hope once asked 1966 Australian Open champion Arnold Palmer.

'I've seen better swings in a condemned playground!' Palmer replied.

A Big Smile

Down at the mortuary, the coroner was talking to the chief of police about a very strange coincidence. Three bodies had been discovered in the same city on the same afternoon, all very dead and all sharing one peculiar feature — they all seemed extremely happy when they died.

The coroner explained that there was nothing suspicious going on. He pointed to the first corpse. 'A Frenchman,' he said, 'approximately 65 years of age, died of heart failure while making love to his 20-year-old mistress. That is why he has such a big smile.

'The second man is an American,' he continued. 'Forty-four years old. Just won half a million dollars in the lottery and decided to celebrate by drinking too many gallons of Jack Daniels. He died of alcohol poisoning, but judging by that big smile he was in a good mood up to the very last sip.'

'And the third man?' asked the policeman.

'A golfer,' replied the coroner. 'Twenty-seven. Struck by lightning. He was walking up the 14th fairway when there was this enormous flash and he thought he was having his picture taken.'

Holey Moley

The last round was due to begin but to date there had been no action. There was a dispute over the pin position at the par-three seventh — the tournament organisers had wanted the flag stationed at the front of the green, right behind the big bunker that guarded the right-hand side, but some of the golfers reckoned this was just too hard. Why couldn't it go at the back of the green, as it had been for the previous three days? The course designer got involved, arguing that if the pin went where they wanted, it would be almost impossible for the golfers to get their putts close if the winds raged, and then the executive producer from the television network complained that if the flag was there his coverage wouldn't be as good as it could be.

In the end, the tournament director said, 'I don't care where you put it. I quit! I'm sick of the hole business.'

The Imperfect Round

Nigel was an excellent golfer, but he was also a devout believer in God, so it didn't surprise anyone when he decided to give up the chance to be a professional golfer in order to become a priest. What was surprising, however, was that the faith he chose required him to not just give up wine, women and song, but golf, too. It was not until the elders of the church were convinced that he had the game right out of his system that he was finally ordained a priest.

Unfortunately, a couple of years later, one Sunday morning dawned remarkably serene. It was a good morning for a church service, but a perfect one for golf, and Brother Nigel could not resist. He hopped on his bicycle, rode to the place in the woods where he'd buried his clubs, and then continued on to a secluded course which he knew would be totally empty until 10 a.m. As he stood on the first tee, a gentle breeze brushing against his face and some local wildlife his only companions, he truly believed that God would forgive this very mortal sin.

Up in heaven, however, St Peter was watching. He turned to God and said, 'You're not going to let him enjoy this, are you?'

'No, I guess not,' God replied.

They looked down as Brother Nigel drove off the first tee. The hole was a 385-metre par four, and the shot was amazing, landing about 30 metres short of the green and running up to the flag, rolling one way and then the other before disappearing straight into the hole. A HOLE IN ONE! St Peter looked at God, bewildered. On the second, a short par three, Brother Nigel's tee shot landed at the very back of the green, but then spun back 20 metres into the cup.

ANOTHER HOLE IN ONE! The third was a long par five, but Brother Nigel could not just reach it in one, he landed his drive on the green and the ball landed, bit on the short grass and then dribbled into the hole for ANOTHER HOLE IN ONE!

'Why are you letting this happen?' St Peter asked.

The Good Lord turned, smiled solemnly and replied, 'He's having the round of his life and he won't be able to tell a soul about it.'

Hear Here!

Three old golfers, all well into their 90s (that's age, not strokes), were near the end of their round, when one of them suddenly said, 'Windy, isn't it?'

'I don't think so,' was the reply. 'I think it's Thursday.'

'So am I,' said the third guy. 'Let's go and have a beer.'

A Walk in the Park

Audrey was eight months pregnant. For the past four months, she and her husband Dean had been going to pre-natal classes. Dean was happy to go along, he had told her, so long as the classes weren't on Wednesday afternoons, Friday evenings or Saturday mornings. Those were his golf times. On this occasion, a Monday night, the room was full of pregnant women, and some of their partners, and the midwife taking the class was explaining to the women how they should breathe when the birth was imminent, and also telling the men what they could do and say during these moments. 'Your partner will be in serious pain,' the midwife said. 'She'll want to know you're there to support her.'

Then discussion moved to the latter stages of pregnancy, and Audrey and Dean were paying full attention. 'Ladies, I can't stress enough,' the midwife said firmly, 'exercise will help you. In my view, walking is fantastic. Gentlemen, why don't you find the time to go walking with your partner?'

The room fell silent. The men shuffled in their chairs. The women looked at each other, some with quizzical expressions. Then, quietly, Dean raised his hand.

'Yes?' asked the midwife.

'Is it OK for Audrey to carry a golf bag while we walk?'

Aiming Long

A woman comes to the 18th tee. She pulls a four iron out of her bag, but then stands over her ball for an eternity. She takes an enormous number of practice swings, checks the wind by throwing up tufts of grass, adjusts her visor, goes back behind her ball at least three times, and then, just when she finally seems ready, she steps away from the ball one more time.

All this is driving her partner crazy. In exasperation, she cries out, 'What is your problem? Can you please hit the ball!'

'I'm sorry,' the woman preparing to hit replies, 'but my husband is up on the clubhouse balcony. I'm feeling a lot of pressure to get this shot exactly right.'

'Oh dear, forget it,' the partner replied. 'There's no way known you can hit him from here with a four iron.'

The Hook

A couple were enjoying their second honeymoon, and as part of the excitement the husband decided to take his wife out for 18 holes on the resort's world-famous golf course. On the third tee, the twosome looked out at some very flash houses lining the left-hand side of the fairway, and the husband said, 'Geez, dear, you'd better be careful. If you damage one of those mansions it'll cost me a pretty penny.'

Of course, the wife promptly hooked her drive through a stained-glass window of the biggest house of them all. Soon after, they were knocking on the front door and from inside came a voice, 'Please, do come in.'

When they entered, they saw that an expensive glass bottle was lying smashed near the broken window and a man in a strange Arabic outfit was standing nearby.

'Ah, we came in to apologise for the window,' the husband said.

'Apologise?' the owner replied. 'No, no, no. I want to thank you. For I am a genie who has been trapped in that damn bottle for 1000 years. The golf ball knocked it off that mantelpiece and it broke on the marble floor. Now I am free, all because of you! As I'm sure you are aware, I have the power to grant three wishes, but if it's OK by you I'd like to give you one each and keep one for myself.'

'That sounds fair,' said the husband. 'I want a million dollars a year for the rest of my life.'

'Done!' cried the genie. 'If you check your bank account tomorrow, you will see that the first million has been deposited.'

'I'd like 50 holiday houses all across Australia,' said the wife, 'so I can travel to wherever I want and it won't cost us anything.'

'Too easy,' said the genie. 'The title deeds to all the properties will be in your letter box when you return from this holiday.'

'And your wish, genie?' asked the husband.

'Well, because I've been trapped in that damn bottle, I haven't made love to a woman in 1000 years. I would dearly like to sleep with your wife.'

The couple looked at each other, and the husband said slightly forlornly, 'He did give us a lot of money and all those houses, sweetheart.'

So the wife agreed to go upstairs with the genie while the husband continued on his round without her.

A couple of hours later, the genie and the wife were lying in bed looking at the ornate ceiling, when the genie suddenly asked, 'How old are you and your husband?'

'He's 37, I'm 35. Why?'

'I just wondered. That's a fair age to still be believing in genies.'

Rough Justice

To get away from the pressures of the courts, one of Adelaide's leading solicitors went away on a solo golf tour of country South Australia. He found himself a beautiful little course seemingly miles from anywhere and began to enjoy a blissful round interrupted only by the occasional chirrup of a native bird or the sound of a gentle breeze whistling through the trees. He wasn't playing that well, but it didn't matter, and then on the seventh he duck-hooked his drive way out of bounds into a nearby paddock.

He didn't need to get the golf ball, but there was even something exotic about clambering over the barbed-wired fence and walking through the field to find it, so off he went. He spotted it, and was just about to pick it up when the hefty boot of an old farmer descended upon it. 'I think you'll find that's my golf ball now,' the local said.

'I don't think so,' said the lawyer.

'I think you'll find it is,' the old farmer said menacingly, 'and if you don't get off my property straight away, I'll get you off myself.'

No one spoke to the lawyer this way, least of all some country hick. 'Sir, if we can't settle this amicably, I'll guarantee you that you'll lose this property in court,' he said firmly. 'Now hand over my golf ball forthwith.'

'We don't settle disagreements in court out here,' the local replied. 'We use the "three-kick rule".'

'What on earth is that?'

'The three-kick rule? First, I kick you three times, then you kick me three times, and so on, me then you, until someone gives in.'

The lawyer, a former rugby prop who'd demonstrated some ability in his university days, thought about this for a minute and decided that he could easily beat the bludger. It would make a nice change from humiliating the working class in court. However, the farmer's opening kick planted the steel cap of his work-boot straight into the lawyer's groin and dropped him to his knees. The second shattered the man's nose and bruised his eye-sockets. The third, into the kidneys, almost convinced the city slicker to concede there and then.

But now it was his turn. 'OK, you old bastard, prepare to die,' he spat out through bloodied lips.

'Nah, I give up,' the farmer replied. 'You can keep your golf ball.'

Out of Order

Two male golfers were having an awfully slow round, all because of the women in front, who were each three hundred over par but refused to call the men through. Finally, one of the held-up players decided to do something about it and he marched up the fairway towards the green, determined to give the girls a gobful. But he stopped when he got halfway to them, turned on his heel and returned to his ball as quickly as he could. 'Maybe we should just go back to the clubhouse,' he said to his partner.

'What's the problem?'

'Well, one of those women is my wife, and the other is my mistress!'

'Don't worry, mate, I'll go and sort it out.'

But the second golfer only got halfway to the women when he, too, turned around and hurried back.

'Small world, isn't it?' was all he said.

The Impossible Dream

A man was stranded on a desert island, all alone for maybe 10 years, when one day he thinks he sees something weird in the lagoon out the front of his makeshift home. At first he thought it was a seal or maybe a dolphin, but then he realised it was a woman, a genuine beauty, wearing a black wet-suit and scuba gear. He was going to ask how she got there, but she started talking first …

'How long has it been since you've had a cigarette?' she asked.

'I don't know,' he replied. 'I was washed up here in 1997.'

The woman reached down and unzipped a waterproof pocket on her left leg, and pulled out a packet of fresh cigarettes.

The man took one, lit it, and took a long, long drag. 'Man, that feels so good!' he cried.

'And I suppose it's that long since you've had a beer?' she enquired.

The man could only nod. He felt his eyes fill up with tears as she reached into the pocket on her other leg and pulled out a cold VB. No beer has ever been drunk so quickly, or enjoyed so much.

Then the woman started loosening the long zipper that ran down the front of her wet-suit. 'And tell me,' she said in a tantalising voice, 'how long has it been since you played around?'

The man could not believe it. 'Oh my God,' he shouted, 'don't tell me you've got a set of golf clubs in there!'

12. WAR GAMES

It's a Puzzle

There I was, standing on the beach, wondering why the Frisbee was getting bigger and bigger. And then it hit me.

The Taming of the Lion

A footballer decided to become a lion tamer. 'You're mad,' said a friend, 'what are you going to do if a lion charges at you in a cage?'

'I'll be right,' the footballer replied. 'I'll take my chair and I'll stick it in the big cat's face until he backs away. If he knocks the chair away with his paw, I'll take my whip, and I'll whip him until he calms down. If he ignores the whip, I'll grab my gun and shoot him dead.'

'What if the gun doesn't work? What'll you do then?' he was asked.

'I'll pick up some of the shit on the floor of the cage, and throw it in his eyes and run like hell.'

'But what if there isn't any shit on the floor of the cage?'

'Mate, if there's a lion coming at me, and I haven't got a chair, a whip or a gun, there'll be shit on the floor of the cage.'

Cut Down to Size

Max was renowned as the greatest woodchopper in history, even if he was a tough old bloke who was totally set in his ways. One day he walked into the hardware shop that sponsored him and asked whether they had that new chopping device he'd heard about that could reportedly cut down 15 trees in an hour.

'Max, I think you mean a chainsaw,' said the bloke behind the counter.

'That sounds right,' Max replied. 'But how could it be better than my best axe? Can I check one of these chainsaws out?'

The salesman went out the back and came back with the very latest, top-of-the-range model. 'Why don't you take this out into the forest and see how you go,' he said.

Max looked at the box, nodded his head slowly, and said, 'Thanks very much.'

Next day, he was back, saying, 'No, mate, this thing is no good. It doesn't work. I'm going to stick with the axe. It only cut down one bloody tree and it took me the best part of six hours to finally knock the bastard over.'

'Gimme a look at it,' said the hardware salesman.

He opened the box, pulled out the chainsaw, and started it up. To him, it sounded fine. Max, the great woodchopper, shouted, 'Hey, what's that noise?'

Don't Choke

Two Cowboys fans from North Queensland, Doug and Mick, had come to town for a big game against the Broncos. Their first port of call was a crowded local pub, for a beer, a steak and a chinwag with some mates about the football.

Suddenly, right next to them, they saw a woman at a nearby table choking on her sandwich. Doug looked at her and asked, 'Can you swallow?' It was all the poor woman could do to shake her head. She started to turn blue. 'Can you breathe?' he asked. Again, more painfully this time, she shook her head. Then Mick took over. He made the woman stand, lifted up her dress, pulled down her knickers and then, to the total astonishment of every one in the bar, slowly and methodically ran his tongue from the back of her knee up to the small of her back. The woman was so shocked she spasmed hideously, and as she did so the food that was lodged in her throat flew out of her mouth and across the room. Immediately, she began to breathe again. There were cheers all round, but the two men waved every one away, and resumed their positions at the bar.

'You know,' Doug drawled, as he took another sip on his cold beer, 'I'd heard about that Hind Lick manoeuvre, but that's the first time I've ever seen it.'

Straight Shooter

Back in the days when archery was the No. 1 sport in Britain, Robin Hood was walking through the forest with his merry men when he came across a row of trees. Archery targets had been painted on each of the trees, and smack in the middle of each target was an arrow.

'Gee, Lord Robin, the bloke who fired those arrows must be an incredible shot,' said Little John. 'I was always under the impression that you were the finest archer in all England.'

'In all the world, Little John,' Robin replied, perhaps a little miffed. 'But this fellow does not have to be as brilliant as me to be an amazing exponent of the art. We must find him.'

So the merry men continued through the forest, until they came across a young boy carrying a bow and some arrows. Eventually, the boy admitted that it was he who had shot the arrows plumb in the centre of all the targets.

'You didn't just hammer the arrows into the middle, did you?' Robin asked.

'No, my lord,' the boy replied. 'I shot them from 100 paces. I swear it on my grandfather's grave.'

'You are obviously a master marksman, young lad,' Robin said. 'I would be honoured if you would join my band of brothers.'

The boy accepted. He jumped on the back of Little John's horse, and as they were riding he was asked how he was able to land every arrow smack in the centre of each target.

'Well,' said the lad, 'I find it easier if first I fire the arrow at the tree … and then paint the target around it.'

Things are Looking Grim

The boxer was going so badly that when he asked, 'How am I going?' as he prepared to go out for the final round, his trainer replied, 'If you knock him out, we might sneak a draw.'

The First Bite

It was almost time for the gold medal bout in the heavyweight freestyle wrestling at the Olympics, between Australia's Harry Smith and Russia's Dmitri Piperov. The Australian coach was giving his man some last-minute instructions.

'Son, all you can do is your best,' the coach began. 'You've prepared brilliantly, dedicated your life; everything you've done for the last four years comes down to this moment. I know you won't let me down, let your friends down, your family down, your country down. Just whatever you do, watch out for the Russian's infamous "pretzel" maneouvre. No one has ever escaped the dreaded pretzel maneouvre. The Lithuanian boy he crushed in the semi-final is still on life-support.'

The bout began, but quickly Piperov had Smith in the pretzel. Things looked bleak, the crowd groaned, the coach couldn't bear to look. But then there was a roar, and when the coach looked up he saw the Russian flat on his back, with the Aussie wrestler pinning him to the mat. The gold medal had been won.

After the medal ceremony, the coach asked Smith how he did it.

'Well, coach,' Smith answered, 'when I realised I was in the pretzel I knew I was gone. The pain was incredible, and I could feel the air being squeezed out of my chest. But then I saw this pair of balls in front of my face and I just bit them for all I was worth.'

'Amazing,' said the coach, 'it obviously worked.'

'Sure did,' said Harry Smith. 'It's amazing the strength you get when someone bites your testicles.'

Advice Reputedly from an Infantry Journal ...

'If the enemy is in range, so are you ... if your attack is going too well, you're walking into an ambush ... try to look unimportant; they may be low on ammo.'

Marathon Man

Two men were hunting in the outback when one of them was bitten on the backside by a poisonous snake. Immediately, he broke into a sweat, and his pulse started racing. 'Mate, hang on,' said his partner. 'I'll run and find a doctor.'

And off he ran, like Robert de Castella in an Olympic marathon. Finally, he made it back to civilisation, but the only doctor in town was involved in emergency surgery. 'I'm sorry, I can't leave here,' explained the medico. 'Here's what you have to do. Take a sharp knife, cut a small X in the flesh where the snakebite is, suck out the poison and spit it on the ground.'

So the man ran back, his second marathon on the same day. Finally, he returned, to find that his ailing mate was in agony, a lather of sweat, clearly close to death. 'Where's the doctor?' the victim moaned. 'What did he say?'

'I'm afraid he said you're going to die.'

It's a Knockout

Then there was the boxing referee who got the job counting down before NASA launched its space flights. First problem was he couldn't count from 10 to one because he was so used to going from one to 10. But he didn't get the sack until he started waving his hands, as if to signify a knockout, when he'd counted 10 numbers. The pilot didn't know whether to set off for the moon or abort the flight.

The Woodchop

It was the annual wood-chopping competition at the Royal Easter Show, and the winner was a big lump of a man who no one had ever seen before. His skill with the axe had been simply breathtaking, and he triumphed in every event he entered.

Afterwards he was interviewed by reporters, and the first question was an obvious one. 'Where are you from?' asked a journalist. 'We've never had such an unknown be so dominant.'

'I come from the Simpson Forest,' the big man explained, 'out in the Northern Territory.'

'Don't you mean the Simpson Desert?' a woman asked.

'That's what they call it now,' said the champion.

We're Going on a Deer Hunt

Justin and Glenn were out hunting when Justin shot a big, athletic deer. Glenn raced over, said how impressed he was, and then the pair gutted the deer and began the arduous task of dragging the corpse by its hind legs back to their ute. On the way they ran into their mate, Doug, who expressed his admiration for their prize and then offered a piece of advice.

'Boys,' said Doug, 'you know you'll find it easier to drag that animal if you grab it by the horns. The way you're doing it, those big antlers are catching on the ground and in the bushes. It'll take you hours to get back to your truck if you keep doing it the way you've been doing it.'

Good thinking, thought Glenn and Justin. They put the dead deer's legs down, picked up an antler each and resumed dragging.

Half an hour later, their bodies lathered in sweat, Glenn and Justin stopped for a moment. 'You know, mate,' Glenn muttered, 'Doug was right. It is easier dragging this buck by its horns.'

'Yeah, mate, no doubt about it,' Justin agreed.

'But there's one thing that worries me,' Glenn continued. 'Seems to me that doing it this way, we're getting further and further away from the ute.'

Missing!

Ferdie the fight trainer was worried. His middleweight contender was late for training again. Eventually, he had to go to the phone, and as he walked to his office, he kept thinking, 'I bet it's that bloody wife of his making him do lovey-dovey stuff when he should be focused on his boxing.'

He dialled the fighter's home number and was surprised that it was his man's young boy who answered the phone.

'Hello,' the child whispered.

'Hello, son,' the trainer replied, 'Is your daddy home?'

'Yes,' whispered the small voice.

'I need to talk to him. Can you go and get him for me?'

'No,' said the lad.

Oh, thought the trainer, *that's a bit weird*. 'OK,' he said. 'Is your mummy home?'

'Yes.'

'Can I talk with her?'

'No.'

'Is there anybody else there?' the trainer asked, sounding more than a little exasperated.

'Yes,' whispered the boy, 'there are policemen.'

That changed things. Understandably, the trainer started picturing a domestic dispute, or maybe even a horrible family tragedy.

'May I speak with one of the policemen, please, son?' he asked.

'No, they're too busy,' whispered the child.

'Busy? Busy doing what?'

'Talking to Mummy and Daddy and the firemen,' was the reply.

Firemen! Before the trainer's worst fears could come true, he heard the sound of a helicopter through the phone.

'What on earth is that?' he cried.

'It's a chopper,' the boy said. 'They're bringing in a search team.'

'A search team! What is going on? What are they searching for?'

'Me!' the boy replied, with a bit of a giggle.

13. REST AND RECREATION

The Ace in the Pack

Dave was about to set off on his first solo trek into the wilderness, but before he left his mountaineering tutor gave him some last-minute instructions and then handed him a backpack of 'safety devices'.

'What's inside?' Dave asked.

'There's a two-way radio, a flare gun and a deck of cards,' he was advised.

'A radio and a flare gun, I can understand,' Dave said. 'But what's with the cards?'

'Pretty simple, really,' the older man replied. 'If you don't know where you are, and all seems lost, and the reception is no good so you can't get through on the radio, and the gun malfunctions or freezes so you can't send up a flare, and you feel the frostbite setting in, then what you should do is start playing Solitaire with the cards. It won't be too long before someone comes up behind you, taps you on the shoulder, and says, "Have you thought of putting the black queen on the red king?"'

Gold Medal Speech

It was the opening ceremony of the 2020 Olympics, and the new President of the International Olympic Committee stood up to give his first major speech. He had been a controversial, compromise appointment, following a bitter dispute between the Olympic representatives from America, China and Russia, so it was important he made a good impression. He looked over the 120,000-strong crowd, took a deep breath, and slowly began …

'Oh! … Oh! … Oh! … Oh! … Oh!'

Quickly, a female aide rushed to the podium. 'Ah, Mr President,' she whispered, pointing at the first page of the IOC chief's notes, 'they're actually the Olympic rings you're looking at …

'Your speech starts immediately underneath!'

Cutting Edge

Frank was one of Australia's best snow skiers, but one day there was a terrible accident and someone ran over him just after he'd taken a tumble on some hard, icy snow. All the fingers on both his hands were severed. Now Frank was a tough man, so he didn't call for the snow-ski ambulance; instead, he just stood up, got his balance, and slowly skied down to the chalet. Then he was rushed to emergency, where the doctor said, 'OK, let's have those fingers and we'll see what we can do.'

'Oh, I'm sorry, I haven't got the fingers,' Frank said.

'What do you mean, you haven't got the fingers?' the doctor cried. 'This is the 21st century, man! With modern microsurgery, I could have sewn them back on and made you good as new. Why on earth didn't you bring back the fingers?'

'I couldn't pick them up,' Frank explained.

An Honest Fisherman

'Do you really believe your husband when he says he's going fishing every weekend?' asked Barbara's best friend, Judy.

'Why shouldn't I?' Barbara replied.

'Every weekend! Have you ever thought he might be having an affair?' Judy continued.

'Not my poor husband,' said Barbara. 'He never comes home with any fish.'

Homework

'Dad, I'm running late for swimming training,' said young Kate. 'Will you do my homework for me, please?'

'No, sweetheart, I'm sorry,' responded the father. 'It wouldn't be right.'

'Yeah, I know,' replied Kate, 'but at least it'd be done.'

Bear Hunting

'Have you ever been bear hunting?' the old man asked.

'I've been fishing in shorts,' his grandson replied.

Salty Water

Glenn and Justin had been fishing for hours and hadn't caught a thing. Then, to rub it in, another fisherman walked past carrying a huge barrel of fish. 'Ah, excuse me, mate,' Glenn said. 'I hope you don't mind me asking, but where did you catch all those fish?'

'Fellas, if you just walk downriver until the water isn't salty, there are a million hungry fish,' the successful angler replied. 'More than enough for every one.'

Glenn and Justin thanked their new friend profusely, gathered up their gear, and were on their way. After about 15 minutes of power walking, Glenn said to his mate, 'Fill your bucket up with water and see if the water is still salty.'

'Nope, still salty,' Justin answered after dipping his bucket into the river.

Fifteen minutes later, Glenn asks him to try it again.

'Nope, still salty.'

Another 15 minutes: 'Nope, still salty.' After an hour's solid trekking: 'Nope, still salty.' Another hour later: 'Nope. Still salty.'

'This is not good,' Glenn said wearily. 'We've been walking for two and a half hours and the water is still salty!'

'I know,' Justin responded. 'But at least the bucket is almost empty.'

A Fold-Up

Foxtel have just announced that they have won the rights to show the annual World Origami Championships from Yokohama, Japan. It will only be available on paper view.

The Only Luge Joke in this Book

Why did all the athletes in the luge competition cross the road?

To get to the other slide.

Kick-off Time

A man came home after work, plonked himself in his favourite chair, turned on the television, and shouted to his wife, 'Quick, honey, bring me a beer before it starts.'

The woman was confused, but still brought her husband a beer as requested. The man guzzled it down, and then shouted again, 'Hurry, get me another beer. It's about to start.'

This time, the wife was a bit agitated, but she still brought him a beer. But a couple of minutes later, it happened again: 'Quick, get me another beer before it starts.'

'That's it!' she roared. 'You lazy bastard! You waltz in here, don't even say hello, flop your backside on the lounge, and then expect me to charge around as if I'm some kind of slave. Don't you understand that I cook and clean and wash and iron and look after the kids and put up with your mother every bloody day?'

'It's started,' the husband sighed.

A Plan for the Future

A boat docked on an old wharf near Cairns on the far north coast of Queensland. A businessman from Sydney was watching as the fisherman lifted his bounty onto the wharf, and he made a point of complimenting the angler on the quality of his fish. 'Do you mind if I ask,' he queried, 'exactly how long it took you to catch them?'

'Not very long, mate,' answered the fisherman.

'Why didn't you stay out there and catch some more?' the city slicker continued.

'Because, mate, what I caught was enough for me and my family, and for me to make enough money so we can live as we want to. I can have a kip in the afternoon. In the evening, I can muck around with my children, then go to the pub and have a beer with my mates. Or I can walk along the beach with my wife, maybe watch telly and play a little golf …'

'Sir, if don't mind me saying, you are selling yourself short,' the businessman blustered. 'I have an honours degree in business from Harvard University in the United States, and I can help you! You should be on the water before first light every morning, and stay out on the water until mid-afternoon. Then you sell the extra fish you catch, and with the profits you can buy a bigger and better boat.

'Eventually, you'll be able to purchase a second boat, then a third one. Soon you'll have a fleet of trawlers and you'll be able to buy out your competitors; then you'll have the market cornered and you can increase your prices. The banks will be throwing money at you, and you'll be able to set up your own fish market, and deal direct with all the big seafood companies around the world.

'I can see you opening offices in LA, New York, Tokyo and Hong Kong. You'll have a boat that would make Greg Norman envious, and your name will be synonymous with fishing the whole world over. With your fishing skill and my business acumen, I hate to think how many billions of dollars we'll be worth.'

'That all sounds fantastic,' said the fisherman. 'But what will I do then?'

'Sir, then you can retire into a life of luxury. Instead of working, you'll be able to have a sleep in the afternoon. In the evening, you can muck around with your grandchildren, then go to the pub and have a beer with your mates. Or you can walk along the beach with your wife, or watch TV and play a little golf …'

Not a Patch on the Reel Thing

A tourist in North Queensland decided to go on a fishing adventure with one of those boats you can hire out for the day. When he made the booking, he had no idea what he was getting himself into, but when he arrived he found himself ready to board a beautiful, slick, modern speedboat that appeared to be equipped with the very latest in fishing gear. Immediately, the fellow had visions of catching himself a marlin or two. Only slightly off-putting was the sight of the skipper of the boat, who looked for all the world like a 17th-century pirate, with an eye patch, a wooden leg and a hook instead of wrist, hand and fingers on his right arm.

Soon they were on their way, and the boat really did glide through the water. The skipper was actually the salt of the earth, and before long they were chatting amicably. Eventually, the question had to be asked.

'So where did you get that peg leg from?' the tourist asked.

'It 'appened like this: one day, years ago when the fish weren't bitin', I was 'aving a swim in the ocean and a big Noah's Ark came up and bit me leg off!'

'Geez, you were lucky to survive!'

'That I was, matey.'

'And the arm?'

'Oh, I 'ad a bit o' bad luck with a stingray, and the bastard of a thing sliced it off at the wrist. When I woke up the doctors had me fixed up with this hook.'

'What about the eye patch?'

'One day we were out on the boat and an albatross dropped its load right in me eye,' the skipper said sadly.

'And that cost you an eye?'

'It was me first day with the hook.'

Pet Shop Boys

A bloke from Queensland walked into a pet shop, spied a couple of budgerigars in a cage and said, 'I'd like those two, please.' The salesperson put the birds in a box, and the man left with his new pets and headed straight for the hills. When he got there, he climbed the highest mountain, and at the summit he put a bird on each of his shoulders and then jumped off. The birds, of course, flew away, while the man plummeted 1000 metres to his death, in the process confirming that budgie-jumping is very dangerous.

A few days later, another man walked into the same pet shop and purchased a parrot. He then drove to the same mountain, where he jumped off with the bird in one hand and a rifle in the other. Of course, the bird flew away while the man managed to fire a few shots before plunging to his death. Parrot-shooting is clearly just as lethal as budgie-jumping.

Later that same week, a third man bought a chicken from that very same pet shop. He, too, went to the top of the mountain, where he took a firm hold of the chicken's legs and then hurled himself off the edge. He, too, fell to his death, a victim of hen-gliding.

A Lucky Roll

Two bored casino dealers were waiting for a customer at the craps table. Finally, an attractive woman sidled up to the table and said, 'Hello, boys, I'd like to bet $50,000 on a single roll of the dice, if that's OK. But before I start, I have a special request. I always like to gamble in the nude. I feel luckier that way.'

'Not a problem,' said the first dealer.

'Be our guest,' said the second.

With that, she slowly and carefully took off her clothes, rolled the dice and suddenly yelled, 'C'mon there, you champions, don't let me down!!'

As the dice came to a stop, she leant well forward, squealed and then jumped up and down, her ample breasts bouncing in every direction. 'I won! I won! I won!' she kept shouting. The poor dealers tried to keep their composure as they closely and carefully watched her celebrate her good fortune.

She hugged each of the dealers separately, then both together, collected her winnings ... and her clothes ... and was quickly on her way.

Only then did one of the dealers say to the other, 'What did she roll?'

Lost!

Don's grandad retired when he was 65 and moved to a house near the beach. He made a resolution that since he was no longer working, he was going to walk five kilometres a day. That was 1980. He's 92 years old now, and no one knows where he is.

Dead Seagull

A mother went to a surf carnival with her kids, and when it got a little boring for them, she took them for a walk along the beach. At one point, her four-year-old son ran ahead of her, but then he stopped, dashed back, and asked her to come quick. Then he led her to a dead seagull that was lying in the sand.

'Mum, what happened to him?' the lad asked tearfully.

'Oh, he died and went to heaven,' was the reply.

'And God threw him back?' countered the boy.

Careful What You Wish For

Henry and Mick were experienced fishermen, but one day they found themselves in the stormy waters of

Bass Strait, floating aimlessly after their engine broke down. They hadn't caught a thing, their water supplies were nil, and it seemed they needed a miracle if they were going to survive.

And who'd have thought it, what was that floating in the ocean but a lantern. Jack swam out to get it, in the hope that maybe, just maybe, there'd be a genie inside. When he got back to the boat, Mick rubbed and polished the lamp and finally a genie did appear, but it was soon apparent that he was a cut-price version. 'I'm sorry, lads,' the genie explained, 'but I can only give you one wish, not the usual three.'

Henry was thinking about what form of rescue he preferred when Mick blurted out, 'I wish the entire ocean was filled with Victoria Bitter!'

'If that's what you want,' the genie responded and soon the sea was still and amber, with the top of the waves a creamy froth, while the granter of the wish was nowhere to be found.

Only the gentle lapping of the beer on the side of the lifeless boat broke the silence. Mick put his hand in the ocean, licked his fingers dry and pronounced it the best VB he'd ever tasted. Henry looked at him with a disgusted look on his weather-beaten face. 'You do realise,' he finally said to his mate, 'that from now on we're going to have to pee in the boat.'

Twenty Bucks' Worth

The local bowling club, where Harry was secretary/manager, decided to send Harry and his wife Doreen on a trip to Las Vegas so they could properly celebrate their 40th wedding anniversary. For a couple who'd spent their whole lives in the Sydney suburbs and had never journeyed further than Wollongong, this was one incredible adventure. First night in Nevada, Harry donned his best brown-and-green checked sports jacket, while Doreen wore a classy peach frock to complement the red tinge she'd put through her freshly cropped hair. As they entered the casino and were dazzled by the sea of poker machines, a sweet young girl 'dressed' in a very short skirt was extremely warm in her greeting.

Harry hadn't come down in the last shower, and he ignored the girl's attention. Doreen thought this was very rude.

'Harry, that dear girl was so nice to you and you treated her worse than you treat my mother,' she moaned. 'How dare you!'

'Doreen, she's a call girl,' Harry whispered.

'Oh rubbish! That young thing? Why do you always think the worst of people?'

'I'll prove it to you,' Harry said.

He walked over to the girl, had a brief conversation, and then came back to Doreen and said, 'C'mon, we're going up to our room. This will only take a jiffy.'

Up in their suite, Harry asked Doreen to hide in the bathroom, and soon after there was a knock on the door. It was 'Kitty', the girl from downstairs, and she looked even sexier now than she had in the hotel foyer.

'Before we begin,' Harry said, sweat forming on his brow, 'I need to know what this is going to cost.'

'Two hundred dollars is my basic rate,' Kitty explained, 'but for a little bit more I can make you feel really important.'

'Oh,' Harry sighed, 'I was hoping to only have to spend 20 dollars.'

'Sir, I don't know where you come from but this is Las Vegas! What sort of jackass are you to think you could have me for that kind of money?'

Kitty made sure to slam the door behind her, and Doreen emerged with a shocked look on her face. 'C'mon, dear,' said Harry, 'let's go back downstairs and have a drink and a flutter.'

Later, Harry was at the blackjack table with a beer and Doreen was right behind him, leaning on his shoulders and sipping on a cocktail. Suddenly, Kitty re-emerged, walked up to Harry, looked at Doreen, and sneered, 'There you go, buddy. That's what you get for 20 dollars in this town.'

Sanity Test

Following some rather tasteless comments about professional sportspeople and depression uttered at a sponsor's function, the football club president was invited to a mental-health institution to see first hand what was being done to help people who have psychological problems. At one point during the visit, the president asked one of the doctors, 'How do you know when a person needs to be hospitalised?'

'We fill up a bathtub,' said the doctor. 'Then we offer a teaspoon, a teacup and a bucket to the prospective patient and ask him or her to empty the bathtub.'

'Oh, I get it,' interrupted the football administrator. 'A sane person would use the bucket because it's bigger than the teaspoon or the teacup.'

'No, a normal person would just pull the plug out. Would you like a room with or without a view?'

In Too Deep

A diver was around six metres below sea level when he became aware of a man in his vicinity. The big difference was that this gentleman had nothing more than his swimming trunks on him — no mask, no snorkel, no scuba gear. His ability to hold his breath seemed to be remarkable.

Still, the diver wasn't here to admire humanity; he wanted to see some of the wonders of the ocean. So he dived down to 10 metres, then 15 metres. But the other man followed. This confused the diver, who had expected him to go back to the surface, so he swam over, pulled out his waterproof pen-and-board set, and wrote, 'How are you able to go this deep without scuba gear?'

The guy took the pen and board, erased what the diver had written, and wrote, 'I'm drowning!'

Detention

This is one of those 'true stories' which hopefully did happen. It's also got nothing to do with sport, though it will still strike the right chord with every person who back in their schooldays preferred sport to study.

One day in court, a female defendant charged with a traffic violation was asked for her occupation. She replied that she was a schoolteacher. The judge rose from the bench and said, 'Madam, I have waited years for a schoolteacher to appear before this court.' He smiled with delight, and then continued …

'Now sit down at that table and write "I will not pass through a red light" 500 times.'

Remote Control

As she walked through the electrical section of a major department store, the woman could see that the mass of televisions were divided: about 50 per cent showing the cricket, the other half split between the motor racing and the golf. However, she wasn't interested in the plasmas or the wide-screens; her mission was the designer-clothes section.

Later, after she placed six or seven items on the counter, the shop assistant asked her a question: 'Cash, cheque or card?'

The woman needed to fumble through her handbag, and as she did the shop assistant couldn't help but notice that as well as the tissues, cosmetics, mirrors, magazine, umbrella, coffee voucher, half-eaten donut, nail file, chisel, a purse and so on, the bag also contained a remote control.

'Ah, excuse me, madam, I hope you don't mind me asking,' she enquired. 'But do you always carry your remote with you?'

'No,' the woman replied. 'But my husband refused to come shopping with me, so I figured this was the most evil thing I could do.'

More Remote Control

The shop assistant nodded her head with quiet respect. Then she said quietly, 'You know remote controls are female.'

'Oh, hardly,' replied the shopper. 'How could that be?'

'Well, you think about it,' the saleswoman replied. 'A remote control gives a man great pleasure. He'd be lost without it. And though he rarely knows which are the right buttons to push, he always keeps trying!'

14. CORN CHIPS

Nerves of Steel

A punter won $200,000 in one bet. Afterwards, a journalist asked him if he was nervous when the race was being run. 'No, he replied, 'I was calm and collected.'

A Day at the Zoo

The greyhound trainer went to the zoo, but was disappointed to find that while it had heaps of different animals from all over the planet, it had only one dog.

It was a shih-tzu.

Call Me

When he went to jail for fixing fights and bribing judges, his wife said she'd stick by him, but then when he never contacted her, she decided to find herself a new man.

'How was I supposed to call you?' the ex-husband cried when she arrived at the prison to tell him the news.

'On your cell phone,' his ex-wife replied.

Leftovers

The car racer went fast into a sharp left-hander, but on the point of the corner he was shunted into the wall by a rival car and in the accident that followed suffered some horrendous injuries — his left arm was ripped off at the shoulder, he smashed his left hip, lost the sight in his left eye and, though the doctors fought hard, eventually he had to have his left leg amputated above the knee. For a while he was not expected to survive, but eventually the hospital was able to announce that he was going to be all right.

Just Look After Them

Coach Smith had an assignment for one of his assistants — 'I'm not going to be able to make training until late this afternoon,' he explained. 'I just want you to go and look after them. Make sure they don't get up to anything. If they start mucking around, it'll ruin them for the weekend.'

'No worries, boss, I'm on my way,' the assistant said faithfully. 'I'll just go and get my binoculars.'

'Binoculars? What'll you need them for?'

'Super vision,' the assistant replied.

Last Re-specs

A few weeks later, the second cousin of the assistant coach's uncle died, and the assistant went along to the funeral with those same binoculars over his shoulder.

'What's with the 8x50s?' someone asked.

'He was a distant relative,' the assistant replied.

Lloyd the Leopard

Every four years, the creatures of the world stage their very own 'Animal Olympics'. In the old days, the big cats of Africa were always dominant. The cheetahs won the sprints, the lions were always the strongest, and the leopards were excellent in the long jump. But then, the Australians came to the fore, especially in the jumping events, where the kangaroos reigned supreme. Lloyd the Leopard, the one-time world long jump champion, was so disheartened when he was beaten by Kev the Kangaroo that he decided for the next Games he'd dodge the track and field and instead enter events in gymnastics and wrestling. But he failed to qualify, proving what most experts already knew: that a leopard can't change his sports.

The Mechanic

Marty the mechanic got a job with one of the leading motor-racing teams, and on the first day in his new role he found himself under a magnificent car, treating the engine with a variety of top-range products. At one point, a drop of brake fluid fell in his mouth, and he instinctively spat it out. But then he thought, *That actually didn't taste too bad, much better than the cheap stuff I used in my previous jobs*. So he took a quick sip. Next day, when he hadn't suffered any side effects, he took another mouthful and from then on he was drinking a bottle of brake fluid a week.

One day, a few weeks later, he was caught by the boss having a swig. 'Don't drink that stuff,' the old man advised. 'It'll kill you if you get addicted to it.'

'No, it's all right,' Marty replied. 'I can stop any time I want.'

School Essay

When Tommy, the leading horse trainer, came home from a day at the track, he immediately went looking for his 10-year-old son Bart. He was astonished to find him out in the stables at the back of their mansion, sitting on the family's former Melbourne Cup winner, who had become something of a family pet after a bad leg injury forced his retirement. Not only was Bart perched on the horse, he had a pen in one hand and a notepad in the other, and was furiously taking notes.

'What on earth are you doing, Bart?' his father asked.

'Oh, hi, Dad,' the boy replied. 'I'm just doing my homework. The teacher told us to write a story on our favourite animal.'

Emergency

Freddie the front-rower was frantic. 'My wife Mary is pregnant,' he yelled down the phone, 'and her contractions are only two minutes apart!'

'Calm down, sir,' the woman at the other end of the emergency line responded. 'Is this her first child?'

'No, you fool!' Frank roared. 'This is her husband!'

All Tied Up

A group of footy players on the end-of-season trip strolled up to a nightclub door, but the bouncers said they couldn't enter without a tie. Now this club had quite a reputation, and the lads wanted to get in, so off they dashed back to the team hotel. Twenty minutes later, they were back, all wearing their club ties, except for one bloke who instead now had a pair of jumper leads around his neck.

'All right,' said the doorman, 'you can come in now.

'But you,' he continued, pointing straight at the one bloke with the jumper leads, 'don't you start anything.'

Michelle

Another end-of-season party had a fancy-dress theme, and one forward came along nude except for a woman strapped to his back. They weren't going to let him in until he explained that he had come dressed as a snail.

'So what's with the girl on your back?' someone asked.

'That's Michelle!' the forward explained.

Imaginary Punting

The gambler was travelling so badly he knew he couldn't afford to have a bet. So he just went to the races to watch and place bets 'in his head'. By race four, he'd lost his mind.

A Sticky End

As the fans poured out of the stadium they noticed that, as usual, the Mr Whippy Ice-Cream van was parked right near the car park. The owner would usually be there from noon on match day until the last fan had gone home after 6 p.m., but later that night police were surprised to find the van still there well after midnight. But it wasn't parked illegally, so they assumed the owner must have gone out for a few drinks, or perhaps the van had broken down.

But when it was still there on the following Tuesday, they thought they'd better investigate. There was no noise when they knocked on the door, so eventually they decided to break in, and when they did they were shocked to find the ice-cream salesman dead and lying on the floor. He was covered in hundreds and thousands, chocolate, caramel and strawberry sauce, nuts, small chocolate flakes, wafers and even some of those silly little paper umbrellas that get poked in nut sundaes.

An autopsy revealed the man had topped himself.

The Smiths

Smith was a great tennis player and a fan favourite, but the local sporting media hated him because he was impossible to locate when they needed to interview him, and if a reporter did find him, his answers were rarely helpful.

One day, a journalist spent all day trying different numbers, until finally he ran into him in a pub. 'How come there are so many Smiths in the phone book?' he said.

'Because we've all got phones,' Smith suggested.

The Brush Off

Once upon a time, at the local golf club, there were these two brooms that fell in love and decided to get married. A few weeks before the service, the female broom told her husband-to-be that they were expecting a baby broom.

'How can that be?' the male broom asked. 'We haven't even swept together!'

The First Dalmatian

George, the veteran greyhound trainer, finally thought he'd found the dog that could win him the big race. Only trouble was, the dog was a dalmatian.

George took him to the track, and even got him as far as the starting boxes. But the dog was spotted.

Drunk and Disorderly

Two footballers had a night on the town that went on a few hours too long. Around dawn, they were found drunk in a local park, with one drinking battery acid and the other eating fireworks. Police charged one but let his mate off.

Poetry in Motion

As well as being a famous playwright, William Shakespeare was a rugby player of some renown. He was also something of a party animal, to the point that he had a reputation for misbehaving that spread across much of England. On one end-of-season trip, he walked up to the door of a pub, but the bouncer wouldn't let him in. 'Sorry, Mr Shakespeare,' said the doorman, 'but you're bard!'

The Nobel Prize

One day, when they arrived for training, the boys in the first XI were surprised to see that one of their team-mates had already left the dressing room and was standing on his own at about deep cover point when the bowler was operating from the southern end. What was weirder was that he wasn't moving; he wasn't doing anything. Eventually, the 12th man was sent to discover what was going on.

Soon after, he returned with some surprising news. It seemed their colleague was trying to win a Nobel

Prize. Someone had told him that they were awarded to people who were out standing in their field.

The Steering Wheel

Late one night, a prominent racing car driver walked into a bar in full uniform, which was strange in itself, but what was even weirder was that he had a steering wheel protruding waist-high from the front of his driving suit. The barman poured a beer, but had to ask, 'Mate, are you aware you've got a steering wheel stuck in your pants?'

'Yes I am,' the driver replied, 'it's driving me nuts.'

Burnt to a Crisp

In 2006, the world chess championships were held on the Gold Coast, and hundreds of devotees came from all over the world for the occasion. Of course, with their game being an indoor endeavour, most chess enthusiasts are from cold-climate countries, so it was hardly surprising that when a large group of them went down to the beach for some sun and surf they came back more than a little jaded and sunburnt.

Later that night, they were in the main bar bemoaning their misfortune. Outside, a man went up to reception, pointed to where they were drinking, and asked, 'Who are those people in there?'

'Roasted chess nuts,' was the reply.

No Fun

What's the quickest way to kill the circus?

Go for the juggler.

Tour de Farce

Why can't bicycles stand up on their own?

They're two tired.

Free Tips

If at first you don't succeed, you're probably not suited to skydiving ... There is no doubt that if you exercise every day you'll die healthy ... If you're going to try cross-country skiing, do it in a small country ... Nutritionists advise a diet including lots of natural foods. But most people die of natural causes ... If quitters never win and winners never quit, why would you quit when you're ahead? ... If flying is as safe as every one reckons, why do they call the place you land and take off a 'terminal'?

Muscle Bound

Furthermore, if you want to lose weight, are sit-ups really the answer? When you exercise a muscle, it gets bigger. So doesn't it make sense that you should really only be doing sit-ups if you want a bigger tummy?

Speed Kills

And then there is the old joke — the one about the motorist who was pulled over for speeding and told the police officer he was going as fast as he could because he wanted to get home before he ran out of petrol. Every one knows the faster you go, the more gas you burn. It's the same with your heart. The more you exercise, the quicker your heart beats. It's logical that your heart is only good for so many beats. The quicker it beats, the quicker it wears out, same as everything else. You want to live longer? Take a nap.

Airwaves

A bloke wanted to watch all the sport he could on TV, so he went to the hardware shop and bought the most expensive antenna in the store. Now he could pick up TV channels from all over the country. After he put it up, the little aerial next door fell immediately in love, the feelings were mutual, and soon enough the antenna and the aerial were married. Afterwards, most people agreed that the wedding was bad but the reception was perfect.

Heeling

The tennis player went to the doctor and said, 'I can't put any pressure on the back part of either foot.'

'What have you been doing lately? Have you been training too hard?'

'No, doc, I've been taking it easy. Yesterday was the first time I've been on the court for maybe a month.'

'That's your problem. Time wounds all heels.'

The Cream of the Crop

'I'd say of all of the horses sired by Octagonal in 2003, he'd be the cream of the crop,' the owner said of one particular racehorse.

'What makes you say that?' a friend asked. 'He's never won a race.'

'That's true,' the owner replied. 'But he's been whipped the most.'

Water Worries

We've all heard about the bloke who couldn't learn to water ski because he couldn't find a lake with a slope. But what about his sister, who lost a breaststroke swimming competition because the other swimmers were using their arms?

A Strange Breed

A man purchased a new guard dog. Trouble was, every time someone rang the doorbell the dog ran straight into a corner.

He was a boxer.

Colour clash

A little-known fact from one of the early Sydney to Hobart yacht races was that one year a red boat collided with a blue boat many kilometres off the Tasmanian coast. The crews of both boats had to live for the next six months on a desert island, bemoaning the fact they were marooned.

Unlucky Breaks

'How come Greg isn't playing?' John the winger asked.

'He broke his arm in three places,' George the prop replied.

'I bet he won't go to any of them again.'

His Worst Fear

He was an ordinary conductor of an ordinary orchestra. His biggest problem was the double basses, who were easily the least professional of all his musicians. Now it was the last performance of the season, Beethoven's Ninth Symphony, but this was a performance that needed an extra effort from the basses at the end. He wasn't sure they could do it, and this dread was heightened when he found them on the drink in the dressing room. There were champagne bottles everywhere — a sight that made him so nervous that when they got to the movement where the basses were needed, he turned towards them and knocked his music stand over. The sheet music went everywhere; all he could do was watch it float away in the breeze.

It was his worst nightmare: the bottom of the Ninth, no score and the basses were loaded.

Beer Ban

A golf club walked into a local pub and asked for a beer.

'Sorry, mate, I'm not allowed to serve you,' the barman told him.

'Why not?' asked the club.

'You'll be driving later,' was the explanation.

Brains Trust

The hooker was carried off the field on a stretcher and taken straight to hospital in an ambulance. There, his condition was classified as critical.

'What's the problem?' asked one specialist.

'It looks like water on the brain,' said another.

'What should we do?'

'I was thinking of giving him a tap on the head.'

Career Change

When his life in footy ended, Jack got a job at the drycleaners. But he only lasted a week — it was too depressing. Soon after, he found some work as an electrician. But eventually, the boss found out that he didn't have any qualifications and Jack was delighted.

Mesmerising

The full forward's eyes were transfixed on the bottle of orange cordial. (The label said 'Concentrate'.)

All in the Mind

A hockey player was in terrible form, and his coach thought the problem might be mental, not technical. So he sent him to a psychiatrist.

'What are you thinking about when the ball is down the other end of the field?' the doctor asked.

'I can't get the thought out of my head that I'm a teepee and a wigwam!'

'Ah, there's your problem,' said the doctor. 'You're two tense.'

All Hot Air

An inflatable jockey was given a ride on an inflatable horse that was trained by an inflatable trainer and owned by an inflatable group of owners. It was a hurdle race, but, no, the jumps were rock solid. The horse was leading easily with just one jump to go, and it looked like all the best would come true, but then he clipped the last barrier, went down on his nose and bounced back up (as you do when you're inflatable) — but two chasers got past him and he had to be content with third place.

Back in the mounting yard, the jockey was furious. In fact, he was so mad he grabbed a hairpin from his inflatable girlfriend's hair and stuck it in the beaten horse. Then he jabbed the pin in the trainer and then in all the owners. The stewards grabbed him, but at the subsequent enquiry he managed to get free and stick the pin in himself. The chief steward could only shake his head. He looked down at the rider and said, 'Not only did you let your horse, the trainer and the owners down, you've let yourself down.'

A Matter of Opinion

The chairman of selectors went to the psychiatrist. 'Doc, you've got to help me. No one agrees with anything I say,' he said.

'No, you're wrong,' countered the medico.

Obsessed?

Joe's wife reckoned he was obsessed with horse racing. 'All you ever read about is racing,' she cried. 'All you watch on TV is racing, all you listen to on the radio is racing, all you talk about is racing, all you ever think about is racing. The only movie you've ever taken me to is *Phar Lap*. We live at Randwick, holiday at Rosehill. We don't have bank accounts, only TAB accounts. You called our children Bart, Gai and Makybe Diva.'

'No, dear,' Joe told her, 'you're way off track.'

Not So Hot

The greyhound had a fever, so his trainer took him to the vet. 'Put these on him,' the doc said, handing the trainer a bottle of tomato sauce and a tub of mustard. 'They're good for hot dogs.'

A Pig's Ear

Declan was a tough, rugged tight-head prop who had the misfortune to lose an ear in a ruck. There were allegations that the ear had been bitten off, but no one could prove anything and, worst of all, the evidence had been stolen — there was no ear to be found. All the doctors could do was replace it with a pig's ear, and though it didn't look too good (not that that mattered, what with him being a front-rower) it worked a treat so every one was happy. Or they were until Declan started hearing a buzzing sound. He went back to the surgeons to complain, but they said there was nothing to worry about, it was just a bit of crackling.

The Nude

A security guard at the cricket was 'doing the rounds' when he saw a naked man down at the boundary fence. It was clear he was about to jump over the fence and dash out onto the field. So the guard ran down, grabbed the fan by the hair, pulled his head back and poured a bottle of some kind of liquid down the unfortunate fellow's throat.

'What was that you made him drink?' a concerned bystander asked.

'Windex,' the guard replied. 'Stops streaking.'

A Bloody Cut

The caddy made the mistake of walking behind his man just as he was swinging on the practice fairway, and was clobbered and left with a horribly large gash across his forehead. At the course, they tried to help him but nothing could stem the bleeding. The ambulance officers did their best, and at the hospital they tried to save him with an IV.

It was all in vein.

Too Much Lip

The coach had been doing it tough, and after his team had put in a disgraceful effort on the training track he went back to the club for a beer or two. The poor bloke didn't have a cent to his name, so before he could enjoy an ale he had to get a few dollars from the Automatic Teller Machine. Up to the machine he went, but before he could insert his card the ATM suddenly said, 'You've got a hide showing your face in here, you fat slob!'

This was too much. The coach stopped, put his card back in his wallet and marched up to the bar to complain.

'Sorry, coach,' said the barman, 'that ATM's been out of order for a couple of days.'

Health Warning

The rugby league coach was sitting in his office, watching a video of his team's next opponent, when there was a knock at the door. When he answered, a big, black cockroach wearing a NSW State of Origin jumper dashed in, punched him between the eyes and scurried away.

That night, the same man was home with his family when the doorbell rang. When he opened the door, the same cockroach, still wearing his Blues jumper, was there again. This time, the cockroach not only threw a punch, he kicked the coach, too, then landed a karate chop and a stomp on the back of the head, and finally lodged a knife in the coach's chest. Then the crazy cockroach raced out into the night.

It was all the coach could do to crawl to the phone and call an ambulance. He was rushed to hospital, where doctors managed to save his life.

Next morning, the coach asked what had happened.

'We're not exactly sure,' the doctor replied. 'But it looks like there's a nasty bug going around.'

The Polar Bears

Two polar bears walked into the main bar of a soccer club. One went up to the bar, and said …

'Bourbon …

'and …

'Coke …
'and …
'a …
'VB …
'please …'

'Why the big pause?' asked the barman.

'We were born with them,' replied the polar bear.

Peanuts

Charles Schultz, the creator of the Charlie Brown and Snoopy cartoon characters, once reputedly said to his fellow Americans, 'Don't worry about the world coming to an end today. It's already tomorrow in Australia.'

Is that supposed to make us Aussies feel more relaxed?

15. MORE FOOTY FUN

The Kookaburra

A Fremantle Dockers fan walked into a bar with a kookaburra perched on his shoulder. The barman looked at him and said, 'Wow, that's not bad, where did you get that?'

'Perth,' the kookaburra replied, 'there're thousands of them over there.'

Miss Right

During the off-season, Steve started dating a new girl. She seemed OK. His team-mates' concern grew when he started describing her lovingly as 'Miss Right'.

Then the autumn came, and his mates asked how the romance was going. 'Not too good,' he replied. 'It wasn't until the footy started that I realised her first name isn't Kylie, it's "Always".'

Re-Tired

As well as being one of Australia's finest AFL footballers, Maggie's husband, Claude, was something of a male chauvinist. Even though Maggie had a full-time job while Claude's only source of income was his football, her husband never helped around the house. That, he constantly explained, was women's work!

Then one night Maggie arrived home from work to find their children bathed and fed, the washing machine and clothes dryer both working, the place vacuumed, a roast in the oven and the dining table set. Something was up, she immediately thought. But after he put the kids to bed, he explained that one of the girls in the footy club's front office had told him that women who work full time and also have to do their own housework are usually too tired for lovemaking. Claude wanted to fix that.

The meal was wonderful, not just because the meat was perfectly cooked, but also because the lit candles and soft music in the background added to the romantic mood. Afterwards, Claude insisted on putting the dishes in the dishwasher, while Maggie put on something comfortable and then lay gently on the lounge, sipping her chardonnay.

The next day, she was asked how the rest of the evening went.

'It was perfect,' she explained. 'Claude was so tired he went straight to bed, so I got to stay up and watch three hours of trashy television.'

Dying Days

Four old footballers are sitting at the bar, when one suddenly says, 'When your time is up, and you're at your funeral lying in the casket, and all your family and friends and the fans are there in the church mourning you … what would you want them to say about you?'

One of the trio replies, 'I'd like them to say, "He was one of the greats, the finest player of his generation."'

'No,' said the second, 'I'd like them to say I was the fairest, most honest footballer to ever pull on a jumper.'

The third man then said, 'I'd like them to say I was the toughest, hardest, bravest man to ever play the game.'

The fourth man, the one who'd asked the question, took a quiet sip on his beer. 'All I'd want them to say,' he laughed quietly, 'is … "Shit! He's moving!"'

Sleeping Soundly

Two married footballers are out drinking one night when one turns to the other and says, 'Mate, I have no idea what I should do. When I go home after a long night out on the grog, I always turn the headlights off before I drive into the driveway. I turn off the engine and glide into the garage. I take my shoes off before I walk into the house, and I sneak up the stairs, get undressed in the bathroom and get into my side of the bed as quiet as a mouse, but the bloody wife still wakes up every time and screams at me for staying out so late! Do you have that problem?'

'No, mate, you're going about it all wrong,' said his friend. 'I screech into the driveway, high beams blazing. I slam the garage door, stumble up the steps, toss my shoes into the back of the cupboard, jump into bed, usually on the wrong side, slap the missus on the backside, and slur, "How 'bout it, luv?" Every time, without fail, she's fast asleep!'

The Great Maldini

The club had lost all its matches in all grades over the first six rounds, and the coaching staff was shattered. Nothing had worked, so as a last resort they decided to bring in a hypnotist. They weren't sure if it would do any good, but at least it would look like they were doing something.

So one day all the club's players were brought into the big change room under the main grandstand, and then they were introduced to the 'Great Maldini', hypnotist to the stars.

'Welcome, gentlemen,' the Great Maldini began. 'Today, I will explore your inner thoughts, find out what is troubling you, and hopefully get you working more as a team. Let us begin …'

The Great Maldini took a beautiful antique fob watch from his waistcoat. 'Gentlemen, I am going to put you in a deep sleep, using this very, very special timepiece. My family have been hypnotists going back five generations. We have all used this watch.'

He began swinging the watch gently back and forth, quietly chanting, 'Watch the watch … watch the watch … watch the watch … you are sleeping … sleeping … sleeping …'

The players were quickly mesmerised as the watch swung back and forth. Seventy pairs of eyes followed the watch intently, but then suddenly it slipped from the hypnotist's grasp and fell to the floor, shattering into a thousand tiny pieces.

'Shit!' cried the Great Maldini.

It took them four weeks to clean up the changeroom, during which time the club failed to win a single match.

Flying South

The young, often cheeky rover from Melbourne was going on a secret flight to discuss a deal with one of the interstate teams. On reaching his seat in business class he was surprised to see that a galah had been strapped into the seat next to him.

Soon the stewardess was asking him if he'd like a drink. 'Any chance of a coffee, please?' he asked.

'Certainly,' she replied, before turning to the parrot. 'And you, sir?'

'Get me a bourbon, you fat ugly cow!' squawked the parrot.

Within 30 seconds, the flustered stewardess returned with the bourbon, but though the footballer waited patiently there was no sign of any coffee. Finally, when he caught her eye, he said quietly, 'I'm sorry, but I think you've forgotten my coffee.' But before he received a reply, the galah shrieked, 'C'mon, woman, gimme another bourbon, you tart.'

The same thing happened. The bourbon was brought immediately, but the clearly ruffled girl forgot the coffee. Again, the rover was polite when he reminded her, again the galah was horribly rude as he demanded another bourbon, and again the bird got what he wanted while the footballer did not.

So he decided he'd try the galah's method. 'Hey, sweetheart,' he shouted, 'why don't you stop gossiping with your repulsive girlfriends, and get on those billiard-table legs of yours and bring me my damn coffee.'

But there was no coffee. Instead, two burly security guards stormed down the aisle. They grabbed the rover and the galah, dragged them to the front of the plane, opened the emergency door, and threw them out, shouting as they did so, 'That's what this airline does to rude bastards like you!'

As the rover began his plunge to a certain death, the galah looked at him and smiled, 'Geez, you've sure got a bit of lip for someone who can't fly!'

Spelling Bee

Coach: OK lads, a simple question before we get started. Shane, how do you spell the word 'CONCENTRATION'?

Shane: K-O-N-S-E-N-T-R-A-Y-S-H-U-N.

Coach: Geez, Shane, that's not even close!

Shane: You asked me how I spell konsentrayshun, and that's how I spell it.

Hijacked

Little did the terrorists know that the plane they were hijacking was actually full of player-managers, all on their way to the taxpayer-funded, all-expenses-paid, annual player-manager conference-stroke-junket to Tahiti. With the plane in the air, the pilots handcuffed and the player-managers cowering in their seats, the hijackers held a conference in the cockpit.

'I think we have to change our strategy,' said the leader of the terrorist gang. 'I'm going to contact the authorities, and threaten to release one player-manager every hour until our demands are met.'

Know Your Brands

Herbert wasn't the most sensitive person in the world. It was the one thing his wife Wendy didn't like about him, but after 20 years playing and then coaching grade footy, maybe this toughness wasn't so surprising. Eventually, though, it became too much and, at Wendy's instigation, they found themselves in the marriage counsellor's office. Poor Herbert was bored in no time, as the counsellor rattled on about all the latest theories and concepts that apparently make for a happy marriage, until he heard the bloke declare, 'It is vital that each partner in a relationship is aware of what really matters to the other.'

He looked at Wendy and asked, 'Can you tell me what's really important to Herbert?'

'The Adelaide Crows!' she sneered in a high-pitched voice. 'Nothing else, unless you count drinking at the pub after watching the Crows play. Or ringing up his mates to talk about the Crows.'

The counsellor was disturbed. He could sense both by Wendy's answer and the tone of her voice as she gave it that this was going to be difficult. He changed tack slightly.

'Now, Herbert, can you tell me the name of your wife's favourite flower?'

'Gee, mate, that's not easy,' Herbert shook his head. 'I'd have to say "White Wings Self-Raising".'

If You Make Your Own Bed …

A footy team went away on their end-of-season trip, having decided to make the adventure up as they went along. Part of the reason for this was that fundraising hadn't gone well, so they were travelling on the cheap. On the first Friday night, they needed to find somewhere to stay, so they walked into an ordinary-looking pub, and asked the old guy behind the bar, 'How much for a room for the night?'

'Fifteen dollars each, fellas, or five bucks if you make your own bed.'

'That sounds OK, we'll take the five-buck deal.'

'Righto, I'll get you some nails and wood.'

The New Coach

Back in the 1980s, the local football club suffered a bad run, finishing last for five straight seasons. These failures were blamed mostly on the local party girls who were always distracting the players. In desperation, the club committee decided to appoint an old army sergeant as its new coach, and he was duly introduced to the supporters at a pre-season launch. All the players were in attendance at this event, as were their many girlfriends, and after the function had been going on for a couple of hours one of the ladies sidled up to the new coach.

'Ah, excuse me, Sergeant … should I call you "Sergeant" … or is it "Coach"?' the pretty blonde said with a smile. 'You seem to be a very serious man. Is there any way I can help you?'

'Negative, ma'am,' the sergeant replied. 'I'm just serious by nature.'

'Every one is saying you've seen a lot of action,' the girl giggled.

'Yes, I have, ma'am,' the sergeant said curtly. 'I've seen a lot of action.'

'Maybe you should lighten up a little, relax a bit, enjoy yourself.'

The sergeant just stared at her, and didn't say a word. Finally, the young lady said, 'I hope you don't mind me asking, but when was the last time you had sex?'

The sergeant looked straight ahead, and then replied, '1955.'

'Well, there you are,' the girl purred. 'You really need to chill out. No sex in all that time?'

She took his hand and steered him into a nearby storeroom, where they stayed for the next half hour. Afterwards, the girl was panting for breath, her hair all over the place, while the sergeant was as stern and straight as ever, offering no indication of the passion he had just enjoyed.

Before they went to rejoin the party, the girl grabbed his arm and whispered, 'Wow, Sarge, you sure haven't forgotten anything since 1955.'

'I should hope not,' the new coach said flatly as he glanced at his watch. 'It's only 2130 now.'

The Gates of Heaven

He arrived at the gates of heaven still wearing his Bulldogs guernsey, and St Peter's first question was, 'What was your main claim to fame on earth?'

'I was the star full-forward for the Western Bulldogs,' the man replied.

'And does anyone moment stand out for you?' St Peter asked.

'Well, yes,' the man muttered. 'One year, we needed to draw in the final round to make the semi-finals. With time almost up and the Bulldogs trailing by two points, I marked 15 metres from goal, right in front. As I went up to take the shot at goal, I heard the siren go in the background. It was all down to me. The 85,000-strong crowd at the MCG went silent. Many Bulldogs prepared to run out onto the ground in jubilation … But then I sliced the kick so badly I didn't even get a behind.'

'When did this happen?' St Peter enquired.

'Oh, I don't know. Maybe 90 seconds back …'

Salary Capped

A very successful multi-millionaire was also the president of a struggling AFL club. One day he came up with a genius idea to get around the salary cap. The club's veteran rover was coming to the end of his existing contract, and now the president personally offered him a half share in his own furniture business if the player would accept a hefty pay cut.

'I see where you're coming from,' the rover said. 'Gimme that contract.'

So pen was put to paper and then the president added, 'Now to keep this above board with the AFL, I'm going to need you to come down to the factory and learn a little about how the operation works.'

'Oh no, I hate factories,' the rover said. 'I can't stand all that bloody noise.'

'I see,' muttered the president. 'Well, we'll have to put you in head office, and you can do some clerical work.'

'No way, mate. I'm a footballer. Just thinking about doing time behind a desk makes me crook.'

The president was totally exasperated. 'What am I going to do with you then?' he cried.

'You could buy me out,' the wily rover replied.

Wide But In

Geelong's high-profile forward Billy Brownless went into the 1993 season carrying a little bit of weight. He was still easily good enough to play in the firsts, and one day was down in the forward pocket when a ball sailed over his head and appeared to go out on the full. But the boundary umpire ruled otherwise, a decision which Brownless debated long and furiously.

According to author Geoff Davie in his book *Cats on the Prowl*, the man in white reacted to Brownless's tirade by saying succinctly, 'Well, if your fat bum wasn't in the way, maybe I would have seen it better.'

There's not much you can say in response to that.

Best Wishes

Two women had a night on the town, got themselves incredibly drunk and then on the walk home developed a desperate need to go to the toilet. This occurred as they were going past the local cemetery, so they jumped the sandstone fence, snuck in until it was pitch black all around them and then relieved themselves behind a headstone.

Being girls of some class, they needed toilet paper. Of course, there was none to be found. So one of them took off her knickers, dried herself with them, and then threw them away into the gloom. The other was wearing her favourite underwear — the ensemble her husband had given her for their 10th wedding anniversary — so instead she grabbed an elaborate ribbon off a wreath that was lying nearby and used that. Then they were on their way.

The next day, the women's husbands were chatting on the phone. 'You know, Mike,' one of them said, 'I reckon we should keep an eye on our wives. Mine came home last night without her undies.'

'You've got nothing to worry about, mate,' responded the other. 'Mine woke up this morning with a card stuck to her bum that read: "From all the boys at the footy club. We'll never forget you."'

Maths Test

The coach of an AFL club was told that unless his star recruit's high-school studies improved, he'd have to take him off the team. The No. 1 problem was mathematics, and when the kid failed a half-term exam, he was in big trouble. But the coach pleaded for the player to have one more chance, and the compromise that was reached was that the kid would be given a maths test before Saturday's game, and if he passed it he'd be allowed to stay.

Now, even though that gave the coach a chance, it was a pyrrhic victory because the lad was so dumb that he'd fail whatever was thrown at him. But for a while it looked like the plan might just work, until only an hour before the first bounce, the club's education officer asked if the exam had taken place. The coach said no and was told that unless it occurred the player was out.

There was no time, so the coach raced into the rooms where the team was getting ready. 'Jason,' he cried out, 'I've gotta ask you a question. If you get it wrong, you can't play today. Mate, what's two plus two?'

'Aw, gee, coach,' the teenager replied, 'it's four, isn't it?'

'Four! Did you say four?' The coach was stunned and thrilled that he'd heard the right answer.

And then, suddenly, in unison, the boy's teammates started shouting, 'C'mon, coach, give him another chance.'

Science Test

So that was the maths problem fixed up, but then there was a problem with the young man's science studies. This time the question was a toughie, but it had to be asked: 'How many seconds in a year?'

The lad asked for time, and the coach was happy to give it. In his heart, though, he knew the boy wouldn't be playing again, and this seemed to be confirmed when a few minutes later he came back with his answer …

'Twelve!'

'Twelve?'

'Yeah, coach. Twelve! January second, February second, March second …'

Capital Punishment

'Your honour,' said the defence lawyer, 'we concede that my client was speeding, but he was only trying to get to training on time.'

'And did he make it?' asked the judge.

'Well, no, your honour,' the lawyer continued. 'He was pulled over by the highway patrolman. That is why he is here before you this day.'

'And for whom does the accused play?'

'The St Kilda AFL footy club, your honour.'

'Oh dear, case dismissed,' the judge sighed. 'This man has suffered enough.'

The Rat

To fully appreciate this story, which the great Hawthorn player Dermott Brereton told about his team-mate, Brownlow Medal-winning rover John Platten, in Platten's autobiography, *The Rat*, you need a picture of Platten: short, nuggety, with long frizzy brown hair well over his shoulders and a hairy body to match. It was an end-of-season trip in Hawaii, and the players had dared each other to cover themselves in sunscreen, then roll about in the sand, and then stay that way for an hour.

Platten jumped at the chance. He lathered himself up, threw himself enthusiastically onto Waikiki Beach, and then sat himself up at the bar. The sand caked on his hairy body had him looking like a piece of chicken schnitzel, and his long, sand-caked, curly hair only added to the look, which was hardly flattering. Yet when the 60 minutes was up, Platten was happy to let the joke continue.

'We stood around that pool bar for about three hours,' Brereton recalled. 'Every time it was his shout, the bar would empty!'

Home Discount

The Melbourne AFL supporter walked up to the ticket office at the Melbourne Cricket Ground and said, 'I'd like a half-price ticket for Saturday night's game, please.'

'Half price?' cried the woman behind the counter. 'We don't sell half-priced tickets!'

'But I only want to watch one team,' the Demons fan replied.

Those were the Days

The coach decided to have a little fun. When he realised that every one of his players had been born in the 1980s or later, he sat them down in front of a whiteboard, drew a greater-than sign (>) and a less-than sign (<) on the board and asked, 'Do any of you blokes know what these mean?'

Nathan was the first to raise his hand. 'Too easy coach. The first one means "fast-forward" and the other means "rewind"!'

All Booked Out

A couple entered one of the finest restaurants in the Melbourne suburb of Collingwood. 'I'm sorry,' apologised the maitre d', 'but unless you have a booking we won't be able to fit you in tonight.'

'Ah, excuse me, my friend,' the man responded. 'You do realise that I am one of this city's finest cricketers.'

'I am sorry, sir, but there just isn't a table available this evening.'

'I bet if Eddie McGuire came in and asked for a table, there'd be one available for him.'

'Ah, well, yes. That is true. I suppose we would have a table for Mr McGuire. But he is, after all, the president of the Collingwood Football Club.'

'But he isn't coming tonight. We'll have his table.'

Work Experience

As part of the AFL's policy that young players should get some work experience rather than just sit around all day playing computer games, Carlton's star recruit, young Lachlan, got himself a job as a trainee house painter.

On his first day in the job, the coach decided to go down and see how he was doing and was surprised to see the lad on top of a ladder, brushing away, while wearing what appeared to be a dentist's white gown over a heavy-duty army jacket. It was the middle of January and the temperature was in the mid 30s.

'What's with all the clothes, Lachie?' the coach called out.

'It does seem weird, coach,' Lachlan replied. 'But on the can it says, "For best results, put on two coats".'

Close Knit

A police car pulled alongside a speeding vehicle on the motorway from Brisbane to the Gold Coast. As the officer did so, he was astonished to see that the woman behind the wheel of the speeding car was knitting. So focused was she on the task that she hadn't even noticed the flashing lights or the wailing siren.

'Hey, lady!' cried the policeman. 'Pull over.'

'Oh no, officer,' shouted the surprised driver, 'it's a Lions scarf.'

Two Worlds Collide

One Saturday afternoon there was a car crash on the Coburg Road in Melbourne, which saw a car driven by an Essendon fan collide with a vehicle driven by a Carlton supporter. Both cars were wrecked, but fortunately the two men escaped uninjured.

Observers wondered if the two would get into a barney, but instead they seemed pretty relaxed about what had just happened.

'Are you OK?' asked the Bomber.

'Yeah, I'm all right,' said the Blue. 'How about you?'

'I'm fine.'

But then the Carlton fan stopped, and bolted for his car. 'Geez,' he cried, 'I've got a case of VB in the boot. They'd better not be smashed.' He forced the boot open, looked in, grabbed a bottle, and then gave a huge sigh of relief.

'Mate,' he said to the Essendon fan. 'This has got to be a sign. Why don't we have a beer to celebrate our survival?' He ripped the top off the beer, handed it to his new 'friend', and watched while it was quickly skolled from top to bottom.

'Aren't you having one?' asked the Bomber as he wiped the last remnants from his lips.

'No, mate,' said the Carlton supporter. 'I'll wait until after the cops have come and gone.'

The Devil

Hamish Lincoln, player-manager to the stars, was stunned one day when he received a visit from the Devil. 'OK,' said Satan to Lincoln, 'I can make you richer, more famous, and more successful than any of your competitors. I can see to it that you dominate not just the AFL, but the NRL, the Rugby Union, the A-League, the NFL, Major League Baseball, the NBA, the Premier League, whatever you want. I can make you the greatest and most feared player-manager there ever has been or ever will be.'

'That sounds all right,' replied Lincoln. 'But what do I have to do in return?'

The Devil smiled, 'You have to give me your soul,' he chortled. 'But not just your soul, I want your parents' souls, your wife's soul, your children's souls, your grandchildren's souls. I want the souls of all your descendants for 20 generations.'

'Hang on a minute.' The player-manager reacted cautiously. 'Where's the catch?'

Wealth is Better Than Health

Charlie, the first-team coach, was a fitness fanatic. George, his brother, was a slob. So no one, least of all Charlie, was surprised when George collapsed and died of a heart attack a few weeks after he turned 50.

Soon after, the family was gathered for the reading of George's will. 'To my darling wife, Debbie, I leave our house and 10 million dollars,' the lawyer began. There was a gasp from the gathering; people knew George was OK financially, but they didn't realise he was that rich.

'To my son, Norman,' the lawyer continued, 'I leave my Mercedes, the beach house and the greyhounds.'

'To my daughter, Susie, I leave my yacht and $250,000.'

'And to my brother, Charlie, who told me time and again that health is better than wealth, I leave the top-of-the-range exercise bike he gave me for my 50th birthday.'

Fool!

The team was losing and the coach was copping it from all corners — not least from the fans, who wanted him gone. He was receiving a stack of hate mail, and one of them was a single sheet of paper on which was written just one word, in thick, black Texta: FOOL!

The coach looked at this letter, and then showed it to the other blokes in the room. 'Isn't it amazing,' he said. 'With most of the letters I've been getting, the people have been forgetting to sign their names. This goose signed his name but forgot to write a letter.'

Team Selection

'Lads,' said the coach, 'for the first few rounds of this year's competition, each of you is going to have a game off.'

'But, coach,' said the team captain, 'that's not going to help us find our best form.'

'That might be right,' replied the coach, 'but this is the best way I know to learn which ones of you we can do without.'

Your Drought

Wally went to his doctor because he was suffering from lethargy and headaches. The doc had a good look at him, and then wrote out a detailed prescription.

'Wal, I want you to take the red pill with a large glass of water when you get up in the morning. Then take the yellow pill with a large glass of water after lunch and the blue one in the evening, also with a large glass of water.'

Having to take all these pills worried Wally who was keenly aware of the AFL's anti-drugs policy. 'What's wrong with me, doc?' he asked.

'Not much, mate,' came the reply. 'You're just not drinking enough water.'

16. SCRUMS AND SEND-OFFS

Dancing in the Dark

The boys were on their end-of-season trip, and had rocked up at the local RSL club disco. Things were moving a little slow for their liking, so to rev things up they decided on a competition — each of them had to try to dance with an ugly girl, with the man judged to have jived with the ugliest girl being crowned as the winner. Norman, the 30-something front-rower with the pot belly, billiard-ball haircut, Merv Hughes moustache, and with a nose that had been broken more times than it should have been, fancied his chances, and sure enough he was soon out on the floor with a fat, bespectacled middle-aged woman who looked as if she'd had three or four facelifts too many. For the rest of the footy team, this was a no contest, and they quickly conceded defeat. Meanwhile, Norm continued to strut his stuff, as he and his new 'lady love' danced their hearts out to the tune the DJ had specially selected: Benny Hill's classic tune from 1971, 'Ernie (The Fastest Milkman in the West)'.

When the song finally ended, Norm came back to his mates and was greeted by high-fives all round. But at the same time something strange was happening on the other side of the auditorium. Norm's 'girlfriend' had rejoined her friends, and they were laughing themselves silly. Billy, the team's half-back, was sent over to find out what was going on. When the news came back it reduced the boys to tears of laughter. Well, all except their big prop.

It seemed that the girls had been playing the same game … and Norm had won twice!

The Good Old Days

Here are a couple of true stories from Sydney rugby league's early seasons. In the game's first year, 1908, Newtown were playing Balmain and the Newtown centre Frank Cheadle had a shot at a field goal. But as he kicked the ball, it burst — and instead of sailing through the posts it just went a few metres, first wobbling like a wounded seagull and then dropping straight to earth. First to react was the Newtown centre, Bert Andrews, who ran in, picked up the sorry, deflated bladder, and dived over for a try.

Balmain captain Bob Graves started to protest the try, but even he had to concede that while the circumstances were bizarre, the try was legal. But then he had a brainwave — didn't the try have to be converted using the same ball that was involved in the scoring of the try? The referee and his linesmen had a conference, and while they conceded that was what the rule said, it would be ridiculous to make the Newtown kicker use the busted ball. Graves continued to protest, a new ball was called for, and the Newtown kicker was so put off by the kerfuffle that he promptly missed the simple conversion.

Two years later, in a reserve-grade game, a fellow known only as 'Thompson' scored an excellent try for Easts against Norths, beating the fullback and running 30 metres to put the ball down. Only trouble was, as one newspaper reported, 'To show his contempt for the opposition, he half turned around whilst running to make fun of them.' Big mistake. His behaviour might have amused the spectators and the reporters, but not the Norths forwards. The newspaper went on to reveal that less than a minute after the try was scored, Thompson was flattened in an off-the-ball incident and was carried unconscious from the field.

The Three-Tackle Test

Of all the great philosopher coaches in the history of rugby league, George was renowned as the best. But one day a group of his players heard a rumour that they knew would upset their mentor, and they resolved that they had to tell him about it.

'Coach,' the team captain said quietly after they'd asked if they could have a moment, 'we need to tell you something we've heard about one of the other team's coaches.'

'Before you say anything,' George replied with much authority, and the hint of a kind smile, 'this information you want to give to me needs to pass what I call the "three tackle" test. This will help you understand the difference between fact and gossip.'

'The three-tackle test?' answered the players in unison. 'What's the three-tackle test?'

'Well,' the great coach continued, 'the first of these tackles is "truth". Are you totally certain that what you are about to tell me is true?'

'Well, um,' the captain mumbled, 'not *totally* certain.'

'All right,' said George. 'So you don't *really* know that it's a fact.'

'No.'

'Now, the second tackle. This is goodness. Is what you want to tell me about one of my rivals something good?'

'Well, er, no,' said the captain. 'On the contrary.'

'So you want to tell me something bad about him, and you're not sure if it's true,' George responded, every word seemingly full of wisdom. 'That's two tackles down. Now the third tackle, the tackle of usefulness. Is what you are about to tell me going to be useful for me?'

The players thought for a moment. 'Ah, not really, coach,' one of the players muttered. The others nodded their heads in agreement.

'Well, if what you want to tell me is not true, not good and not useful, why tell me at all? There must be more important, more productive things that we can worry about.'

So the players went on their way. They had just experienced first hand why George was renowned as a great philosopher, and why he was so well regarded, and loved by all who came under his care.

They also knew that he would probably never discover that his greatest coaching rival was having an affair with his wife.

Sorry

After a St George–Eastern Suburbs game, a Roosters supporter returned to his BMW to discover the car's headlights smashed and considerable damage to the grille. There was no sign of the offending vehicle or the driver, but at least there was a piece of paper stuck under the windscreen wiper. It read:

Sorry. I just backed into your Beamer. I note there is a Roosters sticker on the back window. As I write this note, the witnesses who saw the accident are nodding approvingly and smiling at me because they think I'm leaving my name, address and other particulars …

I'm not.

Sports Speak

'You've played a couple of trials now,' the reporter said to the coach. 'What do you think of your new star signing?'

'I just cannot say enough positive things about the bloke,' the coach replied. 'He is always trying. Whatever he attempts, he does it without any effort. In team meetings, his comments are always critical, and we're always asking him if he's got any idea. There is nothing you can teach a player like him. If he ever leaves the club, it'll be hard to find another one like him.'

'You mean there's a chance he's going?' asked the media man.

'Judging by what we've seen so far, come the start of the season, he'll be fired with enthusiasm.'

A Close Contest

Back in the 1970s, the decade when international rugby league declined from its previous position as the ultimate form of the game, Australia was due to play Great Britain near the end of a long Kangaroo tour. The boys were tired and didn't really want to play, and given that they'd thrashed the Poms in the preceding Tests the result wasn't in doubt.

'Look, fellas,' said the captain. 'We all know the Poms are garbage, but we've got to play the game. If we don't we'll have to cop all the papers bagging us about ignoring the traditions of the game, and how we're arrogant and only here for the grog.'

'I've got an idea,' said Billy, the team's half-back. 'Why don't you blokes all go down to the pub and I'll play 'em on me own. I'm good enough to beat these bastards by myself.'

No one disagreed, so the plan was put in place. On the day of the game, the rest of the team went to the pub and were playing pool in the back room when word came through that at half time Australia was leading Great Britain by 10 points to nil. 'Good old Billy,' every one cheered. 'He'd have to be a chance for the man-of-the-match award,' someone laughed. The guys went back to their pool and their pints and didn't give the Test another thought until about an hour later, when Billy walked in looking downcast.

'What happened, mate?' someone asked. 'How much did we win by?'

'I'm afraid we didn't win,' Billy said quietly. 'It finished a 10–all draw.'

'How could this be? It sounded like you had things under control.'

'I did, mate, I did. I was all over them until just after half time when one of their forwards had a swing at me. I punched him back and the ref sent me off.'

Chance Meeting

It was the start of a new season, and a Sydney paper sent one of its reporters out west to Parramatta to get a gauge on the Eels' chances. The journo began by asking one of the club's officials, 'Well, you'd have to agree that this competition is so open it looks like a lottery.'

'No, I wouldn't,' replied the official. 'We'd have a chance if it was a lottery.'

Midlife crisis

The coach looked at his wife in the kitchen one day and said, 'Darling, 25 years ago, when I was captain of the footy club, we had a tiny apartment, a bomb of a car, slept on a mattress on the floor and watched television on a portable black-and-white set. But I got to sleep every night with a beautiful 25-year-old blonde.

'Now, I'm the coach, we have a big house, flash car, king-size bed and plasma-screen TV. But I'm sleeping with a 50-year-old woman. Seems to me you're not holding up your side of the bargain.'

'Sweetheart,' the wife replied. 'I love the fact you're still at the football club. Why don't you go there tonight and find yourself a hot 25-year-old blonde. And if you get lucky, I can guarantee you'll soon be back living in a tiny apartment, driving a bomb of a car, sleeping on the floor and watching television on a portable black-and-white set.'

Brains not Brawn

The coach of the local football team was sick of his players making dumb mistakes every weekend, so before training on the Monday he put up a sign that said 'THINK!' above the hand basin in the men's toilets next to the change rooms. He wanted to remind his players that they had to make smarter decisions on the field, to use their brains against the opposition as well as brawn.

After training, he went into the gents himself, and was a little disappointed to see that someone had put another sign above the dispenser that was located next to the hand basin.

It read: 'THOAP.'

Death Notice

A player-manager renowned for driving a hard bargain, and for leaking information to the media that made it look like his clients were about to sign big contracts for different clubs, suddenly died of a heart attack. Though his passing was widely reported in the media, his agency kept getting calls for him, to which the receptionist always responded, 'I'm sorry, he's no longer with us.'

After a while, the woman taking these calls realised it was always the same person at the other end of the line. Eventually, she had to ask, 'Why do you keep doing this?'

'I'm sorry, dear,' said the caller, 'but I'm one of the club officials your former boss liked to mess with. I just like hearing you say, "He's no longer with us."'

The Other Cheek

Little Benny was renowned as a cheeky half-back on the field and he was just as devilish off it, even if he was well past his 30th birthday. One day at home he was watching his wife putting cream on her face, and he asked, 'Why do you do that?'

'To make myself beautiful, dear,' his wife replied.

The half-back kept watching, and soon his wife was removing the cream with a tissue.

'What's the matter?' Benny asked. 'You're not giving up?'

Man in Black

In 1971, NSW played Queensland at Lang Park, and because the game was being played in Brisbane, a Sydney referee was handed the whistle. The man in white was no less than the former champion half-back Keith Holman, who is one of the few men to have played in as well as refereed a Sydney premiership Grand Final.

It turned into a controversial game from the moment a Queensland forward flattened a Blue counterpart with a stiff-arm and not only admitted that he did it, but also explained that he'd meant it for Bob Fulton. Four players were sent off, three of them locals, and the crowd was filthy. One irate Maroon supporter tried to invade the field, the mood was extremely hostile, and at full time Holman needed the help of the NSW forwards to get off the field in one piece.

Afterwards, two commentators of the game for Sydney radio stations, Frank Hyde of 2SM and 'Tiger' Black of 2KY, wanted to interview Keith Holman, but when they got near the referee's change room they saw that a big and still angry crowd had assembled outside. Black, a former hooker, volunteered to go first, and Hyde followed, hand on his comrade's shoulder. But it was tough going.

Suddenly, Hyde had a brainwave. 'Make way, please,' he called out. 'Make way, please, for Keith Holman's father.'

It hardly helped, but Black did eventually get out of there alive.

Fifteen years earlier, Tiger Black was covering the Kangaroos in England for 2KY and sent back a report on the winger Don 'Bandy' Adams, who had been hospitalised with a back ailment. Adams was recovering well, Tiger reported, and 'had taken a turn for the nurse'.

Crooked Feeds

Another funny yarn concerning Keith Holman was originally told in the book *Fatty and Chook: Laughing at League*, a collection of league stories featuring Paul Vautin and Johnny Raper. One Saturday, Holman played half-back against Great Britain at the Sydney Cricket Ground, and starred in a match won by Australia after the local referee Darcy Lawler found plenty of reasons to penalise the visitors.

The next day, Holman backed up in a club game for Western Suburbs, but the first two times he put the ball into the scrum he was promptly penalised for incorrect feeding. 'You're not playing the Poms today,' Lawler told him, without even a hint of a smile.

Mental Arithmetic

As part of one NRL club's new policy to get their players a good education, rather than having them sitting around doing nothing all day, young Josh, who'd left high school when he was 15 because he wanted to play footy for Australia, was enrolled at the local technical college. His first subject on his first day was mathematics, and almost straight away — probably because his student was a famous footballer — the teacher tried to embarrass him.

'Joshua, can you tell me what's 1, 5, 28 and 50?'

'That would be TV1, Nickelodeon, Cartoon Network and Sky Racing.'

If You Can't Stand the Heat

Billy had a problem. His team had a match scheduled for Saturday night, against a lousy side entrenched at the bottom of the table, and he'd been invited away on a buck's weekend for one of his best mates. He knew what he wanted to do, but realised there was no way he'd get away with faking an injury or just not turning up for the game. The only thing he could think of was insanity.

So when the lads gathered in the dressing room for a meeting before Thursday-night training, Billy snuck in the room and hooked himself up to the ceiling. Then, when the rest of the team arrived, he started whirling around, his arms outstretched like an aeroplane, while making weird 'whirring' sounds.

The coach looked at his star player and shouted, 'What the hell are you doing?'

'Oh, g'day, boss,' Billy replied. 'I'm your new ceiling fan. Let me cool you.'

With that, Billy started spinning around and whirring some more.

'Geez, mate,' the coach said. 'You've been training too hard. You're all stressed out. Why don't you go home, have a good lie down, and don't come back till next Tuesday night. We're playing the wooden spooners on Saturday. We'll manage without you.'

Billy was smart enough not to laugh or agree too quickly. He whirred a bit more, then slowly stopped, jumped down, picked up his bag and walked slowly out. 'OK, coach,' he said softly, 'you're in charge. Good luck on the weekend, fellas.'

Of course, two or three of Billy's team-mates knew what was happening. Billy was not a second out the door, when they collected their things and began to head for the exit.

'Oi, what are you blokes doing?' the coach asked.

'We're not hanging around in these conditions,' one of the departing players muttered. 'It's too bloody hot in here now Billy's gone.'

You're Next

'I used to hate going to weddings involving anyone at the footy club,' said Matt, the team's star and single half-back. 'Every time at the reception, up would come the ex-players to poke me in the ribs or slap me on the back and roar, "You're next."

'It didn't stop until I started saying the same thing to them at funerals!'

A Storm in a Crocodile

A man walked into a pub with a crocodile under his arm. 'Do you serve Melbourne Storm fans in here?' he enquired of the barman.

'Ah, there's not many Storm fans around, mate, but yes we do.'

'Excellent,' said the customer. 'I'll have a beer for me and a Storm fan for the crocodile.'

Correct Weight

The new back-rower was a huge young man: one of those blokes who seemed very, very proud of every minute he'd spent working out at the gym. Soon, he was annoying every one as he bragged about various examples of his mega-strength, and telling anyone who'd listen — and many who wouldn't — that he could outdo anyone in the premiership when it came to feats of strength. He wouldn't stop, going on to make fun of old Ned, the club's veteran prop, who he reckoned 'just isn't in my league'. After several minutes, Ned was sick of it.

'If you're so good, why don't you put your money where your big mouth is?' he said to the young Adonis. 'I'll bet you a week's match payments that I can lug something in a wheelbarrow over to the main grandstand and you won't be able to wheel it back.'

'You're on, old man,' the young bloke replied. 'Let's see what you got.'

Ned got up slowly, walked over to the wheelbarrow, brought it back right next to his challenger, and said, 'OK, jump in.'

Thanks for Everything

The wife of the tough second-rower was a very reluctant draftee into the job of coaching her seven-year-old's rugby league team, but she did such a good job that the boys made the semi-finals. Better than that, there was a real 'family' atmosphere about the team — the kids all seemed happy, the parents enjoyed coming along to not just the games but training too, and the club's reputation in the district blossomed. After the final game, a tough 12–10 loss in the preliminary final, the coach organised a team barbecue, and it was hardly surprising that all the players came along armed with presents for their beloved mentor.

First up was Johnny, the local florist's lad, who had what was obviously a large bouquet covered in wrapping paper in his hands. 'I bet I know what this is,' the coach said excitedly. 'It's some flowers!'

'That's right!' cried the little boy.

Then Scotty, whose dad owned the local lolly shop, handed over a package. 'These wouldn't be chockies, would they, dear?' said the coach.

'They are!' exclaimed the young fella.

Next up was Billy, the son of the local publican. He handed the coach a package, and she saw immediately that it was leaking. But instead of embarrassing the boy, she touched a drop with her finger and tasted it. 'Is that white wine?' she asked.

'Nope,' Billy answered.

'Champagne?'

'Nope.'

'Red wine?'

'Nope.' Again Billy shook his head.

Finally, the coach smiled and said, 'OK, I give up. What is it?'

'It's a puppy!'

The Invisible Man

The Invisible Man agreed to play with the Bulldogs but before he could sign the contract he had to pass a physical. So he went to the club doctor's surgery, where the receptionist greeted him warmly.

'Just one moment, sir,' she said, before speaking into the intercom, 'Doctor, the Invisible Man is here.'

'Tell him I can't see him now,' the medico replied.

God Saved the Kangaroo

On the 1948–49 Kangaroo tour, the Australians got themselves involved in a fiery encounter at Huddersfield. The locals were particularly incensed when the tourists' tough winger, Johnny 'Whacker' Graves from Souths, stiff-armed the home-team full-back Johnny Hunter, and as the end of the game approached there were genuine fears that something ugly might happen. It looked as if the crowd might invade the pitch and attack the Australian miscreant, and sure enough, when the full-time whistle blew, the fans started to charge out onto the field. Then, suddenly, the local band started playing 'God Save the Queen' and every one stopped and stood to attention.

'Quick, Whacker, now's your chance!' called out the Kangaroos' manager Bill Buckley, waving a route to the dressing room. 'Duck in here.'

And Whacker did just that … and survived.

Flight to Fantasy

Brad Brown, after many years as a first-grade rugby league forward, had received an offer to play NFL football in America as a defensive back and was on his way to the States for pre-season training. The money was excellent, the sense of adventure exciting, but Brad didn't quite know exactly what was ahead of him.

The flight to Los Angeles was uneventful, but things started looking up at the start of his connecting flight to Florida, when he spotted a seductive, 30-something woman walking down the aisle in his general direction. He prayed that she'd take the vacant seat next to him, and sure enough his dreams came true. Soon they were engaged in conversation, and Brad learned that she was on her way to a nymphomaniacs' conference in Miami, where she was due to deliver a paper in which she would use personal experience to debunk some of the popular misconceptions about sex.

'Can you let me in on any secrets?' Brad asked.

'I'm sure you're aware that Frenchmen have a reputation for being the world's best lovers,' she offered.

'Of course,' Brad spluttered.

'Well, it's actually the Greeks. And they say that

men from the Caribbean are the best endowed on the planet,' she continued.

'They do,' said Brad.

'Well, it's actually Native American Indians.'

Brad couldn't help thinking this was the smartest, most beautiful, most seductive woman he had ever met. But then he noticed that she might even have been blushing a little. 'I'm sorry,' she said, 'here I am talking to you about sex and I don't even know your name.'

'Tonto. Tonto Papadopolous. It's very nice to meet you.'

Beaten Finalists

Since they last won the premiership in 1979, St George have played in plenty of qualifying finals, semi-finals, preliminary finals and even five Grand Finals, but they've never won another competition. It's reached the point where Oxo have produced a new cube wrapped in white paper with a red V. They're calling it the 'Laughing Stock'.

First Time In

The young half-back was about to go for a knee reconstruction, and seemed strangely happy about it all. 'I'm surprised you're so chirpy,' said the doctor.

'Oh well, doc,' replied the footballer, 'this is my first time in surgery. There's something a bit exciting about it all.'

'That's interesting,' responded the doctor. 'This is my first operation, too, and I'm scared out of my mind.'

Big Artie

After the 1972 World Cup, the Australian team travelled to England for three games, one of which was at Bradford. In the previous match at Wigan, the great Arthur Beetson had suffered a cut above the eye which needed 15 stitches, but after a tough tour he was still required to sit on the bench, as many of his comrades were even more severely injured.

Before the game at Odsal Stadium — which is a huge bowl of a venue, with the field at the bottom and the dressing rooms and press gallery perched high above — 'Whatever you do, don't get sent off,' captain Graeme Langlands advised. 'If you do you're going to have to fight your way up through the crowd all the way to the dressing rooms at the top.' And then front-rower John O'Neill added, pointing at Beetson, 'Remember, whatever happens, no one goes off today. Have a look at Arthur's eye. We can't let him play with that.'

Two things happened. First, Langlands was sent off, and then O'Neill, of all people, came off injured. Beetson was so surprised by this second development that he didn't have time to get a jumper, and had to wear O'Neill's No. 13 guernsey on to the field. The next day, it became clear that many journalists up in the pressbox hadn't seen O'Neill come off, but they must have seen the No. 13 in the action for the entire 80 minutes, because they reported that O'Neill had played strongly throughout. That was bad enough for Big Artie; what was worse was seeing O'Neill lounging around with his legs up, looking, in Beetson's words, 'very healthy and relaxed'.

'We laughed about that game more than once over the years,' Beetson recalled in his autobiography.

Twins

The girl got pregnant, and then had a big argument with the father, who promptly left town and left her to it. Worse still, six months into the pregnancy she was involved in a car accident and fell into a deep coma. When she finally woke, many months later, the first thing she thought of was her baby, and she was horrified at the realisation that she was no longer expecting.

'Doctor, doctor,' she cried frantically, 'what happened to me, what happened to my child?'

'Madam, don't be upset,' replied the doctor calmly. 'It all worked out OK. We stabilised you after the accident, and you had a normal birth. You had twins, a boy and a girl, and your brother came in and named them for you. I'll never forget it, because he came in on the way to a Newcastle game. He was wearing all the red-and-blue gear and seemed in a bit of a hurry to get to the ground before the kick-off.'

'That'd be right,' the woman replied. 'He's an idiot. Why did you let him name my babies? What'd he call them?'

'The girl he called "Denise",' the doctor said.

'Denise — that's actually not a bad name. I like that. Maybe I'm being too hard on my brother. What'd he name my son?'

'Denephew,' the doctor said quietly.

17. AT THE FURLONG

Going Slow?

True story ... in the autumn of 1930, Phar Lap was running in the AJC Plate at Randwick, a high-class race over two and a quarter miles (around 3600 metres). Jim Pike couldn't make the weight, and the much lighter Billy Elliott was riding him, and the horse just took off on him. Elliott couldn't hold him, and Phar Lap went on to break all sorts of records, even though he walked the last furlong (200 metres), which was when Elliott finally got a grip of him. One clocker reckoned the champion ran the first seven furlongs of that race faster than the Randwick seven-furlongs record, in a two-and-a-quarter miles race!

Afterwards the stewards called in Roy Reed, the jockey of Nightmarch, the 1929 Melbourne Cup winner which had finished second, and accused him of not trying to win the race. This turned into one of the shortest stewards' investigations in history. Straight away, Reed pointed out that Nightmarch had just broken the old track record, even though he got beaten officially by 10 lengths (though by most observers' unofficial estimations the margin was closer to 100 yards).

The stewards looked at each other, and then declared the enquiry closed!

Bionic Bess

A man was sitting quietly watching television when his wife walked up behind him and whacked him on the head with a magazine.

'What did you do that for?' he asked.

'I just found this piece of paper in your jacket,' she sobbed. 'This piece of paper with the name "Bionic Bess" written on it.'

'Oh darling, two weeks ago when I went to Flemington, that was the name of the horse I backed that won,' he muttered. 'If I remember correctly, it paid for that night's Chinese takeaway.'

'Oh, dear, I'm sorry,' the wife cried. 'I should have known there was nothing in it.'

Two days later, the same man arrived home from golf to be met by a flying steam iron aimed straight at head. 'What did you do that for?' he exclaimed at his wife.

'Your horse called!'

Wrong Bet

In 1928, Statesman won the Melbourne Cup for trainer Bill Kelso. It was ridden by Jim Munro, but only because Kelso's favourite jockey, Jim Pike, couldn't get down to the eight stone weight that Statesman carried in the big race. Four days later, in the CB Fisher Plate, Pike was riding the outstanding English import Gothic but was convinced his mount couldn't stay the mile and a half of the race, especially against a horse as good as the Melbourne Cup winner. So he put £1000 on Statesman.

And then, demonstrating that he was a great jockey, a man of integrity and a dud punter, Jim Pike went out and nursed Gothic to a clear victory.

The Bet's on Me

A horse walked up to the betting window at the races and put $500 down in front of the operator behind the counter. 'I want to put the lot on myself to win race five, please,' the horse said.

'I don't believe it!' cried the woman as she took the bet.

'What don't you believe?' said the horse. 'That I can talk?'

'No, that you could be such a terrible judge.'

The New Phar Lap

A man purchased a horse, purely on breeding, sight unseen, and after he picked him up he took him to his trainer's stables. After he had unloaded the horse off the float, the trainer came out and quickly saw that this was one of the ugliest horses he had ever laid eyes on. It was pigeon-toed, sway-backed, scrawny and maybe even cross-eyed.

'What are you going to do with him?' the trainer asked.

'We're going to race him!' the owner replied.

'Well, I'll certainly beat him and I think you'll be too good for him as well.'

Happy Honeymoon

A young male jockey and an even younger female apprentice fell in love and decided to get married. They planned the wedding for late June, after the Brisbane carnival, and opted for a honeymoon in a six-star hotel in the tropics. The service was beautiful, the reception perfect, and after a night of partying they flew off for their romantic getaway.

While checking in at the hotel, the lady behind the desk said, 'Congratulations to you both. Now, sir, we have a choice of suites we can offer you, but I imagine you'd want the bridal.'

'No, no, it's all right,' said the jockey. 'I'll just hold her by the ears until she gets the hang of it!'

How Much for the Horse?

Fred hadn't been in Sydney long when he decided to buy a racehorse. He didn't have much money, so he bought a thoroughbred of questionable breeding for $100 and hoped he'd found himself the new Phar Lap. Not quite — when he arrived to collect his new steed, the previous owner had the unenviable task of explaining that the horse had died the previous night. Worse still, because the demise occurred after the sale had been agreed to, it seemed that Fred had done his 100 bucks cold.

'Well, I'd like the carcass then,' Fred said.

'What are you going to do with it?' the previous owner asked.

'I'm going to raffle the horse off.'

'Mate, the horse is dead. You can't raffle a dead horse.'

'We'll see,' Fred said. 'Just get me my horse.'

A few weeks later, Fred ran into that past owner of his horse, and straight away the question was asked: 'How did your raffle go?'

'Not too bad, thank you very much,' Fred replied. 'I sold 500 tickets at $2 each, and I made a profit of $998, which I thought was pretty good.'

'I bet they were happy when they found out that the first prize wasn't in the best of health,' was the response.

'Well, the only complaint I got was from the bloke who had the winning ticket. I had to tell him the horse had died, and naturally I gave him his two dollars back.'

A Melbourne Cup Winner

A horse was drinking at a pub. A bloke walked up to him and said, 'Are you a racehorse?'

'That's right,' the thoroughbred answered.

'Did you ever win any big races?'

'Yeah, I did. I won a Melbourne Cup.'

'You're having me on. What year did you win?'

'I won in 1979.'

'Are you serious?'

'No, Sirius won in 1944. I'm Hyperno.'

Looks Can Be Deceiving

In the early 1920s, a gent by the name of Percy Miller and his brother Bob had five young horses that needed trainers. Two trainers with whom they had a long association, George Price and Peter Riddle, were told that one would get to look after three of the horses, the other man, two. Who would get first pick would be decided by the toss of a coin. Price called correctly, took his turn, then Riddle, Price again, Riddle again, and Price was stuck with as ungainly a colt as you could find, one that had been rejected with hardly a bid at two yearling sales.

He resolved to put him into work as soon as possible, to discover if he had any ability at all, and then to get rid of him when he confirmed he was no good. However, things didn't quite go to plan, for Price discovered that he actually wasn't too bad, a galloper as tough as concrete. Bob Miller would later describe Price as 'the miracle man'. The unwanted yearling was Windbag, which in 1925 proved too good for the champion colt Manfred in one of the greatest of all Melbourne Cups.

Back in 1894, a woman gave birth in the doctor's room of the Members Stand at Flemington during the running of the Cup. The race was won that year by Patron, and the new mother and her husband decided to name their new daughter 'Patrona'.

This is a lovely true story; it's just lucky the unexpected delivery didn't happen in Windbag's year!

A Unique Rabbit

The staff at Angle Park dog track were frantic. Thieves had broken into the complex during the night and stolen all the hares that the club used during races, the ones that the greyhounds chased. For any club this would have been a problem, but Angle Park had been using a different type of hare throughout its long history: the 'unique' rabbit.

'We might be able to find one up in the hills,' said Bill, the club's long-time curator.

So off went Bill and young Jason, the club's work-experience kid, to try and find a unique rabbit. Up in the hills, they ventured into the thick bush, but for over an hour there was nothing. But then, near a tree, Bill saw what to Jason looked like a normal, stock-standard, see-'em-every-day bunny.

'Mr Kennedy,' said Jason innocently, 'is that really a unique rabbit?'

'Aye, it is, son,' Bill replied.

'Well, how are we going to catch it?'

'Unique up on it,' Bill explained.

Time Matters

A man was trying to explain how betting on horse races works to a young woman. First, he showed her the betting ring, and the bookmakers, the bookies' boards and the TV screens that displayed the tote odds. Then he explained, 'If you put five dollars on a horse at odds of five-to-one and the horse wins, then you win 25 dollars. If you back the horse at 10-to-one and it wins you win 50 dollars. And if you back it at 20-to-one, you win 100 dollars.'

'That sounds good,' she says politely. 'So what happens if I back it at exactly one o'clock?'

The Apprentice

As part of the counselling process that came with their parents' marriage breakup, the three children were required to meet with a psychiatrist, to ascertain how they were handling the stress.

'What is the opposite of joy?' the psychiatrist asked the first child.

'Misery,' was the reply.

To the second child, the question was: 'What is the opposite of depression?'

'I would say delight.'

The third child was an apprentice jockey. The mother had hated the fact that her husband had let her little girl enter the dastardly world of horse racing, but as he always said, 'That's what she really wants to do.'

'Now, young lady,' said the psychiatrist, 'what is the opposite of woe?'

'Giddy-up.'

The Pope is Dead

AG 'George' Mulley's ride on the hot favourite, Bernborough, in the 1946 Caulfield Cup was controversial to say the least. Mulley always maintained he was the victim of circumstances, and it did seem that at least a few jockeys were keen to make life hard for him, but that didn't stop the street-corner gossip that the champion had not been allowed to run on its merits.

A little while later, two punters were talking in the pub when one asked the other, 'Did you hear the Pope is dead?'

'I bet Mulley is riding him,' was the reply.

Right Jockey, Wrong Course

At his best, George Mulley was one of the finest jockeys in the business, but he had a reputation for not always taking his job seriously — a reputation not helped by the couple of occasions when he went to the wrong course. As he explained in the book he co-wrote with Frank Hardy, *The Needy and the Greedy*, he got out of the shower at home one morning, picked up a paper to check where the races were on that day, and set off. However, when he got to Canterbury racecourse the place was deserted — he'd looked at a form guide that was a week old — and it wasn't until he found a copy of *that* afternoon's paper that he discovered the races were at Rosehill.

The other time, he set off for Hawkesbury racecourse with plenty of time up his sleeve, but was surprised by the fact that there was no traffic on the road. He was running so early he had time to stop at a service station near the course to fill up, and was surprised when the bloke on the petrol pump asked him where he was going. 'To the Hawkesbury races,' Mulley answered.

It was only then that he learned the gallops that day were four hours away at Kembla Grange.

Something's Missing

The colt was beautifully bred, superbly built, and very fast at trackwork, but at the races he wouldn't go past a filly, which meant he was costing his connections plenty. One day in the stables, his trainer came up and said, 'I'm sorry to have to tell you this, but I've recommended to the owners that we get you gelded.'

'Oh, that's all right,' said the colt. 'That should mean I have a long and successful racing career, and the way I was losing every week you were never going to send me to stud anyway.'

So the visit to the vet was duly organised and a few weeks later the now gelding was ready for his return to the racetrack. He felt different — the fillies didn't interest him anymore and he really felt focused when he went into the barrier. Then the starter said go and he bounced straight to the lead, but after about 20 metres he suddenly stopped, threw his jockey, and went back and seemed to hide behind the barrier stalls.

'What's the matter?' asked the clerk of the course. 'Why did you stop?'

'How would you feel,' replied the gelding, 'if you'd had the surgery I've just had, and in front of 20,000 people some smartarse yells out over the public address, "They're off!"?'

Sweet Dreams

The heavyweight jockey went to the doctor. 'Doctor,' he said, 'you know those pills you gave me to help control my weight? Ever since I started taking them, I've been having these hallucinations.'

'Are you sure you're not imagining things?' the doc responded.

Problem Gambling

After lobby groups convinced the government that the number of race meetings was causing problems in society, race clubs were forced to put up signs at their courses which read, 'If you think you have a gambling problem, please call 1300-PUNTER.'

As the horses went out for race three at Randwick, Billy studied the odds in the bookmakers' ring, looked up at one of those signs, and then pulled out his mobile phone.

'Can I help you?' said the voice at the other end of the line.

'I hope so,' Billy replied. 'I can't decide if I should back the favourite straight out or have a few bob each way on the topweight. What d'ya reckon?'

The Dream Cups

Which leads us on to one of the most famous of all Melbourne Cup stories. In February 1870, while enjoying some drinks with a few racing mates, a Ballarat publican named Mr Walter Craig sought odds about a Metropolitan Handicap–Melbourne Cup double involving a moderately performed horse named Croydon and his own galloper, Nimblefoot. The prominent bookmaker Joe Slack, who was among the group, offered £1000 to a round of drinks, which the publican quickly accepted, not least because the men were drinking in his hotel. A few months later, Craig dreamed every owner's fantasy — Nimblefoot, wearing his distinctive violet colours, winning the Melbourne Cup — but the vision had an eerie sidelight, for the jockey was a wearing a black armband. Therefore, he sadly told his friends the next morning that if his dream was true he'd not be at Flemington to see his horse triumph. Walter Craig was only 45, but later that very day he died.

Croydon duly won the 'Metrop', and then Nimblefoot entered Cup calculations with a sudden return to form in the Hotham Handicap. *The Age* reported the whole astonishing story 24 hours *before* the Cup, and the following day, with jockey Johnny Day wearing a black crepe armband, Nimblefoot prevailed narrowly over Lapdog in a tight finish. On the following Monday, Joe Slack was at the Goydor Hotel in the city, nobly counting out 20 fifties to a gentleman from Ballarat, a friend of Mrs Craig, and the story was entrenched in Cup folklore.

Indeed, Walter Craig's dream established an annual event of its own. Before every year's race, stories circulated of the latest version of the Nimblefoot saga. By Cup Day of 1883, for example, *The Australasian*'s correspondent was writing:

*Dreams on the Melbourne Cup were as plentiful
as ever, and as a matter of course some of them
came right off. The most sensational was that in
which a resident of Hotham saw a vision in
which Martini-Henri was depicted as the winner
of the Derby, Dirk Hatternick as the winner of
the Cup, and that he (the dreamer) died. The
man did die, and Martini-Henri won the Derby.
Then there was a tremendous rush to get on Dirk
Hatternick, but the treble did not come off.*

Dirk Hatternick, a very average stayer from South
Australia, started at the ridiculously short price of
12–1 and finished down the track. One observer
suggested his proper odds were closer to 1000–1.

A similar story was played out in 1898, when a nag
named Clarion was backed in from 12–1 to as little as
3–1 on the back of yet another visionary who'd 'seen'
the finish and then died before the Cup was run.
Every one realised this new 'dream horse' was way
under the odds, but many punters didn't care.
Happiest of all with this development, of course, were
the ever-realistic, non-romantic bookmakers. As the
horses went to the barrier, one bookie chortled to a
colleague in the betting ring, 'I've stood the horse for
a fortune, and I'd like to stand him for another one!'

Clarion, as favourite, finished 10th. The race was
won by The Grafter, which would have an interesting

story of his own. He was sold to race — with some success — in England, but then years later he was recognised by his former trainer in London, pulling a hansom cab. The trainer offered to buy him, but his new owner would have none of it.

'He's the best cab horse I've had in 30 years,' he explained.

18. RUGGERED AGAIN

Rugby Unplugged

The rugby fan was sitting in his usual position: feet up on the lounge, beer in one hand, remote control in the other. Kick-off was just a few minutes away.

Hopeful of a few moments' conversation before the game started, his wife tried to get him to talk about anything but football, but nothing seemed to interest him. Eventually, she made a reference to a newspaper article about euthanasia.

The rugby fan took a sip of his VB, and then muttered, 'Sweetheart, I never want to live in a vegetative state, totally dependent on some machine. If that ever happens, please just pull the plug.'

So his wife got up and unplugged the TV.

As Time Goes By

A woman was sitting in the waiting room of a new dentist. She looked up at his university degree, which was hanging on the wall. It bore his full name, Mark Edward Smith, and the woman chuckled when she thought back to high school in the 1970s and the tall, handsome, highly athletic boy in her class who had exactly that name. He had been the captain of the school cricket and track and field teams, but it was as captain of the school's first XV rugby team that he was best remembered. God, he was hot, she thought to herself, as she recalled that almighty crush she had had on him and how devastated she was when his parents moved interstate. She hadn't laid eyes on him since that dreadful day when he walked out of the school for the final time.

Could this be the same Mark Edward Smith?

When she was called into the surgery the woman quickly discarded that idea. For the dentist was a fairly ugly, chubby, balding, grey-haired man with a wrinkled face and gnarly fingers who was much too old to have been her first true love. If only he'd taken better care of himself, she thought. This wasn't her Mark Edward Smith … or was it? It was a few years ago, and time affects different people in different ways. Who knows what kind of life he'd lived since high school?

With the examination over, she decided to act on her curiosity. 'Ah, excuse me, Mark,' she said. 'Were you ever at North Street High School?'

'Well, yes I was,' the dentist replied, genuine surprise in his voice. 'But not for too long. My parents moved us to Melbourne. Why do you ask?'

'Well, I think you were in my class,' the woman replied, trying to hide her disappointment.

'Really,' the old dentist replied. 'What subject did you teach?'

The Secret to a Happy Life

'You blokes are a disgrace!' the coach seethed at his players after training. 'The great players who starred for this great club in the past would be disgusted by your performance. You could do worse than talking to some of them, to understand the traditions of this place, and find out the secret of what it takes to be a good footballer.'

Next morning, a couple of the young players thought they'd go and find one of these great players. They saw the club secretary down at the ground and asked, 'Who's the greatest footballer to ever play for the club?'

'George Jones,' the official replied. 'He's still about. You could get George's address from the girl in the front office.'

This they did, and soon after they set off down the street to learn about the game. At the right house, they saw a little old bloke sitting in a rocking chair on the front porch. He had a cigarette in his mouth, a half-full glass of beer by his side, and looked very fragile, but happy and content. He greeted the young footballers like long-lost friends. Straight away, he asked if they'd mind going to the fridge and getting him another bottle of beer. 'It's a long way for me to walk these days,' he explained. 'It's a long way from me chair to me kitchen.'

Then they settled down for a chat. Yes, he had been a 'pretty all right' footballer in his day, which he modestly put down to the fact that he was well coached and played with some excellent team-mates.

'I can't help noticing how happy you seem,' one of the players said. 'What's the secret to a happy life?'

'I've smoked three packets of ciggas a day since I was 17, and there hasn't been a day gone by when I haven't had four beers before lunch,' Jones replied. 'I live on hamburgers and pizza, and haven't exercised since I retired from footy. Hardly exercised when I did play footy, except when I was chasin' birds at the club.'

'That's fantastic,' said the young footballers in unison. 'The coach sent us down here to find out what made you such a champion player.'

'Boys, trust your instincts, never your coaches,' Jones explained, as he shuffled painfully in his seat. 'The most important thing is not to get caught. What they don't know can't hurt you.'

'Superb advice, thanks very much, Mr Jones,' said one of the players gratefully. 'By the way, how old are you, sir?'

'Thirty-three, son,' Jones said. 'But I don't care how much they offer me, I'm not making a comeback.'

King Hits

Some of the Test rugby played in Australia in the 1970s was incredibly fierce, with more than the odd king hit and indiscriminately placed boot being part of the 'sport'. Many Australian supporters and even a few players had an odd sense of pride about this, but in other parts of the rugby world people were not so keen on this new Wallaby style.

This view was captured by Bill Beaumont, the highly acclaimed forward, in his autobiography *Thanks to Rugby*. Beaumont looked back on England's tour down under in 1975 and wrote that in his opinion it would have been better if certain Australian players had not been selected. Instead, he argued, they should have been encouraged to turn their attentions to other 'more suitable' sports.

'Head-hunting in Borneo' was one of his suggestions.

The Red Dachshund

A man walks into a bar with a dachshund under his arm. He's wearing a Queensland Reds jersey, beanie and scarf, and so is the dog. 'Sorry, mate!' yelled the barman, 'there're no pets allowed in here! I'm afraid you and the pooch will have to leave!'

'Oh, c'mon,' the Reds fan pleaded. 'My TV's on the blink and you're the only pub within miles that's showing the Super 14s.'

'All right then, you can stay,' the barman said. 'But you'll have to promise that the dog behaves himself.'

'He'll be right, though he might get excited when the Reds score.'

So the game kicked off, and almost immediately the referee awarded the Queensland side a penalty in kicking range. No sooner had the whistle blown than the dog was up on the bar, walking along on its hind legs giving the other patrons high-fives.

'Wow, that's amazing,' said the barman. 'What does he do if the Reds score a try?'

'I don't know,' the owner replied sheepishly, 'I've only had him four years.'

In and Out

A mother had twin boys, whom she and her husband rather curiously named 'In' and 'Out', apparently because they hoped that one day they'd be the centre pairing for the Wallabies. Both did go on to play top-level rugby, and one day they were out on a boys' night out, when In became lost.

For a few hours, no one could find him, until his brother located him unconscious in the local water treatment plant, up to his neck in raw sewage. In had no recollection of how he got there; the only certainty was that he was very lucky he was found when he was, for just a few more minutes and he would have drowned. But why did Out think to look there?

'Instinct,' he explained.

All Tied Up

Back in the days when even the best rugby players needed a job, one of the game's stars worked during the week as a school teacher. One Saturday, this fellow suffered a serious spinal injury, and he was required to wear a plaster cast right around his upper body. But he was still able to don a business shirt and tie, so after a few weeks of sick leave recuperating he was assigned to a new school and was soon in the classroom trying to deal with some rogue students.

During one class, the children became particularly unruly, and nothing the teacher said could quieten them down. Eventually, as a paper aeroplane flew across the room, he moved over to the window, opened it up, took a deep breath in the fresh breeze, and then walked back to the desk. Then he sat down, told the children to 'Shut the hell up, please!' and then started trying to mark some exam papers. The students were giggling and sniggering among themselves, flicking each other with rulers, doing all sorts of things — except read as they were supposed to. The breeze from the wide open window was playing havoc with the teacher's tie. He kept rearranging the tie and the noise from the class kept rising, until he could stand it no longer. He stood up, took a large stapler out of his desk drawer … and stapled the tie to his chest.

From that moment, the children kept very quiet and stayed fully focused on their schoolwork.

A Good Dig

A team of archaeologists had been toiling deep in the Simpson Desert in Central Australia when they came across an extraordinary discovery. By careful digging and brushing away of dust, rocks and sand, they came across what was clearly a football field. They found the remnants of ancient goalposts and a halfway line — even two old stone huts which, judging by their position, were most likely the dressing rooms.

It was the sporting find of the millennium. Imagine, they thought, old Aboriginal tribes playing rugby centuries before William Webb Ellis picked up the ball at Rugby School in England … and ran with it. Any doubt was dispelled when modern computer technologies proved that the diggers had found a fossilised football, and then they discovered drawings of men apparently passing and kicking a ball, and what might even have been an honour board that featured the names of player-of-the-year winners for the years from 200BC to 150BC.

The archaeologists were aware that the local Aboriginal community had a rich oral history, so they asked if they could interview one of the tribal elders to see if they knew anything of this ancient game. Through an interpreter, the old man confirmed that a game had been played many centuries ago, and that it had been extremely popular, with games played between tribes from all over the country. But what happened? Did this oral history say anything about why the game faded away?

The elder nodded his head wistfully, looked down at the dust at his feet and drew a circle in the ground. As the game grew in popularity, it needed more and more rules. It reached the point where the men in charge of the games needed something to try to keep control. So they invented the whistle. But the men in charge loved their whistles so much that they blew them all the time, and the games became boring. People stopped watching, and then they stopped playing.

And so the game fizzled out, and wasn't played again until white men 'discovered' it in the 19th century.

It's All Over

The half-back was suffering from the 'all my friends are getting married' syndrome. 'My problem,' he said after a few beers one night to one of his married forwards, 'is that because I'm still single, I feel incomplete.'

The veteran forward didn't say a word, and sure enough soon after the half-back met a girl, they dated, became engaged and then got married. A few months later, after a few beers one night, the forward asked the half-back how things were going.

'I'm finished,' he replied.

Nothing was said for maybe a minute. Then the forward shuffled in his seat and said, 'I know where you're coming from, son. I never knew what real happiness was until I got married … And then it was too late.'

What Are You Doing Here?

David Brockhoff was a rugby coach of some fame in the 1970s, and something of a firebrand known for rousing pre-game speeches and also for speaking his mind. At a training session with the New South Wales team in 1973, John Lambie made a mistake and Brockhoff quickly called him to account. The language was as blue as a Waratahs jumper, as the coach described all the ways the rookie had failed him. 'When I bloody well tell you to bloody well do something,' he roared, 'you'll bloody well do it!'

But then the man renowned in rugby circles as a great motivator calmed down a little. 'Actually, son, it's not your fault,' he said. Lambie relaxed just a little. 'It's the selectors' fault. They should never have picked you.'

Sex Tip

A rugby front-rower got a second job as a sex therapist on late-night radio. The first question was from Veronica, who asked, 'Doctor, why is it that men always want to marry a virgin?'

'To avoid criticism,' was the reply.

Short Back and Sides

Two rugby coaches went to the same hairdresser at the same time, and found themselves sitting on adjoining chairs. Both requested and received 'short back and sides'. When the cutting was completed, both accepted the offer of a shave, and when that treatment was finished the barbers reached for aftershave to splash on their customers' faces.

'Whoa,' said the first coach. 'Don't put that stuff on me. My wife will think I've been in a brothel!'

'It's OK,' said the other man. 'Put as much on as you like. My wife doesn't know what a brothel smells like.'

The Wombat

A wombat walked into the local rugby club, clambered up to a bar stool, put $50 on the bar and asked for a beer. The bloke doing the pouring looked at the wombat, then at the cash, and said, 'Gimme a minute, mate.' The barman found his manager and told him what had just happened. Straight away, the boss said, 'Go back to the bar, give the wombat his beer, a dollar's worth of change, and see if you can strike up a conversation.'

So the barman poured a beer, placed it on the bar, took the $50 note, came back with a dollar coin, and then said cheerfully, 'You know, we don't get a lot of wombats in here.'

The wombat looked at his change and then his beer. 'Mate,' he replied, 'at $49 a beer, I'm not surprised!'

The Haircut

The football prodigy had just been picked in first grade even though he was only 16 years old. One night, he came home from training looking a little down, and his father asked what was the matter.

'Oh, Dad,' the lad replied, 'all the blokes in the team are bagging me because I haven't got a car.'

'Son, I tell you what,' the father responded. 'If you study hard at school, read the Bible every night and get your hair cut, then we'll think about a car.'

'OK, Dad.'

A month later, the boy was still in the firsts. He'd also just topped the class and memorised the gospels. 'Son, your mother and I are so proud of you. If only you'd had a haircut, you'd be driving to training tomorrow.'

'You know, Dad, I've been thinking about what you said, and I'm a little worried about my hair. In the Bible, most of the characters have long hair. Look what happened to Samson. Moses had long hair, Jesus had long hair, John the Baptist had long hair.'

'And did you notice,' the father interrupted, 'that all of them walked everywhere they went?'

Geriatric Heaven

A former rugby forward, aged 94, and his new girlfriend, just 91, decided to get married. One day, while on their daily five-minute power walk, they saw a massive 24-hour chemist, much bigger than their usual pharmacy, and decided to pop in.

'Good morning, sir,' the ex-forward said to the man in the white coat behind the counter. 'Are you the owner?'

'Yes, I am,' the pharmacist replied.

'We've decided to get married,' the forward said proudly. 'We live not too far from here, and I was wondering if you sell heart medication?'

'Yes, we do.'

'How about drugs for arthritis?'

'Cheap *and* expensive brands.'

'Rheumatism and diabetes?'

'Definitely.'

'Viagra?'

'As much as you need.'

'Jaundice, asthma, Alzheimers?'

'Yes. Yes. Yes. Sir, I think you'll find everything you could possibly need. We help most of the doctors and medical centres in the district.'

'Do you sell wheelchairs and walkers?'

'All speeds and sizes. We also sell walking canes and walking sticks in a variety of styles.'

'Bandages and Band-Aids?'

'I'm sure I will say yes to every question you ask,' the pharmacist said kindly. It all sounded perfect: a geriatric heaven.

'Sir,' the forward announced, as he tightly gripped his fiancée's hand, 'we'd like to use your store as our bridal registry.'

Retaliate First

The old forward was, to put it bluntly, a thug. But he could cop it as well as give it. As he always said, 'Those who live by the sword, have to be prepared to die by the sword.'

One day, he got himself involved in a real stink, which had started when he king-hit an opponent who had a similar reputation for foul play. Eventually, he was slugged himself by a punch he never saw coming. When the melee finally settled down, the referee sent him off, while the player who'd been flattened was carried from the field.

Back in the dressing room, the old campaigner had a shower, dressed in his civvies, and then went into the opposition dressing room to see the bloke he'd belted. He was relieved to see him sitting up, holding an ice pack to the back of his head. 'I'm sorry, mate,' he said with a hint of a knowing smile, 'but as I always say, those who live by the sword, have to be prepared to die by the sword.'

To which the injured man reached into his bag, pulled out a pistol, and shot him.

Slow Training

'He's one of those blokes who always laughs last,' the team president said of his new coach, who he'd personally handpicked only to see the team lose its first four games.

'Is that because he thinks a bit slow?' a committeeman replied.

Watch Your Diet

Some of the fans and committee members were whispering that the team was unfit, so to make it look like he was doing something, the coach organised for a nutritionist to come and address the team. It was a task the food expert accepted with relish. 'The junk you put in your stomachs is stopping you from performing at your peak,' he roared like a bishop preaching from the pulpit. 'Red meat is full of fat. Fast food will kill you. Soft drink ruins the lining of your gut. Chinese food is loaded with MSG. Too much rice or pasta and you'll blow out like a balloon. Chocolate rots your teeth …

'But there is one thing that is the most dangerous of all and from what I hear and from looking at you now, all tired and over-wrought, quite a few have suffered from it. Can anyone here tell me what it is that has no nutritional value and causes pain and suffering for years after it's consumed?'

For a few seconds there was silence. The players looked at each other sheepishly, while one or two peered over at the empty beer cartons still stacked in the corner from the 'wake' after the previous Saturday's big loss. Then, finally, the team's veteran prop put up his hand …

'Wedding cake?' he asked quietly.

Guilty as Charged

The rugby player had been sent off for stomping on one opponent, kicking another, punching a third and biting a fourth. Now, at the judiciary hearing, he'd been found guilty on each charge. It was time to be sentenced.

'So tell me,' the head of the judiciary began, 'what do you think is a fair penalty?'

'I think a warning, sir,' the player replied innocently.

'A warning, eh?' came the response. 'Fair enough. If you come here again, I'm warning you that you will receive another 12-month suspension, just like the one I'm handing you now …

'Next!!'

Sausages

Steve was a very good footballer with a beautiful wife named Debbie and a seven-year-old son named Nathan. Now Nathan was a very good young rugby player in his own right, but his parents were a little concerned because, while in every physical way he was fine, they were concerned about his rather small appendage. Steve knew how cruel footy dressing rooms could be; better to go to the doctor now than wait till the kid was older and more impressionable.

After examining Nathan, the doctor said confidently, 'Just give him plenty of sausages. Any kind will do. They'll solve the problem.'

Next morning, when the boy came down to breakfast, he saw that there was a huge pile of snags in the middle of the breakfast table. 'Wow Mum, are they all for me?'

'No, they're not,' Debbie answered. 'There are two for you. The other 12 are for your father.'

The Sting

In November 1993, the Australian team produced one of its greatest achievements: a 24–3 defeat of France at the Parc des Princes in Paris. And straight after the game, one of the Wallabies came up with an extremely strange post-match effort that has entered the game's folklore.

Before the Test, full-back Marty Roebuck and centre Tim Horan had made a somewhat bizarre bet. As the outstanding journalist and author Greg Growden recounts in his book *With the Wallabies*, at kicking practice the previous day Roebuck had told Horan that he was going to bury a 10-franc coin on the field for luck. Horan asked what would happen if he found it, and Roebuck responded, as he looked around the vast expanse of one of the world's great sporting arenas, by saying that if Horan could locate the coin, he'd give him a million francs.

When the Test finished, all the Wallabies met in mid-field to celebrate. Well, all except one — Roebuck headed in a different direction, to the far corner, where he dug furiously until he found his money. With five minutes to go, and the French attacking the Australian line, Horan had sidled up to his mate, showed him a 10-franc coin, and said, 'I've found it! I've won a million!' It was the longest last five minutes of the full-back's career, as he had to wait until full time before he could check to see if his coin was actually still where he'd buried it, or if he had indeed just lost a cool seven figures.

Roebuck had been fooled. Horan had taken a 10-franc coin out on the field with him before the Test, and kept it in his shorts until producing it at just the right moment.

Forgive and Forget

The sermon was nearly over when the minister shouted, 'So tell me, how many of you have truly forgiven your enemies?'

Perhaps three-quarters of the congregation put up their hands. The minister looked down sternly from the pulpit and then asked the same question again. This time, everyone responded positively except for one gentleman in the front row. It was old Johnson, now 98 years old, whose claim to fame was that back in the early '30s he'd been the best footballer in the town.

'Mr Johnson? Won't you forgive your enemies?' sighed the minister.

'I don't have any enemies,' Johnson replied.

'You don't have any?' the man in the pulpit said scornfully. 'Mr Johnson, back in your day you weren't just the finest footballer in the district. Were you not also the meanest, toughest, dirtiest player going round?'

'That I was,' Johnson said proudly.

'So please tell us, how is it that a man such as you can live to be 98 years old and not have a single enemy in the world?'

'I outlived the bastards!' Johnson muttered, punching the air as he did.

Arthritis

It was after midnight at the club, after yet another loss, and the team captain had his back to the wall. Not only were there whispers that he was about to get the sack, but he was seriously drunk: a sad, sad figure with a cigarette perched precariously on his bottom lip, his shirt half hanging out and almost totally unbuttoned, his face covered in lipstick, his trousers soaked with beer, and a half-empty bottle of bourbon protruding from his back pocket.

Finally, the club president came over to talk to him. Observers wondered whether he was about to offer a sympathetic ear or kick his skipper out of the club there and then. But before he could say anything, the footballer spoke first.

'Hey, el presidente, howyadoin'?' he spluttered.

'I'm fine thanks, Jack,' the president answered. 'Better than you're going, I'd say.'

'Oh no, I'm orright,' the captain said. 'Bodies achin', but I'll be better by tomorrow. But, el presidente, you're a doctor, can you tell me, what causes arthritis?'

'Son, it is caused by loose living, cheap women, too much alcohol and a contempt for your mates.'

'I thought that'd be it.'

'So, Jack,' said the president quickly, thinking he might be about to get some information that would make it easier to make a leadership change, 'tell me, how long have you had arthritis?'

'Oh, I don't 'ave it,' the captain muttered. 'But I know the coach suffers from it, and so does the chairman of selectors.'

Speed Trap

The day Nick signed the big contract he went and bought himself a Ferrari. Of course, he immediately headed for the open road, and as soon as he got there he set out to discover just how fast this baby could go.

And it could go very, very fast. But after just a few minutes of exhilaration there was a speed trap up ahead and a policeman waving the young half-back over.

'Son, I've been waiting all day for a lair like you,' said the officer.

'Sorry, sir, I got here as fast as I could,' Nick answered.

After the policeman finally stopped laughing, he happily sent the footballer on his way, with a warning but without a ticket.

$imon'$ NOte

Simon was a schoolboy rugby prodigy who won a 12-month scholarship to a famous club in the UK. He had only been there a few weeks when he sent this letter home:

Dear Father,

The rugby $ide I'm playing for i$ fanta$ti¢. I've made heap$ of ni¢e friend$ whom I will alway$ be in DEBT to. I am playing mo$tly in the ¢entre$ and a little bit at $¢rumhalf. We've had three ¢lose win$ and two ¢ruel lo$$e$, and $eriously, they $ay I'm a $uper$tar, one of the be$t in the bu$ine$$. The hou$e I'm $taying at i$ very $alubriou$, lo¢ated ju$t near a river BANK, and though I'm $leeping on the $ofa, the $leep I'm getting i$ $eriou$ly enational. I'm eating lot$ of auage$ and $au¢e, so I've $ta¢ked on $ome POUND$. My $tudie$ al$o $eem to be going $uper, though $ome of the tutor$ are a bit $u$$. I ¢an't think of anything I need, $o plea$e ju$t $end me a $imple ¢ard, a$ I would love to $ee how you guy$ are $PENDING your time, e$pe¢ially on $aturday$ and $unday$. Give my love and ki$$e$ to Mum and e$pe¢ially to my $a$$y $i$ter $u$an. I mi$$ you,

Your $on,

$imon.

The father sent an immediate reply:

Dear Simon
 Thanks for your NOte. I kNOw that your
rugby will go well, but please do not igNOre your
studies, especially ecoNOmics, which I kNOw
you enjoy. Do NOt forget that the pursuit of
kNOwledge is a NOble task. You canNOt study
eNOugh.
 With love,
 Dad

19. THE 19TH HOLE

A Master Putter

It was the 'Walrus' — Craig Stadler, 1982 US Masters champion — who said, 'Why am I using a new putter? Because the old one didn't float!'

The Unlosable Ball

Two golfers began a round, and on the first tee one of them sliced his drive into the thick rough. Few players found their ball in that territory, but this fellow just strolled in, stopped for a second, then walked about six paces to his left and put his hand down into knee-high grass and picked out his ball.

His partner just shrugged his shoulders at his mate's good fortune, but on the second hole it got even stranger when the man hooked his tee shot into what was basically a jungle. 'Just hang on a second and I'll go and get it,' the fellow said, which sounded ridiculous until he reappeared a few seconds later with the ball in his hands.

'Exactly what kind of ball is that?' was the question.

'It's an amazing item,' was the reply. 'When I hit it in the rough on the first I just stood there waiting for its beeper to go off, and from there it was just a case of walking towards the sound of the beep and then picking it up. Just now, I walked into the scrub and looked for the light the ball was emitting. In that darkness, the ball was easy to find. Would you like to try it?'

Absolutely, the other golfer thought. The third was a long par five, with a big lake in front of the green that usually stopped players going for the green in two. But with the 'unlosable' ball, this man had no compunction, but his attempt fell 30 metres short, right into the middle of the pond.

'Sorry, mate,' the man said with half a grin, 'I guess your ball is gone now.'

'No, it'll be right,' its owner replied. 'Just watch and see.'

Which they did. After a delay of about 10 seconds, there were some bubbles at the surface, and then the ball suddenly appeared. On each side of it, little oars appeared, and also a tiny outboard motor on the back, and the ball steered itself back to shore. Then the oars and the motor disappeared, and the ball was ready to continue the round.

'That is unbelievable,' said the bloke who'd hit the ball into the lake. 'Where on earth did you get a ball like that?'

'Oh, I found it,' came the reply.

The Toughest Putt

A father and his two sons were about to start their round when a beautiful woman walked up to the first tee.

'Would you like to join us?' asked the father.

'I will,' replied the woman, 'but on one condition. I like to make my own decisions on the golf course. Whenever I play with men, they always think they know more than I do. I want to make my own club selection and decide myself which way the putts will roll. Will you agree to let me do my own thing?'

'Not a problem,' the men said in unison.

They soon discovered that the woman was an excellent golfer. She went through the first nine in just one over par, and then birdies at the 12th and 13th got her into red figures. When she stood on the 18th tee she was still one under the card.

She appeared a little nervous on the 18th tee, and that might have been the reason she sliced her drive into the trees. All she could do was chip out, but a superb four iron gave her a chance for a par four, though an unlucky kick left her with an extremely difficult 10-metre putt if she wanted to finish in style.

It was all downhill, and would break first left and then right, before dipping again to the left in the last couple of feet. She stood over the putt, walked around it, and seemed extremely confused by what was facing her.

'Gentlemen,' she finally said. 'I am so grateful that you have done what I asked and not offered any advice during the round. But, you see, I have never broken par in a round before. I want to make this putt so badly, but I just can't read which way it will go. Can you help me? If you can and I make this putt, I'll sleep with each one of you!'

One of the sons was over there in a flash, looking at the putt from all angles. 'I think you need to aim about two feet to the right of the hole. Try to ignore the dip at the end, but don't hit it too hard or you'll go straight through the break.'

The second son had a good look and said, 'I'm not sure you're right. That slope near the hole is vicious. It's got to be four feet to the right, and you've got to get the pace right.'

Then the father walked over, picked up the woman's ball and said quietly, 'Looks like a "gimme" to me.'

Deep Bunkers

The dapper bloke sitting in the corner sipping on a cup of tea was a new member. He was also at least 80 years old, and to the young punks at the club he looked like a soft touch, and an easy way to make a few dollars. 'G'day, old timer,' one of them said. 'We'd like to welcome you to our club. Would you like to come out for a round?'

'That would be very nice,' said the old man.

'Can you play at all, sir?' he was asked.

'Oh, I go OK for an old bloke,' he replied. 'But I'm having a lot of trouble getting out of deep bunkers.'

The young golfers were good listeners. They knew the course had plenty of sand, even if most of the traps were pretty shallow. Even if the old codger could get out of those, they reasoned, the treacherous bunkers on the 17th would sort him out for sure.

On the first tee, the young blokes asked if the old man wanted to make it interesting, and after a wager was agreed to — lowest score of the foursome takes all — they set off on their round. The veteran was one of those sensible blokes who didn't hit it far but was always straight down the middle, and he managed to keep up on the scorecard. As they stood on the par-three 17th tee, he was leading by a shot, but when he put his four wood in the front trap, the lads knew everything was going to be OK. They were all on the green, though well away from the hole.

The 80-year-old trod very carefully as he slid into the bunker. As he stood over the ball the lads on the green could only see the top of his cloth cap. But he took a perfect swing, some sand flew in the air, and then the ball floated up, landed softly on the fringe of the green and rolled down to about 18 inches from the flag. Suddenly, the boys' putts looked very long and very difficult indeed.

His playing partners were incredulous. 'I thought you said you had a lot of trouble getting out of deep bunkers!' one of them moaned.

'Oh, I do,' the old man replied. 'Would you mind coming down here and giving me a hand?'

Lost and Found

Brett and Anthony, lifelong friends, were on the first tee preparing for a quick nine holes when Brett turned to his mate and said, 'How about we make it interesting. Let's play for $10, strokeplay.'

Anthony agreed and they began their rounds.

Both men were in excellent form, and when they reached the ninth tee it was all square. Anthony promptly hit a perfect drive, but Brett hooked his into the trees and it looked hopeless. He couldn't afford a penalty so he spent a long time looking for his ball. Eventually he got desperate. He glanced over to see if Anthony was paying attention, and when he saw his mate look away he dropped a ball of the same brand and number as he'd been using down on a bare patch with a reasonable view of the flag.

'Found it!' Brett shouted triumphantly.

Anthony was bitterly disappointed, and he didn't

mind saying so. 'Gee, Brett, we've been mates for how long? And you'd cheat at golf for a lousy 10 bucks!'

'What do you mean, cheat?' Brett replied indignantly. 'Here's my ball, sitting right here!'

'And you'd lie to me, too?' Anthony sighed. 'You'd cheat and you'd lie. I cannot believe you'd stoop this low.'

Finally, Brett confessed. 'But how did you know I was cheating?' he asked quietly.

'Because,' Anthony replied, 'I've been standing on your ball for the last five minutes.'

A Golfing PM

Billy Hughes is one of the more controversial figures in Australian political history. He was a former Labor Prime Minister (1915–1916) who left the party after a conscription referendum he backed was defeated, but he remained prime minister until 1923 and was a parliamentarian until his death in 1952. Hughes liked a game of golf, but hated losing balls, and the story goes that one day he and his playing partners were looking for his ball with no success. Eventually, one of his colleagues tired of the search and dropped an almost new ball on the ground and shouted, 'Found it!'

Hughes came up, looked at it and then said, 'No, that's not the one.' And with that, he put the ball in his pocket and kept scouring the area for another five minutes.

No Preferred Lies

To make their round interesting, two blokes agreed that, unless a ball was unplayable, they each would play it from where it lay — even if the rules allowed for a drop or relief. It turned into a close match, despite the fact that one took five to get out of the deep rough and trees on the 12th and the other finished up caked with mud while taking seven to recover from a slice into the river bank at the 15th. Now, as they walked up the last, one man's ball had stopped in the middle of a concrete path. They parked their cart, walked about 10 metres up to where the ball lay, and then the man whose shot it was, nonchalantly kicked his ball off the path and onto the grass.

'Hey, you can't do that,' said the other golfer. 'We agreed to play every shot as it lies.'

'Yeah, but mate,' replied the man whose shot it was, 'if I hit it off the concrete it'll wreck the club.'

'Buddy, I'm sorry. This is golf. Rules are rules.'

So the man picked up his ball and placed it back on the path. Then, while his partner strolled out to his ball in the middle of the fairway, he walked back to the cart, pulled out a club, and then returned to his ball and swung at it for all he was worth. There was a great clunk as club met concrete, sparks flew, perhaps a little of the club head broke away, and the ball speared towards the green, rolling up and finishing no more than three metres from the stick.

'Mate, what a great shot,' said the other golfer. 'What club did you use?'

'Your five iron,' the man replied.

A Bogey Five

A husband and wife were playing in an alternate shot competition. The husband hit a perfect drive, 280 metres and straight down the middle, but then the wife shanked her shot into the trees. Unfazed, the man produced a superb recovery shot that finished just two metres from the flag, but then the woman seemed to jab at the downhill putt and it rolled 10 metres past the cup. The return putt broke both ways, but somehow the husband made it. Even so, he was hardly in a good mood as he walked with his wife to the second tee.

'Sweetheart, we're going to have to do better than that,' he muttered. 'That was a bogey; five strokes.'

'Well don't blame me,' the wife replied indignantly. 'Who hit most of them?'

Devlin's Billabong

Torrey Pines Golf Course is perched above the cliffs that tower over the Pacific Ocean, about 30 kilometres north of San Diego in southern California, and has been a regular stop on the US PGA Tour since 1968. Arguably its most memorable hole is the 18th, a par five that has seen some memorable finishes over the years — not least in 1975, when Australia's Bruce

Devlin arrived at the 18th tee just three shots out of the lead in the Andy Williams San Diego Open. Unless something crazy happened, Devlin wasn't going to win the tournament, but he was certainly looking at receiving a very healthy cheque. But then his second shot found the small pond that guards the front of the green, and the 'fun' started.

Knowing that he needed at least a birdie to have any chance of winning, Devlin opted to try to splash his ball out of the water. And once you start doing that, you can't really stop. Afterwards, course officials wanted to re-name the water 'Devlin's Pond', but the Aussie had a better idea. A plaque was placed near the scene of the disaster, and it is still there today. It reads:

> **Devlin's Billabong** *On February 16, 1975,*
> *Bruce Devlin took six shots from the edge of the*
> *lake in the final round of the Andy Williams San*
> *Diego Open. He took a 10 on the hole, and lost*
> *$3000 in prize money. Dedicated to Bruce Devlin*
> *on Feb. 9, 1976, by the City of San Diego.*

All Tied Up

One day, a husband arrived home to be greeted by his wife dressed in some extremely sexy lingerie and with a piece of rope in her hand. 'Tie me up,' she purred, 'and you can do anything you want.'

So he tied her up, picked up his clubs and went to the golf course.

The Back Tees

Fred was driving off from the back tees. He never noticed that at that precise moment his wife, Charlene, was teeing up her ball at the ladies tee, directly in his path. Sadly, he nailed his tee shot, struck his wife in the back of her skull, and killed her instantly.

A few days later, Fred took a call from the coroner concerning her post-mortem.

'Ah, Mr Smith, it is clear that your wife died from a traumatic blow to the skull. You said you hit her in the head with a golf ball, did you not?'

'Yes, sir, that is correct,' Fred answered. 'The police ruled it was an accident.'

'I understand that, Mr Smith,' the coroner continued. 'But we also discovered a large bruise on her right hip. Do you know anything about that?'

'Yes, sir, I do,' Fred replied. 'Because I'd been so unlucky, the boys gave me a free second tee shot. Unfortunately, I hit one of those daisy cutters that never get more than a couple of inches off the ground.'

The Trophy Wife

Bob, a wealthy, unmarried 73-year-old golfer turned up at his local club with a breathtakingly gorgeous and extremely sexy young blonde, who proceeded to stun every one with not just her extraordinary looks and vivacious personality, but also by the way she stayed on Bob's arm and listened closely to his every word.

His mates at the club didn't quite know what to think. When they finally got the chance, after the young girl announced it was her shout, they cornered him and asked what was going on. 'Bob, how'd you snare the trophy girlfriend?' someone asked.

'Girlfriend?' Bob snorted. 'Fellas, we're just back from our honeymoon. We … whatd'ya call it … we eloped. Kylie's my wife!'

'How the hell did you do that?' a mate enquired. 'Did you lie about your age?'

'That's right.'

'What, did you tell her you were 50?'

'No,' Bob smiled. 'I told her I was 90.'

Mr 59

Al Geiberger was the first man to shoot a round of 59 on the US PGA Tour. He did it on a sweltering hot day in the second round of the 1977 Danny Thomas Memphis Classic, hitting 11 birdies and an eagle for 13 under par. At the start of the 2007 season, only two other men on the tour — Chip Beck in 1991 and David Duval in 1999 — had matched Geiberger's score, and no one had beaten it.

Geiberger's achievement (which came a couple of days after US President Gerald Ford made a hole in one during the pro-am) won him the nickname 'Mr 59'. While he never missed a fairway and chipped in for an eagle at a par five, he made his record score because he had a once-in-a-career day with his putter — he had only 23 putts and of his 11 birdie putts, none was shorter than a metre-and-a-half and the others ranged from two-and-a-half metres to 12 metres. He usually demanded that his caddie change his ball every three holes, but on this occasion his bagman kept handing him the same ball for fear of breaking the spell. Needing a birdie on the par-four last to break 60, Geiberger split the fairway with his drive, then landed a nine-iron three metres from the cup and made the putt.

What is most amazing about the round is how it stands out when compared to other scores in the tournament. Geiberger, who'd shot a par 72 on the opening day, went on to win the event by three strokes from Gary Player, but he couldn't break 70 in either of the last two rounds (he shot 72 and 70). He finished at 273, 15 under, without a round in the 60s. There were three 65s shot in the tournament, one on the first day, one on the second and one on the third, but there was no other score lower than 67 in any of the four rounds. The US Open was played the following week, and Geiberger finished tied for 10th, with one round in the 60s — a 69 on the final day.

The following week's tournament was the Western Open, and Geiberger finished tied for 43rd, after making an 81 on the third day.

So in the space of 15 days, Geiberger shot a round in the 50s, 60s, 70s and 80s. That, in its own way, is kinda funny.

Lifesaver Not Required

A man was having one of the worst rounds of his life, and it culminated with a horrible topped drive from the 18th tee. The ball dribbled straight into the pond in front of the tee, never to be seen again.

It was actually quite a big water hazard, and the poor bloke announced that when they reached the bridge he was going to jump in and drown.

But his caddie thought otherwise. 'I doubt you could keep your head down long enough,' he snapped.

The Leprechaun

An Irish golfer sliced a ball into the forest, but things turned out for the best when he came across a leprechaun as he was searching for his ball. 'As you caught me,' said the leprechaun, 'I have to grant thee two wishes.'

'Excellent!' said the golfer. 'I'd like a beer glass that never empties.'

And with that there was a flash and the man had a pint glass full of VB in his right hand. 'And your second wish?' asked the leprechaun, as he watched the man down the beer in an instant.

'Ahh! Same again!'

Disaster Calls

Lloyd had been interstate on an important business trip for three days. Just before dawn on the fourth morning, his phone rang.

'Hello, sir,' said the voice at other end of the phone, 'this is Diego. I am ringing from the house.'

'Geez, Diego,' the man mumbled to his servant, 'this had better be important. Do you know what time it is?'

'I am sorry, sir,' Diego answered. 'But I thought I should tell you straight away: your dog is dead.'

'Skipped Bale? My Derby winner?' Lloyd tried to stay calm as he thought about his beloved greyhound. 'How could this be?'

'It seems he ate bad meat, sir.'

'Bad meat? From where?'

'From the yearling, sir. I'm afraid he died yesterday, but no one found him in the paddock until this morning.'

'The yearling?' Lloyd was stunned. This was the colt that shocked the racing world when Lloyd went to three million dollars at the recent Easter sales. 'What happened to the yearling?'

'He was exhausted, sir,' Diego said. 'But I had to ride him into town yesterday because the phone was out of order.'

'What was wrong with the phone? Why did you have to ride into town?'

'Sir, your house burnt down after an intruder knocked over a candle and the curtains caught fire. Everything went down. That's why I couldn't call. I had to ride into town to get the police because I had to report your wife is dead.'

'House burnt down … Janice dead!'

'I'm sorry, sir, but I was in the house yesterday and your wife snuck up behind me. I thought she was a robber, so I grabbed your favourite golf club and swung as hard as I could. I struck her in the temple and she died instantly.'

Lloyd was devastated. His dear wife was gone. But then he stopped; his mind was racing … 'your favourite golf club' … 'swung as hard as I could' …

'My favourite golf club!! Diego, if you've wrecked my new square-headed driver, I wouldn't be turning up for work tomorrow!'

Advice from an Expert

'If you drink, don't drive,' advised Hollywood actor and golf addict Dean Martin. 'Don't even putt.'

20. OVER AND OUT!

Who Are You?

The South African cricket team was scheduled to travel to Australia in 1971–72, but after a long and passionate campaign by anti-apartheid protesters and much agonising by the Australian Cricket Board of Control, its Chairman Sir Donald Bradman announced on 8 September, 1971, that the tour had been cancelled. Soon after, Bradman revealed that in its place, a 'Rest of the World' team would play a series of matches against the Australian team during the '71–72 summer.

One of the members of that 'World XI' was a left-handed South African opening batsman named Hylton Ackerman. When he arrived at Melbourne Airport for the start of the tour, Ackerman was met by officials from Australia, one of whom, a short, balding man in his early 60s, kindly grabbed his bags and volunteered to carry them to the team bus.

'Are you connected with the Australian Board of Control?' the South African asked.

'Yes, I am,' was the reply.

'Did you play any cricket when you were younger?'

'Yes, I did.'

'Any Test cricket?'

'Yes, as a matter of fact.'

'Really! What's your name?'

'Don Bradman.'

Fail-safe

In cricket, a low score by a batsman is called a 'failure'. One day, a batsman went out to bat but was soon struggling to score at a time when his team needed quick runs. So the captain asked him to get out for the good of the side.

'You want me to fail?' asked the batsman.

'That's right,' said the captain.

'So if I get out, will I have failed or succeeded?'

Perfect Delivery

An expectant father was stuck at work while his wife was in the process of giving birth. A combination of stress, excitement and embarrassment got him all confused when it came time to ring the hospital, and instead of ringing 'Melbourne Maternity' he called 'Melbourne Cricket Ground'.

'What's happening?' he asked as soon as he heard a voice at the other end of the phone.

'It's going really well,' came the reply. 'We've got four of them out already, and the last two were ducks!'

The Red Ferrari

It's the first week of January, and a young lady in a Ricky Ponting cricket shirt walks into the Paddington branch of one of our leading banks and asks to speak to the loans manager. This particular branch is located just a couple of five irons away from the Sydney Cricket Ground. After the loans manager introduces himself, the customer explains that she needs to borrow $5000, and wonders if her shiny new red Ferrari, parked right outside, might serve as collateral. That sounded fair enough, so the cricket fan handed over the keys and was handed fifty $100 bills while one of the young clerks drove the car carefully into the bank's very own underground garage.

Later, at drinks after the branch closed for the day, there was much merriment as the woman's actions were recalled. How dumb could she be, putting up a $200,000 car on a $5000 loan?

A week later, the lady returned, again wearing that Ponting shirt, and paid back the loan in full. Interest for the week came to $9.62, and there was a total of $40 in administrative fees and charges. As the loans officer handed back the keys and showed the woman to her car, he couldn't help asking the question.

'Miss, we were very happy to have your business, but as you own a fantastic car like this, there must be other, easier ways of getting $5000 whenever you need it?'

'Yes, there are,' the woman replied. 'But where else can I get a secure parking spot during a cricket Test match at the SCG this close to the ground for less than 50 bucks a week?'

Where You From?

Because of the popularity of Test-match cricket these days, officials from the Sydney Cricket Ground Trust have adopted a stringent approach to patrons who try to reserve seats for their mates who won't be arriving until later in the day. On the first day of an Australia–New Zealand Test, ushers were called after a man in an All Blacks guernsey was spotted lying prone across three seats in the ground-level seating of the MA Noble Stand.

One of the ground officials tried to rouse the Black Caps supporter: 'I'm sorry, sir, but you're only allowed one seat.'

The Kiwi sort of groaned but didn't budge, and the official grew more impatient. It seemed this problem was not about illegal seat reservations but alcohol. It was ridiculous that a man could be this drunk when the Test hadn't even begun. 'Sir, if you don't get up, I'm afraid I'm going to have to call the police.'

The official looked up and motioned to a group of his colleagues, seeking their assistance. But not even this small posse could get any response from the fan, just the now-constant groaning. Finally a police sergeant arrived on the scene, and he leant down and spoke firmly into the New Zealander's ear.

'All right, mate, what's your name?'

'Sean,' the man whispered.

'Where you from, Sean?'

The man lifted his arm about a foot, as if he was trying to point somewhere. And then he groaned, 'The upper deck.'

Ear, Ear!

A cricketer arrives at training one day and quickly notices that one of his long-time team-mates has gone and got himself an earring. What makes this especially strange is that the now bejeweled individual is renowned as a conservative chap, with a fashion sense that is more Big W than big end of town.

'I didn't know you were into earrings,' the first fellow says to his mate.

'It's no big deal, it's only an earring,' is the reply.

That was the extent of the conversation for a while, but after they'd finished their fielding drills, the first guy decided to try again. 'What was going on? How long have you been wearing it?'

'Ever since my wife found it in my kitbag.'

The 12th Man

During Australia's tour of South Africa in 1994, a three-day game was played against Boland at Stellenbosch. One of the opposition players fell crook just after the start of play, and stand-in captain Mark Taylor kindly allowed the local team's original 12th man to bat in the ill man's place. Unfortunately, though, the new man looked out of his league, to the point that Aussie paceman Paul Reiffel cried out in exasperation after yet another delivery went past the outside edge, 'Geez, mate, you should have stayed as 12th man.'

'Well, who did you expect to be 12th man,' the equally exasperated batsman replied, 'Don Bradman?'

The Third Waugh

In similar circumstances came a line from the NSW paceman Richard Stobo, when he was playing in a grade match in Sydney against Bankstown. The batsman was Dean Waugh, younger brother of the famous twins, and as Steve Waugh records in his autobiography, *Out of my Comfort Zone*, Dean was playing and missing a bit too much for Stobo's liking. Finally, the bowler couldn't take it any longer, and he cried at the batsman, in exasperation, 'For Christ's sake, you must have been adopted!'

A Kind Donation

The Very Reverend Stanley Johnson answers his phone …

'Good morning, is that Rev. Johnson?'

'It is.'

'This is the Taxation Department. Can you help us?'

'I'll try.'

'Do you know a Jack O'Reilly, the famous cricketer?'

'I do.'

'Is he a member of your congregation?'

'He is.'

'Are you aware that last year he earned over half a million dollars?'

'I'm not.'

'And paid no tax.'

'I see.'

'Did he donate $50,000 to your church?'

'He will.'

Hard Hearing

During the height of cricket's match-fixing scandal in the 1990s, the following incident occurred, which fortunately cricket officials managed to keep out of the media. It started when one of the leading bookmakers on the subcontinent learned that a leading umpire who was supposed to be on the take had actually ripped him off for millions of rupees. They came face to face in a gloomy underground chamber in Mumbai.

The cricket authorities didn't realise that the umpire was deaf, but the crime bosses certainly did. That was why he was brought on board in the first place; the crook's reasoning being that if he was ever charged he'd be able to use his deafness as an alibi. For this 'discussion', they came prepared — a lawyer who was also an expert in sign language was with them in the room.

The bookie pushed his face only centimetres from the umpire. 'Where did you hide the money?' he was asked. The sign language expert promptly repeated the question, and the umpire, also using sign language, answered, 'I don't know what you're talking about.'

This response was quickly passed on to the crime boss, who reacted by angrily pulling out a pistol from his jacket. He put it to the umpire's sweaty temple, and said slowly, 'Ask him again.'

The lawyer signed to the umpire: 'He'll kill you for certain if you don't tell the truth!'

'OK, you win,' the umpire signed frantically. 'The money is in a locker at the railway station, locker number 365. You'll have to get the key off my cousin Vijay.'

The bookmaker looked at the lawyer. 'What'd he say?'

'He said you haven't got the balls to pull the trigger.'

Getting Square

It was late in the 1954–55 Ashes series, just before the final Test, and the English team was obliged to play a 'return' match against New South Wales at the SCG. The locals won the toss and batted on what proved to be a lively wicket, and when captain Keith Miller came out to bat England skipper Len Hutton walked up to his 25-year-old pace bowler Peter Loader and said flatly, 'I want you to give Miller a few short ones.'

Perhaps Hutton was trying to give his side a psychological advantage before the final Test, or maybe he was just keen to get one back after copping a truckload of bumpers from Miller over the years, but the order didn't exactly thrill young Loader, because he knew that if he bowled a bouncer or two at Miller there was every chance he'd be getting a few in return when it was his turn to bat. However, he did as he was asked. The Aussie hero clearly didn't enjoy it (finally being caught at slip off Loader's bowling for just 11), and NSW were all out for 172 before stumps. But there was still time for two English wickets to fall before the close, and who should Hutton make nightwatchman when the second wicket fell? Peter Loader, of course.

He came out, fumbling his gloves, face as white as the sightscreen, and as he took guard to face his first ball from Pat Crawford, he heard Miller at slip having a quiet chuckle. 'I didn't think I'd be getting square as early as this!' he laughed.

First ball, Loader was hit high on the thigh, and the only relief he felt came when he heard the umpire call, 'Over.' Then he had a bright idea. He appealed against the light. Miller had seemed keen to bowl the next over, and Loader knew that the Australian champion would concede a single to get him on strike, but now he strode up to the umpire and said, 'I think he's right, we should go off.' Loader's reaction was a mixture of shock and pure relief, but then his nemesis sidled up to him and said, 'Now you've got all night to worry about me.'

Next morning, the wicket still had plenty of life in it, but Miller didn't bowl himself. Instead, he gave the ball to Alan Davidson, who promptly bowled the nightwatchman for a duck. All those nightmares about Miller bowling retaliatory bouncers at him had been for nought.

A Good Catch

One day, during a tour of New Zealand, Australia's Michael Bevan was fielding on the boundary. As is the way with Black Cap fans, Bevan was copping the usual abuse from the outer, and again as is customary there was more than the odd lolly or piece of fruit, mostly apples, being lobbed in his direction.

But then, as he was walking in with the bowler, fully focused on what was happening in the middle, he heard and sensed a big thump near his feet. Bevan's first thought was that it might have been a huge rock, or a brick, a full can of beer or even a hand grenade. Imagine his surprise when he looked down to see what he described in his book *The Best of Bevan* as a 'gorgeous four-kilo snapper glistening in the sunlight'.

'Why the fish was wasted on me,' Bevan wrote, 'I have no idea.'

The Sandshoe Crusher

At the Gabba in 1974–75, Australia's Jeff Thomson bowled England's Tony Greig with a yorker that became famously known as the 'sandshoe crusher'. Across the country, young quicks tried to emulate 'Thommo', first with a series of bouncers and then with a fast fully-pitched delivery aimed straight at the batsman's feet.

In one game, a bowler did the trick perfectly, and straight afterwards the poor batsman was writhing on the ground in agony, holding his Dunlop Volleys. He couldn't walk, and there was general agreement that at least a few bones had been broken, so one of the team-mates said, 'Should we call an ambulance?'

And someone else said, 'No, I reckon we need a toe truck!'

Only the Names Have Changed

That joke reminds us of one of cricket's most repeated yarns — a story that has involved a variety of leading characters, such as Harold Larwood, Fred Trueman and Dennis Lillee, depending on the era in which it was told. Each time, it starts when the bowler (Larwood/Trueman/Lillee) fires in a rapid yorker at the hapless batsman, who is struck on the foot and collapses in agony. Up walks the bowler …

'Are you all right, young fella?' he asks kindly.

'Yes, I think so,' replies the batsman through clenched teeth, 'thank you very much.'

'Can you walk?'

'Yes, thank you.'

'Good, well you can piss off to the pavilion, because you're out LBW.'

Another story that has been played out more than once involves a punchline delivered in South Africa by the Victorian fast bowler Ernie McCormick in 1936 and by the legendary Dougie Walters in 1970. English fans from between the wars recalled a similar story involving the accomplished left-arm spinner Hedley Verity.

In the McCormick yarn, recalled by the prolific cricket-book writer RS Whitington in his biography of Bill O'Reilly, *Time of the Tiger*, the famous spinners, O'Reilly and Clarrie Grimmett, were bowling against Transvaal at the Old Wanderers Ground in Johannesburg, when a pair of late-order batsmen, 'Buster' Nupen and 'Chud' Langton, started smashing sixes. To save time, as both teams were trying to end the game that evening rather than have it drag out to the next morning, each time a ball disappeared out of the ground, a new one was called for. This occurred something like seven times in the space of two overs.

In the Walters version, remembered by Ian Chappell in his book *Chappelli has the Last Laugh*, Ashley Mallett was bowling to the great South African all-rounder Mike Procter in a tour game against Western Province at Cape Town. One delivery ended up in a nearby brewery, another landed in the railway yards outside the ground and was last seen disappearing on a goods train bound for East London, and three other balls also sailed over the boundary fence.

Back in 1936, McCormick sauntered up to his captain, Vic Richardson, to make his crack. Walters went straight to Mallett. 'Well, Vic/Ashley,' they said with a straight face, 'that's the end of the reds. Now we can move onto the colours.'

Dougie

Few cricketers have had more of their stories — whether they be lines cracked by them or yarns about them — repeated down the years than Kevin Douglas Walters. At least some of them are undoubtedly apocryphal, such as the joke that when it was his turn to bat he'd place his cards face down on the table and mutter, 'Leave them here, I'll be back in a minute.' It was often suggested that he didn't practise very hard, yet his cricket constantly proved that he was very fit, never more so than when he became the first man in cricket history to score a double century and a century in the same Test match (242 and 103 versus the West Indies in Sydney in 1968–69) and when he scored the highest Test score ever by a No. 6 batsman (250 versus New Zealand at Christchurch in 1977). He was criticised for being inconsistent, yet his career Test batting average of 48.26 was bettered by only Greg Chappell among his Australian contemporaries. And further, he was a true match-winner, and also a genuine team man, one of those blokes who made the side better just by being who he was. When Walters suffered a poor sequence of form in England in 1972 and had to be dropped after a seven-year run interrupted only by army service, captain Ian Chappell worried about the impact the axing of such a popular stalwart might have on the colleagues. But when the side for the final Test was announced at a team meeting, Walters muttered in a voice just loud enough for every one to hear, 'Thank God, now I won't have to get up for practice.' Given the circumstances, it wasn't flippant; rather, it put every one at ease, and Australia went on to win the Test to level the series.

When, during the Centenary Test at the MCG in 1977, Rod Marsh broke Wally Grout's record for the most dismissals by an Australian keeper, Walters went up to his great mate and cracked, 'If you'd held all those catches you dropped in your first Test, you'd have broken the record months ago.' Four years later, when Dennis Lillee took his 249th Test wicket to break Richie Benaud's Australian record, Walters (who was a good enough medium pacer to take 49 Test wickets at the highly respectable average of 29.08) took the time to tell him that he'd 'given up the chase'. When a press report quoted Rodney Hogg saying that he'd stopped concentrating on his batting as a teenager to focus on his fast bowling, Walters wondered aloud how quick he might have been if he'd done the same. Yet the pad was on the other leg when, after arguably his most famous innings — the hundred in a session at Perth in 1974–75 that ended with a pulled six off the last ball of the day — his captain Ian Chappell decided that, rather than have his comrades greet the returning champion with the customary cheers and backslaps, they'd retire to the showers. So the room was quiet and very empty when Dougie and his partner, Ross Edwards, entered.

Walters, by all accounts, didn't bat an eyelid. He just put down his bat and went for a smoke as he always did, and eventually his great mates came back and shared in his joy. He never played for laughs, but he generated plenty.

A Cricketing Duck

It is a little-known fact that back in the 1950s, Daffy Duck was selected in the USA's national cricket team. A duck making any cricket team is interesting enough, but Daffy found that all those days out in the sun fielding for those terrible American bowlers was causing him grief, because he kept getting burnt lips. Eventually, the team doctor told him to go and buy some kind of lip moisturiser.

So Daffy walked into a pharmacy and requested the most effective brand. 'Will that be cash or credit?' asked the chemist.

'Put it on my bill,' Daffy replied.

Gotcha!

'Stumper' was an ordinary club wicketkeeper, but a cheeky young bloke all the same. His team was an ordinary club team. In the opposition was a former international (we'll call him 'George') who had decided to have one last season 'on the park' and was scoring centuries every week.

When George came out to bat he looked the part — perfectly creased creams, top-of-the-range gear, Australian team practice cap. He didn't bother taking guard from the umpire; instead he cracked some joke about 'playing here before'. Then, just before his first ball was delivered, from behind the stumps came the chirpy voice of our mate Stumper. 'Geez, you're lookin' good, Georgie,' he said. 'How 'bout a wager on your dig? An even hundred says you won't make a hundred.'

George was taken aback. Who was this punk daring to take him on? 'Son,' he sneered, 'with that sort of attitude I'll take your cash and score 200!'

'OK then,' continued Stumper. 'But to make it fair, you've gotta give me two "gotchas".'

'A gotcha?' said George. 'What's a gotcha?'

'You'll see. I'll use one on this first ball so you know what they're about, and then I'll keep my second one for later.'

And so the bet was on. First ball was well pitched up, and George was just about to drive it through the covers away for his first runs when he reeled away in pain, as if he'd ripped a groin or torn a hamstring. 'Are you all right?' the opposition captain enquired as he came running in, but the former Test star waved him away. He went down on his knees for a minute, and then composed himself in readiness for the next delivery.

For the next 40 minutes, he was anything but an ex-international batsman. He scratched around as if the wicket was a minefield, and seemed very hesitant to go back on his stumps, or to lean too far forward. It was almost a relief when he was finally dismissed, for just eight. Stumper had his hundred bucks.

Back in the dressing room, his usually admiring team-mates asked George what had happened. He told them about the opposition keeper, the bet, and those bloody gotchas. 'When I went forward on that first delivery, that bastard of a keeper had taken his right glove off, and he leant forward with me, grabbed my crotch and cried, "Gotcha!" And then the keeper added, "Remember, I've still got one more that I can use a little later." After that, I was no chance. The only balls I could concentrate on were my own.'

Jonah and the Cricketer

An international cricket team was on a long flight. Because of some confusion with the booking, one of the players was sitting away from his team-mates and next to a middle-aged woman who seemed to be extremely nervous. She was shuffling and shaking, and constantly reading verses from the Bible she clasped firmly in her hands.

Trying to be friendly, the cricketer chuckled, 'You don't really think all that stuff in there is true, do you?'

'Of course I do,' the woman replied indignantly. 'It is the Bible.'

'So that story about the dude being eaten by the whale and surviving, that's true is it?' he asked.

'Jonah?' she said. 'It is in the Bible, so yes I believe it really happened.'

'Lady, don't you think you should get real? How the hell can a man survive all that time in a whale's gut?'

'I don't really know,' the woman said firmly. 'When I get to heaven, I will ask him.'

'And what if he ain't in heaven?' the cricketer asked, his voice dripping with sarcasm.

'Then you can ask him,' the woman replied.

Time for a Change

Johnny Douglas, the captain of the England team that toured Australia in 1920–21 and lost all five Tests against Warwick Armstrong's side, had a bigger opinion of his bowling than many of his team-mates did. One day, the home team's great No. 3, Charlie Macartney, was coming out to bat when Cecil Parkin walked up to his leader and said, 'You come on now and bowl Macartney in, and I'll come on at half-past four and bowl him out.'

Another time, one Englishman suggested, 'Perhaps it's time for a bowling change.' Douglas had been bowling for hours, for little effect.

Hearing this, Parkin was quick with a suggestion. 'Aye, skipper, why not go on at the other end,' he said. 'You'll get a better view of the scoreboard from there!'

Keeping Count

Bruce Francis, the NSW and Australian opening bat who later organised the 'rebel' Australian tours of South Africa in the mid 1980s, had a season of county cricket with Essex in 1971. Before one match late in the season he found himself talking to another Australian, Cec Pepper, who'd moved to England to play league cricket not long after World War II and was now a first-class umpire. During their conversation he explained that the season had gone pretty well, and that he was enjoying county cricket except for the fact that he'd been trapped leg before wicket no less than 16 times.

As a cricketer, Pepper had been quite an extrovert. Once, after watching a batsman struggle to read his mixture of wrong 'uns, toppies and leg-spinners, he reputedly called down the wicket, 'All right, lad, you can open your eyes now. It's over.' On this occasion, Francis was quickly struck on the pad, and the bowler shouted out a loud appeal, to which umpire Pepper shot up a finger and cried, 'That's 17, Bruce!'

How close?

Another good umpiring story concerns an apparently true exchange between a bowler and an official after a delivery had struck the batsman on the pad.

Bowler: (innocently) Was that close?

Umpire: Yes, it was close.

Bowler: (slightly interested) Very close?

Umpire: Yes, very close.

Bowler: (shouting, hands in the air) How was it then?

Umpire: Not close enough.

True Grit

One more umpiring yarn from England concerned a gentleman named Alec Skelding, who was good enough to officiate in first-class matches and was also able to establish quite a reputation for his rare (for an umpire) sense of humour. One day, Skelding responded to a tight run-out appeal by saying, 'Gentlemen, it's a photo finish, and I haven't got time to develop the photo. Not out!' Another time, in a county game, a bowler accidentally spat out his dentures in delivering the ball, which left him unable to shout out an appeal when the batsman was hit on the pad.

All the bowler could do was swing his arms and mime an appeal, while Skelding made out that he couldn't understand what he was saying. This pantomime went on for a few moments, with the bowler's face getting redder and redder, until in exasperation he leant down, snatched his dentures out of the scuffed-up area around the bowler's footmarks, and shouted out a dirty and gritty, 'How was that?'

'Not out,' replied umpire Skelding.

The Great Unknown

One fellow who never needed to worry about that scenario was the former Victorian opening bowler, John Power, who was known for taking his false teeth out and using them to mark the start of his run-up.

Power might not have been the keenest aficionado of the game's goings-on, but he wasn't a bad bowler, and in a game against New South Wales at the Melbourne Cricket Ground in 1959–60 he had the rare experience of taking the first three wickets of the visitors' innings — Warren Saunders, Brian Booth and Neil Marks — in one over.

The big crowd was buzzing. New South Wales were struggling at 3 for 22, and at the end of the over, as the spectators stood and applauded, Power sidled up to his wicketkeeper, Len Maddocks, and asked seriously of his victims, 'Len, were any of them any good?'

A Change of Practice

It was Wednesday, the usual day for cricket practice, but Tom decided to give practice a miss and get home at 5 p.m. However, after he walked through the door he discovered that it had not been one of his wife's better days. Nothing the poor fellow said or did seemed to be right.

By 7.30, the mood hadn't changed, and Tom made a suggestion. 'How about we just forget the last two and a half hours? I'll go outside and pretend I've just got home, and we can start all over again.'

So Tom went back to his car, walked down the drive to the front door, came through the door, into the kitchen and with a big smile announced, 'Hello, honey, I'm home!'

'Where the hell have you been?' she moaned. 'Just once, could you give bloody cricket practice a miss and come home and give me a hand?'

A Question

Why do they call them grandSTANDS when they're full of seats?

Chicken and Mash

One of the problems 'Anglo' cricketers used to suffer on tours of the subcontinent was an upset stomach, the dreaded 'Delhi Belly'. Different players tried various strategies to try to keep the lurgy at bay, and the method adopted by the former England player, Alex Stewart, was to take no less than 43 separate portions of chicken, mashed potato and broccoli on tour with him, one for each day. He ate little else.

Laugh at Stewart if you want, but the fact is he got through the tour without so much as a tummy rumble. Unfortunately, though, when he arrived home the first meal his wife cooked for him was … chicken with mashed potato and broccoli.

It's Your Mother!

The captain's mother-in-law rang the doorbell to her daughter's house and when the skipper opened the door, she said softly, 'Hello, son, can I stay here for a while?'

'Sure,' he said, as he quickly shut the door.

What Does Your Dad Do?

It was the first practice of a new season for the under 12s, and inevitably there were a number of kids making their debuts. There was also a new coach, and in order to make the new players feel more comfortable she began her first team-talk by saying, 'Hi guys, my name's Diane and I'm a schoolteacher during the week and a cricket coach on Saturday. I thought you might like to introduce yourselves and tell us something about your cricket and your dads.'

Diane then pointed to a boy sitting at the front of the group, and he said, 'Hi, I'm Dylan. I'm a wicketkeeper. My dad's a doctor and he saves people's lives at the hospital.'

The next boy stood up and said, 'I'm Tom. I'm a fast bowler. My dad's a fireman. He drives the red fire engine and rescues people from burning buildings.'

A third boy: 'My name is Lachlan. I'm captain. My dad is in the navy. He's in charge of a battleship and sometimes has to go and end other countries' wars.'

This goes on. Opening bat Nicholas's father is a park ranger; No. 3 Nathan's dad is a policeman; spin bowler James's father is the local mayor. Finally, Diane has heard from every one except young Jack. He is new to the team, and doesn't know anyone. 'Well, Jack,' the coach said, 'what can you tell us about your dad?'

Jack shuffles his feet, looks up at the sky, starts to speak, stops, and then says, 'Ah, miss, my dad's dead.'

Silence. Diane is taken aback, but quickly she decides the best thing to do is to persevere. 'I am so sorry, Jack. I'm sure your dad was a fantastic man. What did he do before he died?'

'Well miss ... he ... um ... he sorta went ... *ah ... aaahh ... aaaaaaaaahhhhhhhhh!!!*, and then he just keeled over and Mum called the ambulance.'

Bibliography

Geoff Armstrong and Peter Thompson, *Melbourne Cup 1930*, Allen & Unwin, Sydney, 2005

Mike Atherton, *Opening Up*, Hodder & Stoughton, London, 2002

Arthur Beetson, *Big Artie*, ABC Books, Sydney, 2004

Michael Bevan, *The Best of Bevan*, Allen & Unwin, Sydney, 2002

Ian Chappell, Austin Robertson and Paul Rigby, *Chappelli Has the Last Laugh*, Lansdowne Press, Sydney, 1980

Geoff Davie, *Cats on the Prowl*, HarperCollins, Sydney, 1994

Bob Dwyer, *Full Time*, Pan Macmillan, Sydney 2004

Barry Fantoni (editor and compiler), *Private Eye's Colemanballs*, Corgi, London, 1982

Greg Growden, *With the Wallabies*, ABC Books, Sydney 1995

Chris Handy, John Lambie and Jeff Sayle, *Well I'll Be Ruggered!*, Ironbark Press, Sydney, 1993

Frank Hardy and Athol George Mulley, *The Needy and the Greedy*, Libra Books, Canberra, 1975

Frank Hardy and Fred Trueman, *You Nearly Had Him That Time*, Hutchinson, Melbourne, 1978

Max Howell, Lingyu Xie and Peter Horton, *Stan the Man*, Celebrity Books, Auckland, 1997

Peter Jackson, *Whatd'ya reckon!*, Ironbark Press, Sydney 1992

Brian Johnston, *The Wit of Cricket*, Leslie Frewin, London, 1968

Robert Lusetich and Frank Arok, *My Beloved Socceroos*, ABC Books, Sydney, 1992

Neil Marks, *Great Australian Cricket Stories*, ABC Books, Sydney, 2002

Mark H. McCormack, *The World of Professional Golf*, Angus & Robertson, Sydney, 1978

Jack McHarg, *Stan McCabe: The Man and his Cricket*, Collins, Sydney, 1987

Muir MacLaren (editor), *The Australian Golfer's Handbook*, Muir MacLaren Pty Ltd, Sydney, 1957

John Platten, *The Rat*, HarperSports, Sydney, 1997

Jack Pollard, *The Tennis Player Who Laughed*, Hutchinson, Melbourne, 1984

Ricky Ponting, *Captain's Diary 2006*, Harper*Sports*, Sydney, 2006

Tom Raudonikis, *Rugby League Stories*, Methuen Australia, Sydney, 1981

Paul Salmon, *Fish Tales*, Viking, Melbourne, 2002

Phil Tresidder, *The Golfer Who Laughed*, Hutchinson, Melbourne, 1981

Paul Vautin and Johnny Raper, *Fatty and Chook: Laughing at League*, Lester Townsend Publishing, Sydney, 1990

Paul Wade, *Captain Socceroo*, Harper*Sports*, Sydney, 1995

Steve Waugh, *Steve Waugh's South African Tour Diary*, Pan Macmillan, Sydney, 1994

Steve Waugh, *Out Of My Comfort Zone*, Penguin Books, Melbourne, 2005

RS Whitington, *Time of the Tiger*, Hutchinson, Melbourne, 1970

Mike Whitney, *Quick Whit*, Pan Macmillan, Sydney, 1994

Mike Whitney, *Whiticisms*, Pan Macmillan, Sydney, 1996

Kenneth Wolstenholme, *The Wit of Soccer*, Leslie Frewin, London, 1971